The Script is finished, Now what do I do?

The Scriptwriter's Resource Book & Agent Guide

K CALLAN

© K Callan 1998
Second Printing 1998
ISBN 1-878355-04-X
Library of Congress Catalog Card Number ISSN 1068-5162

Other books by K Callan
An Actor's Workbook
The Los Angeles Agent Book, 2nd, 3rd, 4th, 5th editions
The New York Agent Book, 1st, 2nd, 3rd, 4th, 5th editions
How to Sell Yourself as an Actor, 1st and 2nd editions
Directing Your Directing Career
The Life of the Party

Cover: Barry Wetmore
Photography: Capital Cities/ABC, Inc.
Editor: Kristi Nolte

Read the Directions

Most of us buy an appliance and never read the instructions. We might use the equipment for years before we find out that in addition to its basic function, it also sings and dances.

Though you are eager to skip through the book to the agency listings and begin sending out query letters, be patient: this book also sings and dances. There is valuable information here that can enhance the effectiveness of your submissions when it's time.

Many agents complain that writers seek agents before they or their material are ready. This book can begin to give you an overview of how the business really is. It can help you understand the need to focus in order to succeed.

This book can help you determine if you can have a career from Peoria and/or penetrate the fence to gain admission somewhere inside the system if you do move to New York or Los Angeles.

If you decide to study, you'll discover which classes can enhance your business opportunities as well as your script. You'll find out about contests, scholarships, The Writers Guild, The Dramatists Guild, informative Websites, managers, lawyers and other details before focusing on agents.

The Script is finished deals with query letters, meetings, writer/agent relationships and how to nurture them; what the writer has a right to expect and what is too much to expect; the relative value of no agent, a star agent and discerning which is the agent with whom you would have the most fruitful relationship. There is a list of books you might find helpful for your reference library and sound ideas on when it's time to change your work habits instead of your agent; all this before you ever get to the agency listings.

Each chapter informs the next so if you digest the main dish before you get to dessert, the dessert gets better.

One of the most important things I learned in my research is how much form means to agents. They do judge your work by whether you took the time to learn the format and do it right. They also judge you by the form of your behavior. Calling or walking in cold will not impress. Bad behavior no matter how great the talent is not a positive calling card.

Begin to practice patience and form now by going a step at a time.

Good luck.

Table of Contents

1 Knowledge is Power

The ability to write is the smallest part of the talent puzzle that produces success as a scriptwriter. The bottom line to becoming part of the show biz system is possessing the grit, drive, ingenuity, talent, craft, patience, professionalism, stability, wit, style, grace, faith, hope and stamina to separate yourself from the pack and become an income tax paying member of the artistic community.

This book is written to give you as much information and insight as possible into how the business really works so that you can make an intelligent determination about your future as a screenwriter.

The quotes in the book are gleaned from interviews with scores of agents in Los Angeles and New York who represent writers for theatre, film and television. The agents reveal their ideas on how neophyte writers might enter the marketplace, help themselves, attract agents, and move toward their career goals in the most timely and intelligent manner.

If you have not already pondered the following, this book is going to expand your knowledge by helping you consider:

☞ the single most important attribute for success in show business

☞ what your chances are of actually making any money as a scriptwriter

☞ the importance of a writing focus

☞ if there is any market for what you want to write

☞ how you can enter the system

☞ what you can do for yourself

☞ why it does or doesn't make sense to study

☞ whether you can sell your work if you don't live in New York or Los Angeles

☞ whether or not you need an agent

☞ what an agent really does

☞ what attracts an agent

☞ what you should look for in an agent

☞ how to research agents

☞ what you have a right to expect from an agent

☞ what the agent has a right to expect from you

☞ the best way to approach an agent

☞ how to have a mutually rewarding relationship with your agent

Wrap Up

Research is essential
✓ writing is the easy part
✓ ask yourself informed questions
✓ this book can help you focus

2 What Are Your Chances of Making Any Money?

Is it worth it to you financially to pursue a career as a scriptwriter? Just because a few superstar writers make millions of dollars for their scripts is no guarantee that you will. Don't become intoxicated by the possibilities and ignore the realities.

In 1992, only 51% of the 8,500 members of the Writers Guild, made any money at all. Of those who *did* make money, 20% made less than $4,000 and only 10% made over $7,000.

These numbers represent the last in depth research the Guild conducted relative to detailed earnings, but WGA Special Affairs Chief, Chuck Slocum told me that as of July 1997, the median earnings of a working member of the Guild was $75,000 a year.

Before you get out your wordprocessors, Slocum stressed that this is the *average* income of scriptwriters who make millions of dollars figured along with those who make one dollar in any calendar year.

In any given year, half of the members of the Writers Guild of America will make no money at all. Slightly down from the detailed numbers in 1992.

As in the other entertainment guilds, the money is made by white men. And it is made by young white men.

• *A new five-year study about writer employment in Hollywood shows that the industry is not making any great strides in terms of overcoming racism, sexism and ageism.*

White Male Pens Still Busiest
Kathleen O'Steen
Daily Variety
June 15, 1993

• *...while males' share of total employment has declined by just under 2%, they still account for over three-quarters of the writers working in the industry. Women account for just over a fifth of all employed writers, increasing just slightly from 20.7% employed writers in 1987 to 22.3% in 1991.*

...the share of employment going to writers over 50 declined from 24.4% to 20.3% between 1982 and 1987 and declined further to 16.9 % in 1991.

While just over half of the membership (52.5%) was not employed in

1990, *unemployment varies by gender, minority status and age. The lowest rate of unemployment continues to be for non-minority males aged 40 and under, at 40% (up slightly from 35% in 1987). The unemployment rate is close to 50% for both non-minority women and minority writers under the age of 40. Among writers over the age of 40, the percentage of writers not employed ranges from 72% for minority writers, to 59% for non-minority writers, regardless of gender.*

The 1993 Hollywood Writers' Report
William Bielby/Denise Bielby
June 1993

Ageism

There's much conversation these days about ageism, particularly in television. The consensus among many is that since the heads of networks are quite young, (Jamie Tarsus head of ABC Entertainment is in her early thirties) they prefer to hire writers in their own age group. Undoubtedly, that is part of it, but there are other facts that are more pertinent.

Last season, a fifty-something actor friend of mine who had been making his living in another field, anxiously handed me his short film: *I am becoming a writer/director. Here is my film. Let me know what you think. I'm having a hard time with it because of ageism.*

Supportive of my friend, I viewed the film immediately and instantly had new insights about ageism. Looking at John's film, I thought, *if John were twenty, this would be a promising film. I would want to keep an eye on him to watch his progression.* But, John is not twenty. At 50+, if I watch his progression for twenty years, he might be seventy by the time his developmental process puts him in the position to have a credible place in the business as a writer or director.

My thirty-something friend Tom is a senior exec in the field of computer research. One of his duties is sifting through high powered resumes in search of leaders for his company. His eye recently caught the resume of a fifty-nine-year-old whose experience in a particular area was compelling. He was disappointed that some of the newer computer language skills were missing, but called the man anyway. When he asked the man what assets he might bring to the job, the prospective employee was vague. In response to questions about the newer computer languages, he mentioned that he had *played around* with them, but his answer showed no real interest in having kept himself sharp in that area.

Not surprisingly, he didn't get the job.

I asked Tom if there was anything the man could have said that would have resulted in a job. Tom's answer provides clarity regarding age, experience and ambition: *If he had said,* Well, I'm 59 years old. I'm nearing the end of my career. I'm not going to be one of your hot shots, but I can provide leadership and excellence in some of the less glamorous areas that your hotshots wouldn't want, and I can help you train the new hotshots that you do hire. I am also actively learning the new languages, and by the time I get to you, I will be up to speed on them, *I would have hired the man over the phone.*

The best people, at any age, are the best because they like what they're doing, they have a vision of where they and the business are going, and they are enthusiastic. They enjoy what they're doing.

There is a sense of entitlement that comes with age sometimes. In all careers, one must keep sharp and productive in order to be competitive. With the world changing so quickly, knowing where you are in the scheme of things and addressing it, is key in any area of business.

• *For a new writer who is older, yes, age is a factor. For an established writer, not necessarily. I represent many writers over 45 or 50 for that matter who are successful and making lots of money.*

I would think hard before taking on a television writer who is getting up in years, I wouldn't care on a feature film. I don't think there is as much age discrimination with a feature film. They don't care if my mother wrote it. Everyone wants to get their hands on a hot feature script.

Rima Greer
Above the Line Agency/Los Angeles

• *I think some ageism is legitimate. I think the perception of people over a certain age might not be relevant to the marketplace. But, I think more often than not, ageism is unfair. When they say,* How old is the writer?, *if they're not in their 20s or 30s or 40s, it can be a problem.*

There's a certain place in your career where it doesn't matter, but if your last produced credit was 10-15 years ago and you're 50 something, you're in trouble.

I used to be outraged that if you're older and you want to pitch Encino Man at Disney, well, they're not going to hire you. Can a 50 year old write it? Well probably, but they're going to go with a younger writer.

On television, it's even more noticeable. With Steven Bochco and David

Jacobs and Steven Cannell, that's fine, but I have an older client who is trying to get her half-hour read and when they ask how old she is, I say, she's really good.

I know any number of men and women who have made a good living in television and if they get to a certain age and if they are not really successful, they have a harder go of it than people 10 or 15 years their junior. It's sad and true.

Writers that used to sell 2 or 3 episodes a year free lance making $40,000-$50,000 a year, now I can't get them an episodic assignment because most shows are staff written. Out of a 28 show series, they buy maybe one free lance script, but if you get on a series, it's the key to the bank.
　　　Lynn Pleshette
　　　Pleshette/Millner Agency/Los Angeles

● 　*I think ageism is a reality. Unfortunately there comes a point where if you have no credits, it becomes a lot harder to find work. It's a lot harder to start an older writer who doesn't have credits than a young writer who doesn't have credits. There is a preference in this town for youth.*
　　　Jim Preminger
　　　Jim Preminger Agency/Los Angeles

● 　*Age is more of a problem in television. In film, you can be hot at any age.*
　　　Debbee Klein
　　　Paradigm/Los Angeles

Older writers may just need to reevaluate their thinking, because it's not chronological age that attracts or puts off buyers. Elliot Stahler thinks age isn't the issue:

● 　*Everybody is looking for what's sexy. What's sexy, almost by definition, is what is new and exciting. When someone is new to the business whether the writer is 20 or 50, that's sexy. Those new ideas inspire us to get the buyers excited to see the new material, someone who can take this new person and sell him to his superior. It's about what's new and exciting.*
　　　Elliot Stahler
　　　Kaplan Stahler/Los Angeles

There are times however, when only experience will do:

● 　*I think there are many cases where producers are looking for people with a track record and you can only develop a track record with age.*

Jim Preminger
Jim Preminger Agency/Los Angeles

- *I've studied the situation pretty closely. It all depends. If you are in television and the show is Beverly Hills 90210, common sense tells you they're not likely to be hiring somebody 60 years old for that show or something where it's an ensemble of kids or people in their early twenties. If it's a screenplay, hey, you can be 18 or 80, if it's good, it's good. I think that think is exaggerated, just as, The women are* hired for this and that and whatever. *I really and truly have not found that to be a problem. Someone is going to write most scripts regardless of gender. If it's a television series about guys in the tank corp, there's not going to be too many women.*
    Stu Robinson
    Paradigm/Los Angeles

Women and Other Minorities

Women writers are beginning to make more inroads into the business, but the WGA tells me the earnings gap is still there. If a man is making $60,000 for a job, a woman will usually be paid $50,000 for the same job. Of course, if you are Linda Bloodworth Thomas, Marcy Carsey or Diane English those ratios no longer apply. These women are all now powerful producers, but they all started at the beginning:

- *Born in Buffalo, New York, [Diane English] started her career as an English and drama teacher, then decided to become a writer for television. She began working at a PBS affiliate in New York and distinguished herself as a writer with a television adaptation of Ursula K. LeGuin's* The Lathe of Heaven, *which she cowrote and for which she received her first Writers Guild award nomination. From there, it was a short hop to writing MOWs and then on to half-hour comedy.*
    TV's Top Twenty
    Kathleen O'Steen
    Emmy
    October 1996

Although women have no old boy network to look to for guidance, Carole Black, president and general manager of NBC 4 in Los Angeles, says having a mentor is essential:

- *Women need to have someone willing to take a chance and be supportive.*

Choose your boss carefully.
> *Gaining Ground*
> Kathleen O'Steen and Jennifer Pendleton
> *Emmy*
> October 1996

Being a woman in the business has its drawbacks. Being a woman and being black makes the hill that much steeper.

• *Winifred White Neisser, a vice-president of movies and miniseries at Columbia TriStar Television who, incidentally, was an honors grad from Harvard-Radcliff, concurs about having to work twice as hard to sometimes get half the credit.* As a black and as a woman, I'm sure I've had doors slammed in my face. And maybe I would be further along in my career if I was white or male. But who has the time to worry about it? I say keep moving forward.
> *Black by Popular Demand*
> Alan Carter
> *Emmy*
> February 1997

• *The determined [Suzanne] DePasse started her career as creative assistant to legendary Motown Records president Berry Gordy, rising through the ranks to eventually become president of Motown Productions. She was the executive producer of* Lonesome Dove, *the landmark miniseries for CBS. But after twenty-two years at Motown, DePasse struck out in 1992 to become an entrepreneur. DePasse Entertainments' sitcom* Sister, Sister *is entering its fourth season and is being sold into syndication for fall 1998.* Smart Guy, *another family sitcom with a primarily black cast, will be a midseason replacement on the WB.*

As one of the few powerful African-American women in Hollywood, DePasse feels an obligation to help others like herself get started. She participates in a mentor program at USC in addition to offering internships at DePasse Entertainment to promising newcomers. DePasse believes women have gained ground in the television industry. But, *she insists,* many challenges remain. It's deeply entrenched and almost subliminal, *she says of the sexism in the business.* There's this all-pervasive attitude that the game belongs to the guys.
> *TV's Top Twenty*
> Kathleen O'Steen
> *Emmy*
> October 1996

- *A recent survey by the WGA reported that of its 7,768 members, 235 (3 percent) are blacks who describe themselves a working in TV.*

  By the Numbers
  Alan Carter
  Emmy
  February 1997

Money Talks

The only way that anyone makes inroads into the business is by seizing the initiative and doing the work.

Spike Lee, Robert Townsend and John Singleton not only wrote and directed their first films, but in most cases, raised the money for their projects as well. Robert Townsend, who wrote and directed *Hollywood Shuffle* became a show business legend by financing the film with credit card advances.

The twenty-four year old writer/director/producer of *El Mariachi*, Robert Rodriguez, is another creative fundraiser. He not only managed to make his first feature for $7,000, but raised the money by participating in medical experiments. Rodriguez wrote the script while lying in bed hospitalized for the tests and even cast from the hospital bed, choosing a fellow guinea pig for the film. He ended up landing CAA as his agent.

Rodriguez wrote a book about the experience called *Rebel Without a Crew: or how a 23-year old filmmaker with $7,000 became a Hollywood Player.*

Because the public is unaccustomed to seeing people of color at all, these examples appear to be great progress. And they are. But they still represent a very small percentage of the overall pie.

Higher black employment has nothing to do with affirmative action, talent or fairness. Higher black employment reflects two things: the expanding economic clout of the black community and the growing number of black artists who have become entrepreneurial about their careers.

- *The DGA (Directors Guild of America) and the WGA (Writers Guild of America) have committees set up to monitor minority hiring, but both unions say they are not a hiring hall or employment office. They do, however, work toward opening doors and increasing the number of blacks who work in the business. Each union has a steering committee that holds occasional networking sessions, works toward pro-moting diversity, and in the case of the DGA, has established a minority training program.*

By the Numbers
Alan Carter
Emmy
February 1997

The only way minorities are going to find work in the marketplace is by finding ways to finance their own projects. Of course the white male establishment is going to fill the marketplace with their own propaganda, it's their money. If minorities are to have success, they must have the motivation and the vision to tear down all the barriers standing in the way of their progress. Money comes to those who pursue it and believe they deserve it. With that headset, perhaps other stories will be told that will begin to reflect what happens to those people who are not white men under 50.

Wrap Up

Earning potential
✓ young white men make the money
✓ 30-year-old white men are the largest fraction of Guild membership and are the most likely to find employment
✓ older writers must have a true vision of their talents and their place in the business and use that information to focus their careers and keep current
✓ a good screenplay is the best ticket

Women and other minorities
✓ have no old boy network
✓ need to initiate their own projects
✓ need to raise their own money
✓ make less money for same work
✓ opportunities increase if you are entrepreneurial

3 Focus/Homework

Now that you know more about your earning potential, the next tasks are to do the homework that will enable you to present yourself as a professional and to become focused on the genre in which you intend to write.

- *The biggest problem with new people is that they are not prepared. People don't do their homework. I was speaking at a seminar at Northwestern. I was on the panel. I was in the information booklet, and people would raise their hands and go: How do you spell your name? What company are you with? Excuse me, they should know my favorite color. They should be nice to my assistant, he decides who I talk to.*
  Rima Greer
  Above the Line Agency/Los Angeles

- *If you see a screenplay and the names of the characters are justified to the left, you won't read the script because you think this person doesn't understand.*
  Howard Sanders
  United Talent Agency/Los Angeles

- *Know the market, know your craft. Live so you have something to write about. Learn the business, immerse yourself in it. I have a major deal happening for one of my writers. He told me, I don't want to see the deal. You just do it. I told him to learn the business. To learn what's in a contract. To learn what an agent is and how to interact with the agent. To learn what a producer is, a network executive. To take acting lessons. To take directing classes. To learn all the other sides.*

  To learn what's in a contract so that you know if you're in the ballpark, because you know, in this town, the game for the buyer is to get what he can for as little as he can. There's no respect in it. You just have to be a little wiser so that you can laugh and have a sense of humor so that you don't go home and start crying.

  You have to learn to face rejection head on. To learn how to take rejection positively. Learn the elements of the industry. Learn the personality of the producer.
  Bob Hohman
  Hohman Maybank Lieb/Los Angeles

- *A writer should put his best foot forward right off the bat and look like a professional even if it's his first time. He should not look to the agent to give feedback on whether or not the material is ready. Even if he is going to work with an agent or an editor, he shouldn't count on their participation. The material should be polished and professional when it's turned in.*

  Sheree Bykofsky
  Bykofsky Assoc. Inc./New York

- *You'd be surprised at how many writers turn in hand written material on torn up ragged sheets or letters with major typos and improper grammar. Although I know that writers have to move to writing in the style of human speech in dialogue, that's not the way you present yourself in an introductory letter. Show us you can spell, punctuate and present your material professionally.*

  H. Shep Pamplin
  Oppenheim-Christie/New York

- *Do your homework thoroughly in whatever field you are trying to penetrate. Before going to a publisher, make every effort to get an agent.* The Insiders Guide to Book Publishing Editors and Literary Agents *by Jeff Herman is a great resource.*

  Sheree Bykofsky
  Bykofsky Assoc. Inc./New York

- *People come in and write spec scripts and it's clear that they have never seen the show. This is not thinking. Format signifies you did your homework. In television, this means if you are going to write a* Murphy Brown *script, that you go to WGA and read* Murphy Brown *scripts. It all goes back to school,* Does neatness count? *The answer to that is,* Yes, neatness does count. *If there are a ton of typos, yes, of course it makes a difference. If you haven't done your homework, that makes it harder for us to take you seriously.*

  Anonymous Agent

- *A writer should do his or her homework before he comes to town with a script. Learn the industry format for scripts. Go to the library. Get samples. Font, length of script, even covers are important. Don't try to make the script look different. Don't try to reinvent the wheel because it only makes you look like a novice. The most experienced and professional writers work within a certain accepted format.*

  Barbara Alexander
  Media Artists Group/Los Angeles

- *Most TV movies are made for a predominately female audience, while the marketing of feature films is predominately male-directed.*

  Ken Raskoff/MOW Producer
  Ken Raskoff Productions/ABC Films

- *It's a great market for new writers now. There are no closed doors. It's better for women than it ever has been. Have a portfolio with one or two spec scripts, variety sketches, original sketches.*

  Don't vacillate between comedy and drama, decide what you want to write and go for it. Variety sketches are the hottest thing in town.

  Debbee Klein
  Paradigm/Los Angeles

- *People look for agents too soon. There's this myth that is fueled by the exceptions. 20 years ago, actors and directors were all caught up in the Sylvester Stallone/Rocky craze. Judging yourself by that criteria, you felt like a failure. There are always students right out of school that suddenly makes a big splash. 99% of writers don't get sold on their first script. I think people start to look for an agent before they have a body of work. The only way you get better at writing is to write. You have to hone your skills and be able to write.*

  Writers need to have two or three scripts with 12 rewrites on it before they show it to anyone. They need to have every friend that they know read the script until they think it's the very best they can do. They need to have three of those in each genre they're looking to move into. It's a very unusual situation where your first script gets picked up. Agents want depth. You send a script out, the agent likes the writing, you do a lot of work on it and they don't sell it. What else do you have? You've done all this leg-work for this person and that's the end.

  Jonathan Westover
  The Gage Group/Los Angeles

Focus Your Energy

Although you will want/need to have several different kinds of writing samples in your bag when you are ready to talk to agents, making a decision as to the particular niche of scriptwriting you want to call your own will enhance your chances.

- *I find it very difficult for those writers who walk in here with a drama sample and a comedy sample and they don't really know which way to go. You must*

decide which way you want to attack this career and go for it 150%.
    Rima Greer
    Above the Line Agency/Los Angeles

    Film choices include romantic comedies, action/adventure, drama, film noir, science fiction, slap-stick comedies, animated films, etc. Television offers situation comedies, daytime soaps, nighttime soaps, drama, reality, animation, interactive, game shows, news writing, etc. The Internet brims with categories that are still being formatted. Many agencies have entire departments dedicated to New Technology. Theatre runs the gamut from comedy, drama, musical comedies, revues, skits, variety revues, one-person shows to performance art.

    Not only does each genre have a particular formatting style, structure and length requirements, but there are more opportunities for new writers in some areas than others.

- *The best thing you can do is write something you truly believe in. If you spend your time trying to create what you think sells, you're dead in the water. In my case, it was only when I wrote something from the heart, something extremely personal, that people in the industry took notice. And then, lo and behold, they began to think of me for all sorts of things. They even took a second look at my old scripts they previously had thrown in the trash. You must write for yourself first.*
    Jonathan Tolins playwright/screenwriter
    Twilight of the Golds

    You might be interested in a few statistics generated by Casey Hoelscher, publisher of *Development Source*, a database used by studios, producers, agents and managers to track films in production. Out of 3839 films in development, 17.8% (685) are comedies, 14.5% (560) are dramas, 10% (385) are thrillers (with 81 of those being action thrillers), 9.7% (373) are classified as action), 2.2 % (85) are science-fiction, 1.5% (57) are family films, 1% (39) are horror films, 1.28% (46) are either westerns, animation or musicals and the other percentage lacked genre classification.

    At this point, you might just be saying, *I don't care. Just pay me to write and I will be happy.* But in order to get paid for writing, you must stake out your piece of the turf and research it mercilessly. Who are the people who are writing the kind of material that interests you? Who are their agents? How did they get started?

Watch credits carefully. Learn the names of those writers and producers who are working in your area of interest. Go to the Writers Guild and look at scripts. Study the format. Haunt the WGA webpage (http://www.wga.org). There is a lot of information there.

• *Writers should be very careful about the story they want to tell. They should really work on the story before they even put pen to paper. They should tell their story to people they respect and are close to and those they are not so close to and get the reaction. It's harder to ask a friend to read a 120 page script. It's not so hard to go to lunch with them and tell them a story. See if they are still awake by dessert.*

It's not necessarily true that a story is interesting because it's true. My mother went to the store and she broke her leg. *So what?*
Lynn Pleshette
Pleshette Millner Agency/Los Angeles

• *The best thing for a writer to do is to try to get somebody who knows somebody who knows somebody who knows somebody to read his work.*
Elliot Webb
Broder.Kurland.Webb.Uffner/Los Angeles

Have You Written a Million Words Yet?

You can only get better with practice. A writer friend of mine promises that once you have written a million words, you will sell your material.

• *Write and keep writing. I had one client who wrote about 8 scripts before he mastered screenwriting form. I could see the person was extremely talented. In the first script he wrote great characters and no plot, and the next script had an exciting plot and weak characters. Suddenly, it all came together. He ended up with an overall deal, including a corner office with a parking place downstairs, $100,000+ a year salary, and most importantly, the ear and the eye of all the executives at the studio.*
Ken Sherman
Ken Sherman Agency/Los Angeles

• *The inspiration for those who want to break in is to see how much second-rate material is around. That's a clue to the fact that there is room. The clue isn't,* Oh, I could be just as bad. *It should be an inspiration to say,* Oh, I could do better. *We have some writers who are wonderful and we have some writers who are mediocre. I don't think we should kid ourselves. The reason for that is that there are a lot of pedestrian writers and very few good ones. The best are writers who have been writing since they were young. They just write. Writers write — whatever it is, poetry, fiction, they just write and some of them have the talent and some of them just don't. People can learn the skills if the talent is there.*

> Lynn Pleshette
> Pleshette Millner Agency/Los Angeles

• *It's very important not to send your material to producers or studios until you have an agent. It is so important, I can't even tell you.*

> Rima Greer
> Above the Line Agency/Los Angeles

• *The life of the writer is rewrite. The first draft sent to us by a new writer, should be what they consider their third or fourth draft. We want to represent the writers who write because that is what they do.*

> Fredda Rose
> Monteiro Rose/Los Angeles

• *As soon as they finish the first script, they should start on their second one, as soon as they finish the second one, they should start on their third. They should write and write and write. What happens too often is that a writer turns in the script to the agent and then sits on his hands and waits for the agent to call and say,* Guess what? I sold your script for a million dollars. *It doesn't work that way.*

> Howard Sanders
> United Talent Agency/Los Angeles

• *I'd appreciate it if writers did not call cold. I won't take the calls if I know it is someone asking about representation. If they get to me anyway, I'm a nice guy so I'm not curt or rude. I'll chat with them and explain the situation to them. I'm nice that way, but it would be better if people would not call cold. The best thing is an inquiry letter and if I'm interested, I'll respond to them.*

> Stuart Jacobs
> CNA/Los Angeles

• *A lot of writers think they have to sell their script right now. Although that would be pleasant and we're all spending a million hours writing it and want to sell it right away in order to eat, actually, it's much better to make yourself a part of the*

community and it's also important for us to support each other.
Robin Moran Miller
New York

•   *I do all the reading myself which is much better than having an outside reader because you're actually getting the agent to read the stuff. The downside is that I have reading stacks that literally are a mile long. If the writer wants to follow up, he should take that into consideration and wait longer. I'm not going to get to it any sooner because of the phone call. When I read it, I will call you, if I am interested.*
Stu Jacobs
CNA/Los Angeles

Your task is to hone your craft to a particular niche in the marketplace. This does not mean that action/adventure is hot right now, so you decide this is going to be your specialty. It means isolating what it is that you are most suited to write. Once you have made that decision, then focus your material into that form and begin to do research in that area.

•   *Write, write, write. Until you have made it, don't try guessing what's trendy, write for quality whether for series television or feature films. If you are going to write series television, write spec scripts for the best shows. For feature films, try to write layered screenplays with fully dimensional characters, unusual stories, something that feels real. Real does not rule out science fiction, etc., just the reality of that.*
Jim Preminger
Jim Preminger Agency/Los Angeles

•   *Don't second guess the buyer. Write what you have to write, then it's the agent's job to find the right venue for it.*
Jonathan Westover
The Gage Group/Los Angeles

Scriptwriter/teacher Robin Moran Miller, who was a literary agent at DGRW in New York brings special insights to the subject:

•   *I always know that a writer is not very good when he/she doesn't want to tell me what his project is about because he thinks I'm going to steal the idea. Good writers know it's not the idea, it's their voice. No one can steal your voice. David Webb Peoples who wrote* Unforgiven *can say,* I'm writing this script about an old gunfighter who reformed because of his wife, and now she's dead and he's got to go back to gunslinging for the money to feed his kids. *That doesn't sound like much. It's how you tell the tale. So when a writer says,* I have this idea, but I don't want anyone to steal it, *I know from the get-go that he's not a real writer or he wouldn't even be worried about it.*

What you have to offer as a writer is your voice telling the story and the way you're going to tell the story. The way you're going to tell Romeo and Juliet *is different from the way Shakespeare told* Romeo and Juliet. *It's your way of telling whatever story you tell. That is what makes you special.*

Robin Moran Miller
New York

• *I cannot overemphasize the need for writers to figure out the business of the business and how to be perceived as someone with whom people want to work.*

Ken Raskoff/MOW Producer
Ken Raskoff Productions/ABC Films

In addition to choosing the area you want to write in, researching the marketplace will point you even more specifically toward those areas where you have the best chance of breaking into the system.

• *There are those parts of the business that offer greater opportunities for females. Cable TV has many more women in its ranks than traditional broadcast TV. Turner Broadcasting, for example has a 47% female workforce. It offers an array of family-friendly benefits and is currently building a child-care facility at its Atlanta headquarters.*

Gaining Ground
Kathleen O'Steen and Jennifer Pendleton
Emmy
October 1996

• *Daytime is a very specific and demanding medium. You've got to prove you can do it without having a nervous breakdown, and once you prove yourself, very few of these jobs open up. They tend to go back to the people who have proven themselves in the past, and those people tend to shift around from show to show.*

Black by Popular Demand
Alan Carter
Emmy
February 1997

•   *Writers get my attention by being good. You become good by understanding every part of the business. Take an acting class. Take a directing class. When you empathize with the actor and the director, the material reflects that.*

Debbee Klein
Paradigm/Los Angeles

•   *The best thing to do is to write. Too often, you get someone who wants to come in. Let's say they have a feature script and it's okay. Say we sign them and then we make the effort to get the script out to try and sell it, but also to use it as an introduction of this person to everybody around town.*

Then they come in, I've got an idea. I want to go pitch it. *Well, no, you need just to keep writing. You need to write and write and write and write. Realistically to sell a pitch, to sell a treatment, that comes with a track record. People do it, young writers sell treatments all the time, but to give yourself the best advantage in being able to show off your work in various areas, you have to hone your craft, you just have to keep writing.*

In feature films, that means spec scripts, in television, you keep writing samples (specs). As opposed to someone who has no track record and they say, I've written a great pilot. *Who cares? Let it be a great pilot. I don't care.*

In a lot of ways, it's easier to break into feature films. If you have a feature script and it's good, people will read it somewhere along the way. There is such a lack of great material. Logically you'd think there is so much more television production than feature film production that they would be the ones screaming for new material...not so. It's actually (from my perspective) harder to break a new person in television. It's much more of a closed club. Let's face it, they're all scared to death and to bring somebody in that they don't know, and they're thinking can we trust them? will they deliver? *It's ludicrous, but that's the case.*

Anonymous Agent

•   *If you want to write MOWs, start watching them. Form must be observed. I've always felt the worst films give the best advice because it's easier to articulate what didn't work than what did. Good art is seamless. Bad art is obvious.*

Ken Raskoff/MOW Producer
Ken Raskoff Productions/ABC Films

Read Read Read/Write Write Write

If your interest is situation comedy, begin to analyze every comedy on television. Watch the good and the bad. Tape them and watch them over and over. Why is *Seinfeld* appealing? Does it have more jokes? More interesting characters? Does the story unfold more quickly than on a show you don't like as well? Or does that even matter?

Scripts from *All in the Family, M*A*S*H, The Mary Tyler Moore Show* and other classic shows that defined the form are all available at the Writers Guild library and are a must for any student. Watch *I Love Lucy* reruns, compare them to *Seinfeld* and check out their similarities and differences.

• *Two friends of mine who are incredibly successful writers each probably have 3 or 4 scripts that have never seen the light of day. When they started out writing screenplays, the thought was never about selling them, it was about telling a very interesting story. No one has ever seen these scripts and no one ever will, because they are not very good, but they are rungs to a ladder.*

Richard Green
United Talent Agency/Los Angeles

• *Samuel French publishes screenplays. It's hard for me to believe that you can't get hold of screenplays someplace. Also, it's so easy to rent the films. But they should read for the form, for how writers have professionally solved problems.*

Lynn Pleshette
Pleshette Millner Agency/Los Angeles

Would be film writers should read *Casablanca* and *Chinatown* and other classic scripts. If you can't get copies of the scripts, tape from television or rent videos. Watch them once for entertainment value and then begin to *study* them. It's your job to figure out what's so appealing about them.

When encountering a really bad movie on television or in a theatre, don't turn it off or leave; keep watching and try to figure out how it could have been better. If you sit down and write a better scene, you've gained something from the experience.

Just because you have written one or two or even three scripts, doesn't necessarily mean that you are far enough along for an agent to be interested in reading your material. How many rewrites did you do? There are a couple of millionaires out there who managed to sell their very first script though probably not the very first draft, but they are extremely rare.

- *I think a writer's best bet is not to write a script and then immediately try to get an agent which is what most writers do. In New York, there are lots of ways of getting your work read or produced and the more you do that, the more likely an agent is going to want to look at your work.*
  Robin Moran Miller
  New York

A playwright frequently goes through a long, arduous process before he's written what will be the final draft.

- *Before a play is submitted to either agents or producers, agent Susan Schulman suggests that it probably should have been through some kind of workshopping or reading process — not for the public's benefit, but for the playwright's benefit — to hear how the actors respond to the language of the play, how long it is, and whether or not the individual voices of the characters are clear and the way that the author intends them to be. Since it's an oral tradition, I don't see how one could possibly write without hearing it.*
  Literary Agents
  Ben Alexander
  BackStage
  October 2, 1992

Although readings are an accepted procedure, there is disagreement among playwrights as to their effectiveness. Some feel the process is the only way to get a play auditioned while others believe that an endless amount of readings can be disheartening and destructive. And it's not just the playwrights who think readings are questionable.

- *Some plays do not read well and others only read well. When I ran the Back Alley Theatre and we had a play we were not sure of and staged a reading, we never ended up producing that play. If we liked a play, we produced it. Readings only point up the flaws in material.*
  Laura Zucker
  Executive Director, Los Angeles Arts Council

Playwrights

The most fruitful avenue for a playwright involves forming his own relationship with a theatre where his material is staged on a regular basis. It's advantageous for the playwright and for the theatre.

Bruce Graham is a successful screenwriter who has managed to forge a relationship with a theatre where his plays are staged annually. He had a three picture deal at Universal and was offered a staff position on the number one show on television while continuing to live in Bucks County, New York.

New York City is still thought of as the place for a playwright to ply his trade, but Los Angeles is beginning to draw its share of writers for the theatre, although as this article points out, the possibilities of living on royalties (if you are fortunate enough to get any) seem pretty slim:

• *Despite the fact that Los Angeles is home to a growing number of playwrights — some guess upwards of 2,000 — few actually get to see their work on stage, and fewer still make any money at their chosen craft... The Dramatists Guild alone has 1,200 members here, and there are more than 40 organized playwright groups in Los Angeles.*

...The average playwright royalty on the Taper [The Mark Taper Forum] mainstage for a six to eight week run may range from $35,000 to $50,000, but the average royalty for the same number of weeks at a 99-seat theatre is $600-$800.

...A commission at the La Jolla Playhouse is $5,000 and generally goes to an established writer. A 99-seat theatre might pay $100 for a reading or $500 for a workshop and some even ask for money from the playwrights themselves.

To Live and Write in L.A.
Barbara Isenberg
The Los Angeles Times/Calendar Section
February 14, 1993

Adding People to Your Team

It's also mutually beneficial to cultivate relationships with free lance producers who are interested in helping develop new material. As you begin to accumulate a body of work (even if only in your portfolio) that is being read by various folk in the business, *one* of those various folk will read it and take an interest.

The process will then begin to include not just you alone with your word processor, but an interested second party who is either ready to buy or willing to advance money to encourage the developmental process.

It's easier to get agents, producers, would-bes, will-bes, and anyone else walking by, to read your movie or television feature than any other area of the business. In the past, that meant preparing a treatment for submission; today, however, fewer and fewer deals are being made from treatments except for those writers with extensive backgrounds. In a precarious economy, the buyers want to know exactly what they are getting.

Although the doors are harder to penetrate, agents say television comedy is where the real money is. Since nearly twice as many writers are employed in television as in feature film (and because the money can be staggering), the snob line between film and television writers is becoming less and less distinct.

Films for television run the gamut from disease of the week to star vehicle to thoughtful treatments of subjects that the big screen (usually for economic reasons) is too timid to deal with. The quality is as varied as the subject matter, and as more prestigious film writers are writing for cable and even for the networks, the standards are becoming higher (along with the stakes).

Spec Scripts

Isabel Nagy Storey worked in local news and reality based TV shows, but had never written until she had a maternity leave in 1991. She sent her spec script to producers and agents and within four days got a call from CAA:

• People often hawk stories about real-life events but few get nods from agents and producers, *said Dick Berg, a producer at Viacom Pictures, the company to which Storey sold her script.* But he said Storey stood out because she took the uncommon step of not just pitching an idea but also writing a script about it.

What she's done is extraordinary, *he said.* She put up her own money, she researched it and to cap it off she wrote a script with style. She spent 22 months and $2,000 on developing and marketing the work.

Writer's First Script Draws a Speedy Response
Walter Hamilton
The Green Sheet
February 8, 1993

Since Ms. Storey was already in the system, she was not only connected at some point, but had an overview of how things work. Her ability to write a first-rate script was enhanced by her willingness and entrepreneurial ability to research and develop. When buyers see that level of executive ability, they want to be in business with that person.

- *The samples for television have to be great. They almost have to be better than the shows themselves.*

    Jonathan Westover
    The Gage Group/Los Angeles

- *The core of a successful TV series remains the ability to bring viewers back week after week, and more than anything else that relies on characters. Even TV's best series don't turn out gems for all 22 or 26 episodes.*

    TV characters must bond with the audience in order to succeed, either positively or negatively, while film characters need only to intrigue or visually dazzle them for the two hours they're on screen.

    Character's the Thing That'll Catch the TV Viewers
    Brian Lowry
    Daily Variety
    June 24, 1992

The name of the game in situation comedies and one hour dramatic shows is being able to write excellent spec scripts for existing television shows. There's a difference of opinion about what show to choose as a specimen. The majority of agents tell me that the best shows to write for are those that, whether or not they are garnering big numbers, have the respect of the industry — *Chicago Hope, NYPD Blue, The X-Files, ER, Friends, Seinfeld,* etc., but there are other points of view:

- *Write the spec script. And don't write for the season's hot show, they already have brilliant scripts. Write a brilliant script for a show that's not brilliant. Think how happy they would be to see a brilliant script.*

    Elliot Stahler
    Kaplan-Stahler Agency/Los Angeles

If you write spec scripts for deceased shows, this makes people think you are not tuned into what's happening. They are right. It is necessary to have numerous excellent current scripts to showcase your ability.

One last item about focus comes from an article about Brandon Tartikoff that shows how he learned to put his career in focus.

• *There's nothing like cancer to get you focused on what's important, the first time around, I just felt that I had this bad card dealt to me. I was in my mid-20's, tremendously cocky, and what the illness did was bring a humility to the situation. I'm not saying that I'm a poster boy for humility right now, but it changed me. With no bad card dealt, I might have become a reasonably successful local television manager. I had 18 balls in the air — acting at the Second City Workshop in Chicago, writing plays and writing free lance articles for* New Times *magazine.*

Afterward I just focused. You know you're sick, and you've got to do this and that to try to get the result you want, and you put on blinders and plunge right ahead. I definitely bought into the concept that the cancer was curable and to look ahead this year and next year.

Tartikoff Examines
Bernard Weintraub
The New York Times
October 13, 1992

Tartikoff's words made a big impression on me. Although it is advantageous to learn all aspects of the business in order to augment our specialties, having too many balls in the air may prevent our dreams from coming true. Tartikoff pointed to a truth that none of us wants to know: you really cannot have everything. Nobody has it all. It's like going into a room with the most fabulous food in the world. You can put it all on your plate, if you want, but you can't possibly consume it all without becoming sick.

Wrap Up

Define your goals
✓ write from the heart
✓ determine your values
✓ pick your genre and stick to it
✓ write to form - neatness counts
✓ study the classics
✓ have lots of material
✓ know the marketplace

✓ keep writing
✓ keep networking
✓ you really can't have everything so focus

4 Does It Matter Where You Live?

Can you be a viable client without moving to New York, Chicago or Los Angeles? When I asked agents the first thing a writer should do when he got off the bus, I wasn't surprised when a couple laughed and said, *Get back on.* They were joking, but there's always truth behind a joke.

Since what you are selling is primarily you and your way of looking at life, it just might be a more valuable look if it's not tainted with a show biz point of view and is still pure with the Cleveland, San Antonio or Ft. Collins air.

• *I think they should not get off the bus before they figure out what they want to do when they get here. You don't have to be in Los Angeles to be a writer. Maybe you need to stay at home and write. Everybody is looking for a new novel because it is an original voice. Writers from out of town are original voices because they are not reactive to the movie business. Sometimes novelists do not become screenwriters because it's a whole different skill. One reason buyers want novels is that they are people's experiences that are not from this particular place.*
    Lynn Pleshette
    Pleshette Millner Agency/Los Angeles

Even if you want to write for television, there is no reason to leave a protected environment until your writing has reached a marketable level. You can be writing *Larry Sanders, Friends* and *X-Files* spec scripts in Iowa with the same zest and much less overhead. Rejection won't be so expensive, you'll have an emotional support group for comfort and you'll be bringing a fresher outlook to the proceedings.

Even if there seems to be nothing in your own environment comparable to the bright lights, those bright lights are not going anywhere and they are a lot more attractive when you have the money to pay for your own electricity.

You can write from jail, a convent, or a cruise ship. You can write from any place. If you want to be a scriptwriter, it is not necessary to incur both the financial and emotional expense of moving to a totally new environment to experience rejection; you can do it at home.

Criminal defense attorney John Grisham (who wrote *The*

Runaway Jury, The Client and *A Time to Kill*) lives in Oxford, Mississippi, coaches Little League, never studied writing and wrote his books in longhand on yellow legal paper:

Grisham's agent Jay Garon (Jay Garon-Brook Associates) is the man writers dream of. He actually responded to a blind manuscript that arrived at his office.

David Webb Peoples, Academy Award nominee for *Unforgiven*, is another successful scriptwriter who never moved to Los Angeles. He has lived in northern California since he graduated from Berkeley in 1962. Working as a news and documentary film editor, he struggled for years to sell screenplays. His big break came in the late 1970s when his writing partner read one of his scripts and handed it over to his brother (Ridley Scott), who asked Mr. Peoples to help write *Blade Runner*.

Peoples' agent Martin Shapiro has been his representative since 1982 when another client introduced them. Shapiro has several clients who do not live in Los Angeles.

• *With faxes and modems and airplanes, a writer can live anywhere. It helps if the agent is Los Angeles based, but it's not mandatory.*
Ken Raskoff/MOW Producer
Ken Raskoff Productions/ABC Films

As mentioned earlier, Bruce Graham manages to be successful in both theatre and film. Even so, he says that it was a lot harder to make things happen from where he lives and he had to turn down television offers which would necessitate his relocation to Los Angeles.

It was difficult to turn down the money possibilities from television, but Bruce said that his most important consideration is living with his wife and children on the same street on which he grew up.

It took him a long time to get to a place where he could give up his day job teaching college and make a full time living as a writer, but he says that it can be done and he is happy with his decision.

Some agents say it's not only easier to be in town, but they require it:

• *Although it is possible to have a career from out of town, it's difficult. I won't represent anyone from out of town. I did it once and I won't do it again, unless they are a very major player. I represent New York people. You can get them meetings in New York and they can fly out here for specific things. It's a lot tougher when they are sitting in Timbuktu. So much of what our writers do to get work and to jump-start a career is not just me sending their work out, but them following up with meetings.*

What often happens is that a producer will call me up and say, That was a great piece of writing. What a wonderful writer, does he have any ideas to pitch? We can't do that story, it's too close to something else, but this is a writer that I really must be in business with. *So they go in and they have a meeting for two hours and maybe they end up developing a project together.*

Then, again, it's possible that they can go in and have a meeting and hit it off and they don't have anything, but two months later, the producer will call me up and say, you know that writer that we were talking about? I have a project that's right for them. *If that meeting had never happened, I would have never gotten that phone call. So by a writer being in Timbuktu, you can't make that happen.*

If someone wants to be a staff writer on a show and they are in Timbuktu, you can't get them a meeting with a producer or with the network. They need to be in town. It needs to be on the page, but relationships count, too. A producer is not going to hire someone as a staff writer unless they think they are going to work well with them, they're going to be an asset to the team and it's going to be a pleasurable experience.

Stuart Jacobs
CNA/Los Angeles

Lifestyle

If you do leave your roots for the big city, one of the most comforting things you can do for yourself is put together a cozy light place to live and make it your own. Spend money on a coat of paint, if it needs it: you need a place of shelter from the storms. Living a free lance life, as most artists do, requires that you build into your life a routine, a support group, financial security, decent food and an atmosphere that nurtures you.

If you intend to write every day from 9 to 3, do it, but also, be sure to go to the gym or walk from 7:30 to 8:30 or participate in some other activity that includes both exercise *and* regular contact with people. If your writing habits dictate that you write before all else fine, just don't skip the all else.

Fight the temptation to eat junk food. It is more convenient, but your mind and body both pay for it later. If all you have in the house is carrots and celery, that's what you'll eat. At least make it harder on yourself to get candy and Fritos by not keeping any on hand.

If you don't have a nest egg to tide you over for a while, get some kind of job, preferably in the industry. Even if you do have enough money to survive for a while, a job puts you in the company of other people, gives form to your life and enables you to keep your forward motion (or lack of it) in perspective.

Success is reached over time. Great success begins with a series of little successes starting with getting situated in town and being financially secure. That doesn't mean you have to be rich, but you do have to have a job.

If you are in an impossible relationship or if you have any kind of addiction problem, the business is only going to intensify things. Deal with these things first. Show business takes even balanced people and chews them up and spits them out for breakfast unless they remain extremely focused and provide another life for themselves. Even if you are balanced, tenacious, driven and talented, take time to get your bearings before you attack the marketplace and vice versa.

Friends

Life is easier with friends. Begin to build relationships with your peers. Some people say to build friendships with people who already have what you want. Although I understand the thinking, it's not my idea of a good time. It's easier to live on a shoestring and/or deal with constant rejection if your friends are doing the same thing. If your friend is already on staff on *The X Files* or already has her feature optioned and has plenty of money while you are scrambling to pay the rent, it is going to be harder to keep perspective about where you are in the process.

It takes different people differing amounts of time to make the journey. Having friends who understand that will make it easier for all of you. Whatever else you do, commit to being positive. It's one of the most important things you can do for yourself.

Actress-writer Ruth Gordon had great perspective,

• *Life is getting through the moment. The philosopher William James says to cultivate the cheerful attitude. Now nobody had more trouble than he did — except me. I had more trouble in my life than anybody. But your first big trouble can be a bonanza if you live through it. Get through the first trouble, you'll probably make it through the next one.*

The Careerist Guide to Survival
Paul Rosenfield
The Los Angeles Times
April 25, 1982

You create your life by the choices you make in how to spend your time. You can be happy or depressed. There is no value judgment. If you choose to spend your time being depressed, which takes more energy, that's your business. It is beneficial to note that this is *your* choice. If you don't get something out of being depressed, you will take some action to change that state.

If you are already a member of the Writers Guild, check for support groups and/or become involved with one of their committees to help someone else. This will engage you in a productive activity with your peers on a regular basis.

Writers can besiege the marketplace from home and never leave. Of course, if one of the reasons you are writing is that you want to leave home and move to the land of palm trees or subways, then it may be time to buy your plane ticket.

Wrap Up

Reasons to stay home
✓ protected environment
✓ cheaper to live
✓ emotional support group in place
✓ may end up with better material

Home away from home
✓ get a place to live with good light
✓ cultivate a routine
✓ get a job in the business
✓ exercise and eat well
✓ see people every day
✓ get involved in a support group

5 Ways Into the System

If you've decided you can make money, you know what you want to write, you've written some spec scripts and you've decided that you and/or your material are moving to the big city, you will now have to be more than an ingenious writer to get someone to read your material. Other than saving Stephen Spielberg from getting run over by a bus or being related to someone in the business, getting agents and/or producers to read your material will tax your creative ability to the max.

Although this part of the process is extremely frustrating, if you can bear to look at it from the agents' perspective, you'll be more understanding and appreciative once you have made it into the exclusive club of represented writers, knowing your agent's attention is on you and not on searching for your replacement.

• *I've been in Los Angeles seven years, and in that time have been more or less consistently repped by four separate agents — none of whom has ever gotten me a scrap, not even the teensiest, grottiest little speck of work. I know an agent at Gersh (not one of my agents), a great guy and a real straight shooter, who summed things up pretty niffity when we spoke last year.*

To paraphrase, he said You know, I'd be just the right agent for you. But I'm not gonna represent you. Know why? 'Cause right now, I've got a bunch of guys earning seven figures. Now, if I bring you aboard, I'd have to work four times as hard to get you noticed, which would take time away from my guys making ten times more money. Now is that fair?

Can a Screenwriter Achieve Success & Happiness Without an Agent?
Jim Cirile
Written by...
April 1997

And unfortunately, the agent is right. The good news is that this is just the guy you want representing you, once you get in the system. The bad news is that you are just going to have to represent yourself a little longer until you get to that place.

- *Writers shouldn't get angry with agents because they won't read their material. Busy agents already have a full time job keeping their present clients serviced.*

    Daniel Ostroff
    The Daniel Ostroff Agency/Los Angeles

Though your writing may be the best thing since *Casablanca, Death of a Salesman* or *The Mary Tyler Moore Show*, if you can't get anyone to read it, no one will ever know.

The trick to getting your material into the hands of a buyer is to put yourself in a position to pass your material on to someone in the business who counts. You've arrived in Los Angeles from Podunk and don't know anyone who counts? There are still ways.

- *Be as aggressive as humanly possible. Don't waste your breath giving your whole pitch over the phone. If it's an office you really want to be with, go after everyone there until it's read. Find out each agent's name. Find out the assistant's name. Call him up. Send him a script. The eager assistant may try to sell the script.*

    Raphael Berko
    Media Artist Group/Los Angeles

- *Part of getting into the system is being out there all the time. The single most important factor may be the persistence factor. I believe in trying to meet as many people as possible.*

    Miriam Stern
    Miriam Stern, Esquire/New York

David Mills is an Emmy nominated writer because he was in the right place at the right time and spoke up:

- *Mills was on the staff of* Picket Fences *when he read a news account of a 1994 conference attended by* NYPD Blue *exec producer David Milch. Milch was quoted as saying that he doubted blacks could write successfully for TV, adding that many were mediocre. Over breakfast, Mills took Milch to task and was offered a script assignment and later a job.*

    Black by Popular Demand
    Alan Carter
    Emmy
    February 1997

I hear all of you saying, *No fair. He's already in the system.* That's true, but the kind of thinking and activism displayed by his interaction with Milch is the kind of behavior that contributed to his being in the system in the first place.

Industry Jobs

The most successful method of entry is to get *any* kind of job at any studio. Many studios have temp pools of over qualified people to call when an employee calls in sick. Your assignment could be anything from picking up an actor at the airport and delivering him to the set, to working in the mailroom, being a production assistant or driving a producer to appointments. I know of several people who worked as drivers who managed to pass their material on to staff writers who became their advocates.

There are temp agencies that specialize in providing workers for networks and studios, although Movie of the Week producer, Ken Raskoff, who entered the business through temp work as a secretary, said he got more access to creative people via a regular temp agency.

Although there is more opportunity for show biz related jobs in Los Angeles, there are jobs in New York as well. You can end up working at WMA, ICM, Paradigm, CAA or any of the big agencies, production companies or networks.

You don't get to choose where you are going to work if you go through an employment agency, of course, but any destination will be illuminating.

Check the temp ads in the trades or call a studio yourself and ask if there is an in-house temporary employment pool. Many temp jobs work into regular employment if you strike the fancy of your employers and are clearly motivated. In that case, not only do you have a chance to pass your material around, but you will begin to meet other writers who are already in place, as well as producers, directors, and actors, the very people you want to be doing business with.

When I was working on *Lois & Clark* which we filmed at Warner Bros., every single person working in the production office was a writer: every secretary and every assistant. These people were not only in a position to get read, but they had a first hand view of how the business really works.

I don't want to imply that getting a show biz job is a piece of cake, but if you apply yourself, you can do it. No matter what city you live in, there is some kind of show biz community of work. Check out your local opportunities.

• *Betsy Borns, a former writer-producer on* Friends, *started her Hollywood career in the network executive ranks at Fox Broadcasting, but she soon recognized the quickest avenue to success was not the corporate maze.* I looked at women like Diane English and Linda Bloodworth Thomason and realized the real creativity and power was in writing. These women were actually getting to do shows. So I wrote a spec script.

    Gaining Ground
    Kathleen O'Steen and Jennifer Pendleton
    Emmy
    October 1996

    Pam Veasey, the head writer/coproducer of *In Living Color*, got her start by working as a receptionist for the Nell Carter show, *Gimme a Break*.

• *Veasey wrote a script for another half-hour show and submitted it to the* Break *producers* — just so they could tell me if I was even close. *She was close. They fired her as a receptionist and hired her as a writer, and she went on to write for* Break, What's Happening Now! *and* The Robert Guillaume Show *before linking up with Keenan Ivory Wayans on an earlier CBS pilot that didn't pan out. She later submitted sketches for* In Living Color.
    I camped out in Keenan's office for thirty minutes without an appointment so I could say, Please hire me or let me submit some other work, *laughs Veasey. He said,* I've already hired my staff this year. *I went,* Great, *and came back again and said,* Here are some more sketches. *And ultimately, I got hired.*

    Below-the-line
    Rip Rense
    Emmy
    October 1992

Producers

Producers are easier to contact than agents because producers can't make a living if they don't have scripts to produce. Even though the producer may have 200 projects in development, he can always use one more. Connected show biz lawyers have entree and also pick up the phone more easily. If you paid agents every time you queried them, they'd probably be happy to take your calls, too. So, if you have money, a lawyer might be your answer. Just make sure he really is in the system. Many charge just to read your material. That always makes me suspicious. Do some research. Define their avenues of access.

• *Frequently people who are not recognized as bona fide production entities make their way into the business through attaching themselves to production companies, by pitching their ideas to producers who will make a deal to allow the production company to own the film if it gets made. Many producers look for ideas this way.*
> Ken Raskoff/MOW Producer
> Ken Raskoff Productions/ABC Films

Many producers are actively looking for material:

• *Arthur Chang, the 32-year-old Taiwanese multimillionaire who founded Kingman Films, wants to provide a platform for Hollywood aspirants who lack experience or connections, or have unconventional ideas. *Each Thursday afternoon, in a scene lifted from Frank Capra's* Mr. Deeds Goes to Town, *the Kingman office in Glendale is open by appointment to anyone who wants to come and propose a film, which Chang will seriously consider producing. In a similar Cinderella scheme, Chang has already given away $1.5 million to the winners of a screenwriting competition that he sponsors.*
> *Wild Pitches*
> Jaime Wolf
> *The Los Angeles Times Magazine*
> January 12 , 1997

*Contact information for Kingman Films is on page 47.

• *A lot of my friends who are screenwriters got their foot in the door through a specific director that they may have met at some school or along the line, who has liked a script of theirs. When the director got development money, he said* I want to do this script.
> Robin Moran Miller
> New York

Many people try to rewrite the rules with varying results. Zak Penn and Adam Leff dug their own tunnel into ICM by creating a buzz about their work using low level studio or agency employees they knew who also knew the agent in question. Each friend called (supposedly unbidden) to recommend the script. By the time the agent learned the truth, he had already signed the writers and the script was hot.

Retitled and rewritten by several other screenwriters and without screenwriting credit, Penn and Leff did get to take home $500,000 and a less prestigious writing credit (story by) for their idea for the Arnold Schwarzenegger film, *The Last Action Hero,* but there were disappointments along the way and the two no longer write together.

Outrageous in their approach, Penn and Leff researched the action genre, committed themselves totally to the outcome and moved ahead in the business very quickly. It's possible that they moved too fast.

If you are not far enough along in your development that your career has its own momentum, this might be a sign for you to take it easy, otherwise you may not be ready to capitalize on your notoriety.

In the past few years, I've begun to notice the creative energy that some writers expend getting noticed. Mostly, I feel that same energy would have been better served by working on their material.

One of the joys/pitfalls of beginners is that they rarely have developed the insight to know whether the work is their best effort, so enlist the help of a mentor whose taste you trust, who will read your material and keep you honestly apprized as to how far along you are. When you have a prospective buyer's attention, you want to have a worthy product to show them. Remember, you are only new once.

A good example of a writer who had something to show is Jonathan Tolins. I met Jon when he stage managed a play at The Matrix Theatre in Los Angeles. A year later, he produced his own first play. His second play, *Twilight of the Golds* played at The Kennedy Center and Broadway before becoming a successful television movie starring Gary Marshall and Faye Dunaway. Just four years out of college and Tolins was on Broadway, his name in the trades with deals for screenplays with important buyers. Here's a guy who was not only talented, motivated and focused, but very, very smart.

Tolins graduated from Harvard in 1988 with an impressive theatrical university resume. A triple threat, Jon had acted, directed and won a major literary award. When he got to Los Angeles, he got a job writing questions for a game show. He says he wrote *Twilight* while temping at studios. When we were working at The Matrix, he showed me one of his plays.

Within a year, he wrote, starred in and produced a two person play that ran for months in a small theatre in Hollywood. Although he had offers from several theatres in Los Angeles to produce *Twilight,* he passed on them, spending $500 of his own money to stage a reading of the play in order to interest and secure the more prestigious theatre that he wanted.

Jon managed to do all the things the agents tell you to do: write all the time, be visible and work in the industry.

Oh, and be talented.

Another avenue that provides entree plus an important overview and some visibility in the business is getting work as a reader.

- *A job as a reader is a good way to get into the system. The club is a big club. You can get in any which way.*

    Elliot Webb
    Broder•Kurland•Webb•Uffner/Los Angeles

Readers

Because the number of scripts submitted to agents, producers, and others who routinely traffic in the written word exceeds their available reading time, readers are employed who read scripts and make recommendations about the project's viability. Sometimes called story analysts, these folks decide whether the material will move up the food chain to the ultimate buyer.

Although being a reader en route to being a writer sounds like a good idea, when I called the readers union (called Screenstory Analysts), the woman I spoke to said, *if you want to write, then write.* She said becoming a reader on the Industry Experienced Roster is such a hard thing to do and there are so many union members already in place, that your energy would be better served using it to write.

Union readers are paid a range of prices from the low end ($750 weekly) to *whatever you can negotiate.* Some people get jobs from producers who are not signatory to the union and are paid by the script. $50 per script is the going rate for someone with no experience. Depending upon one's reading and comprehension skills, it can take about two hours to digest one script.

Being able to digest, discern and be articulate about your conclusions can give you enormous entree — depending upon your employers — since your name is the first thing the producer sees when perusing the script.

• *If you're well read and willing to work at a job that is unforgiving sometimes in its boredom because you are reading so much junk, being a reader is an invaluable way to get to understand the business better than most people. You will hone up on your writing and reading skills (you will actually get to use your education if you have one to use) and you will get the attention of people in the business. If you can put your thoughts down on paper coherently, you will learn what people are looking for, what is good and what is bad, and you will learn to write your thoughts in a concise and educated form. These papers are not only read by your superiors, they are passed around and your name is the first thing these people see.*

Sidney Iwanter
Director Children's Programs
Fox Children's Network

Script Analysts/Script Consultants

Script analysts (sometimes called script consultants) are those people hired by writers to evaluate and sometimes improve their material. There are two points of view about script analysts: theirs and everybody else's.

The WGA looks unfavorably on those who charge scriptwriters to read their material. So does every professional scriptwriter I queried. All seem to feel charging to read is exploitation.

Analysts counter that if you can get a professional eye to read your material and critique it in a professional manner, you will revise your script appropriately and have a better shot at success.

The sticking point is that if you couldn't get anyone to read your material before, why would it be easier to get this unseen supposedly better script read now. It may have been great before, but you just didn't have entree.

• *There are people who are experts in the field who are screenwriters and teachers who do a combination career counseling and reading. If you find someone who*

has been really recommended and is going to work with you on the script and you are
totally new to this business, then it can be a good idea, but check their references.

Barbara Alexander
Media Artists Group/Los Angeles

A good example of what Barbara is talking about is Dave
Trottier. A produced screenwriter/script consultant, Dave conducts
seminars and practical workshops in many writing areas. Dave teaches
across the land and through correspondence.

Two of the last three winners in the prestigious Nicholl
Fellowship Contest run by the Academy of Motion Picture Arts and
Sciences were students or clients. He has his own webpage and an E-
mail address, so if you are wired, he's pretty easy to contact. His book is
available at bookstores everywhere or from:

Dave Trottier
Box 520248
Salt Lake City, UT 84152-0248
Website: http://www.clearstream.com
E-mail: dave@clearstream.com
The Screenwriter's Bible
($18.95 + $3.50 shipping/handling)

Donie Nelson is a another effective script consultant. A
credentialed professional, Donie has worked with film companies and
independent production companies for feature film and television in the
creative developmental area. A problem solver by nature, Donie's background brings practical career guidance as well as insights into the
creative process for both novice and established writers and producers.

Donie's charges less than a script analyst ($300 for a first read
with reduced rates for subsequent readings of the same material). The
fee includes a read plus a two hour career and/or script conference.
Donie charges $75 an hour for career consultation.

Donie Nelson
10736 Jefferson Blvd. #508
Culver City, CA 90230-4969
310-204-6808/ fax 310-202-1151
E-mail: Wrtrconsult@earthlink.net

Natalie Lemberg has an intriguing business called The Insiders System for writers. Natalie is a professional story analyst who has also worked in personal management. She has experience in writing, evaluating, buying, selling and editing materials for film, television, theatre and publishing.

Natalie has taught in connection with The UCLA Writers Program, The Learning Annex and The American Film Institute. Her business offers a careful review of manuscripts and 6-10 pages of coverage for $175. She also publishes a quarterly magazine, *Writers Showcase* that previews 40-60 new screenplays, novels, non-fiction manuscripts or proposals, children's books, short stories, essays and poetry. The magazine is distributed to 250 agents, producers and publishers. Clients pay $175 to be in the magazine.

Natalie says up to 80% of showcased writers (via proposals in the magazine) have had their manuscripts requested. I saw a copy of the magazine and it's pretty impressive.

Natalie says 55 of her writers have gotten representation as a result of being involved with The Insiders System. That's about 13% of the people who have come to her.

The Insiders System for Writers
Natalie Lemberg
8306 Wilshire Blvd. #7041
Beverly Hills, CA 90211
800-397-2615
E-mail: Insiderssystem@msn.com

As you read the agents' quotes throughout this book, you'll notice a recurring theme: keep writing. Do good work. Somebody who knows somebody who knows somebody will read it — for free. You will be found. Everyone is searching for a good script. Whether you are a playwright or a screenwriter, you must be persistent and creative in your thinking:

• *If you have one reading and send a postcard, people aren't going to come, but if you get two or three and keep informing agents, after enough time, the agent says,* Gee, this guy is getting done a lot, he must be good *and they go.*
Robin Moran Miller
New York

- *It's very important to be out there, be friendly with new theatre companies. If you have a group of actors that you respect and work with and write for, that does help. Everyone in New York goes to showcases.*

   Do presentations and readings. Associate yourself with a group of talented actors. Besides getting to know those people and having those associations, you get to see your work on the stage instead of just on the written page.

   Charles Kerin
   Kerin-Goldberg Associates/New York

- *As a writer, you never know where offers are going to come from. The more out there you are, the better the possibilities. You can't just sit there in your room writing, you need to go to things.*

   Robin Moran Miller
   New York

- *There are many ways to market yourself: teaching, writing, going to industry functions, seminars, wherever the industry you are in congregates.*

   Miriam Stern
   Miriam Stern, Esquire/New York

- *It's your job to get that screenplay on the desk and get it read. Try to get an internship or get a job somewhere in the industry. You've got to know someone to get it on the agent's desk unless you want to wait a year, and maybe not even then. Referrals do help. Get into a writing block. Anything. If you get a job in production as an assistant, there are professionals around that you can show the script to. Of course, you always risk getting ripped off, but referrals help.*

   Anonymous Agent

- *If you write for film, go to film festivals and it's not to go around going,* Here's my script, *but going around saying,* Hi, how are you doin'? I really liked your film. *And then chatting about the film and that's it. Meet people so that a little later on you can say,* Oh, I met so-and-so. He might be interested in that.

   Robin Moran Miller
   New York

- *Writers who want to get an agent should identify agents who are young and just starting their careers. Most of my clients and I grew up together in the business.*

   Daniel Ostroff
   The Daniel Ostroff Agency/Los Angeles

- *Find out everything you can about the agent. Write him a letter. Call him by name. Demonstrate that you know who he is. Agents have big egos. I throw away everything that says* Dear Agent. *Tell him you have been following his career. We're all susceptible to flattery.*

  Raphael Berko
  Media Artist Group/Los Angeles

- *I just sold a script last week. My literary department had turned it down, but the writer got the script to me and I fell in love with it. That's why I was able to sell it. It's all subjective.*

  Anonymous Agent

- *Be persistent without being obnoxious. If someone gives you any encouragement to see your second script, don't forget, follow up. Let them know when it's going to be ready and remind them in your cover letter that they asked to see it.*

  Barbara Alexander
  Media Artists Group/Los Angeles

- *Even before you get to Los Angeles, you should investigate the film schools (AFI, USC, UCLA) and the colleges that have communications departments. Besides the craft-skills to be gained from their programs, internships are invaluable. The best interns I've worked with have been from the communications department with film emphasis from Cal State Fullerton. The smart ones are the ones who say,* I want to be a screenwriter and I hope you'll read my material along the way, but in the meantime, I want to learn everything I can about the business. I just want to learn.

  I always say, if you want to work here, it's better than working in a smaller or medium size production company or studio job where you'll end up filing all day and you'll have little or no contact with other interns, writers, producers, etc.

  I let interns sit in on meetings, read contracts, go through appropriate files and read my clients' work. Anyone wanting to get into the business should take a job, any job, to get in the proverbial door, so that they're not imagining what people do who are writers in the business, but are seeing what they do, first hand, and that it's hard, serious work.

  If you just arrive in town, take an extension course at UCLA or USC. They have major writers, producers and directors in the film and television industries teaching classes, major writers. I've taught at UCLA and at USC, both through extension or respective masters-of-professional-writing department. At least that way, a student can get into the mix. I found one client in one of my classes although I said

I wouldn't read students' material.

> Ken Sherman
> Ken Sherman and Associates/Los Angeles

•   *There are a lot of classes in New York for playwrights. A good portion of them aren't geared to how you learn to write plays, they are for practicing playwrights to meet with their peers. You meet once a week and everyone brings in material. You discuss it and you have a group of intelligent people whose opinions you trust, but also you don't worry about showing them something that might not be as perfect as it should be.*

> Robin Moran Miller
> New York

Another way into a connected environment is to get into an acting or directing class either as a participant or an auditor. As you join in the collaborative experience that produces theatre, film and or television, experiencing the problems of actors and directors, your writing will unconsciously reflect the information and begin to solve those problems.

•   *Go to a lot of theatre, meet a lot of people and when you meet a director whose work you really like, contact the director personally, because directors are always looking for material.*

> Robin Moran Miller
> New York

Contests

Screenwriting and playwrighting contests are another avenue of possibility for scriptwriters seeking to get attention. Whether or not you manage to grab some of the $2.9 million dollars offered in prize money in 1997, if you win, place or show, you'll not only have a credit to add to your resume for agents and producers, but show biz insiders are frequently tapped to judge some of the more prestigious contests like the Nicholl Fellowships sponsored by the Academy of Motion Picture Arts and Sciences.

I interviewed screenwriter, Aileen Murphy who also publishes a resource book about scriptwriting contests and grants.

• *You have better odds of success in contests than through the labyrinthian channels of Hollywood because many contests publicize their winners, giving you public recognition. Your confidence is enhanced through winning and you may even pocket some money. In 1997, there are over fifty contests. Some are big and prestigious, some are small and don't offer much and some are in between. But there are plenty to choose from. Many have special categories of scripts they are looking for. Some smaller, more specialized contests could be a good match for your background, talents and screenplay.*

The downside of contests is that the competition is still tough and you must have a better script than hundreds or even thousands of other entrants. In almost all contests you will have to pay an entry fee, which averages $35. If you enter ten contests, you have spent $350.

Although there have been a few contests of dubious integrity, the vast majority are legit. Also, out of those fifty-two contests there may be ten or fifteen with entry restrictions that make you ineligible.

Aileen Murphy
Writer's Aide

Aileen's book provides a comprehensive and up-to-date source for information regarding screenplay contests and fellowships. Published since 1991, Writer's Aide is constantly updated, evaluates the contests and screenwriting consultants, provides entry forms for many contests and contains other information helpful to screenwriters. *Writer's Aide* sells for $24.90 for U. S. residents, which includes shipping and handling.

Writer's Aide Publishing
1685 South Colorado Blvd., #237
Denver, CO 80222
303-430-4839/fax 303-692-8170

The Dramatists Sourcebook is also an invaluable tool listing about 36 pages of grants, scholarships, contests and prizes for scriptwriters of all kinds. The 1997 edition features an introduction by Tony Kushner who won the Pulitzer Prize for his play, *Angels in America*. *The Dramatists Sourcebook* is available in good bookstores and from:

Theatre Communications Group
355 Lexington Avenue
New York, NY 10017
212-697-5230
E-mail: tcg@tcg.org

Some contests not only charge, but put in writing that if they like your script, they have first option. Some are production companies that use this approach to canvass material. The contest keeps them in scripts and is self-supporting. You could get your material optioned. On the other hand, it might not be a good idea to sign everything away blindly, so research carefully anyone you intend to do business with.

Below are some noteworthy contests and contact numbers.

America's Best/The Writer's Foundation
3936 S. Semoran Blvd. #368
Orlando, FL 32822
407-894-3378

Austin Heart of Film Festival
1600 Nueces
Austin TX 78701
800-560-6894

The Chesterfield Program/Universal Studios
100 Universal City Plaza Bldg. 447
Universal City, CA 91608
818-777-0998

The Chesterfield looks for young, undiscovered story telling talent. They canvass universities through the writing faculties and take recommendations from agents and producers.

The Disney Fellowship Program/The Walt Disney Studios
500 S. Buena Vista Street
Burbank, CA 91521-1735
818-560-1000

The Disney Fellowship has no entry fee.

King Arthur Screenwriter Awards /Kingman Films
801 N. Brand Blvd. #630
Glendale CA 91230
818-548-3456/fax 818-548-3899
E-mail: Kingman@primenet.com

King Arthur Awards have no entry fee.

The Nicholl Fellowships
The Academy of Motion Picture Arts and Sciences
8949 Wilshire Blvd.
Beverly Hills, CA 90212-1972
310-247-3059
Website: http://www.oscars.com

The Sundance Institute
Independent Feature Film Program
225 Santa Monica Blvd. 8th floor
Santa Monica, CA 90401
310-394-4662
E-mail: Sundance@delta net.com

Sundance is not only the most visible means of getting film into the marketplace, it's also the most difficult to penetrate. Sundance is run with an eye toward semi-established talent who have already proven real potential and are usually bringing a project to the table, not just a script.

Classes and Other Support Groups

Whether you are in a formal writing class at a connected institution or gathered with a group you have pulled together yourself, support groups not only provide comfort and a place to blow off steam, but they are conduits of information and access. Some groups are more tied in to what is going on than others, but whenever you enlist others on the same journey, you open the door for possibilities.

More support groups, scholarships, fellowships and contests are available to writers than any other group of artists in theatre or film. Although more writer support is available in Los Angeles and New York, there is also help for writers all across the country.

Independent Features Projects

One of the most connected and effective support groups for filmmakers is Independent Features Projects. IFP's 2000-plus members include writers, actors, grips, sound technicians and anyone else seeking to be involved in independent film. This non-profit group sponsors seminars, classes, screenings, producer series, The Spirit Awards and an eclectic collection of industry resources. It is not necessary to be a member in order to attend events, but the monthly newsletter listing free screenings, get togethers, resources and ads from people wanting scripts is only available to members. Membership fees are $40 for students and $95 for individuals. Members have access to discounted health and production insurance.

Independent Features Projects West
Executive Director: Dawn Hudson
1964 Westwood Blvd. #205
Los Angeles, CA 90025
310-475-4379

Independent Features Projects Midwest
Executive Director: Jim Vincent
676 N La Salle Dr.
Chicago, IL 60610-3784
312-587-1818

Independent Features Projects
Executive Director: Michele Byrd
104 W 29th St.
New York, NY 10001
212-465-8200
E-mail: info@ifp.org

Independent Features Projects North
Executive Director: Jane Minton-Fors
401 N 3rd Street # 450
Minneapolis, MN 55401-1351
612-338-0871

Independent Features Projects South
Executive Director: Richard Seres
PO Box 145246
Coral Gables, FL 33114
305-461-3544

The Writer's Network is an organization started by in 1994 by successful scriptwriters to help those entering the business. TWN holds seminars, produces a magazine, maintains a screenplay library, an agency referral program and an annual writing competition. The Writer's Network has members all over the world who communicate with them via mail and E-mail.

The Writer's Network
Audrey Kelly, Director
289 Robertson Blvd.
Beverly Hills, CA 90211
310-275-0287
E-mail: Fadeinmag@aol.com

Scriptwriters Network is a consortium of writers who gather monthly to give support, share information and rub shoulders with visible writers and producers whom they invite to speak and shmooze.

A prime motivation of the group is to give writers an understanding of how it *really is* in the business. The Scriptwriters Network meets the second Saturday of each month and sponsors an annual contest called The Door Opener Derby. Prizes include guaranteed script submissions to producers, heads of development and agents.

The membership fee is $60. Members are admitted free to all lectures and non-members pay $10 and must make a reservation. They have a website address (listed below) with full information, or you can request information by snail mail by sending a SASE plus two 32 cent stamps to:

Scriptwriters Network/Membership Director
11684 Ventura Blvd. #508
Studio City, CA 91604
24-hour hotline: 213-848-9477
Website: http://scriptwritersnetwork.com

The *Spec Screenplay Sales Directory* lists spec sales by agent and agency. It notes first time sales of screenplays, provides a synopsis of the story and in many instances lists the price. There is also a section listing screenplay spec sales for one million dollars or more.

The book is cross-referenced detailing information on agents making the sales and the number of sales in a given year. The more expensive edition of *SSSD* covers sales from 1990-1997 and costs $59.95 while the edition tracking sales from 1994-1997 is only $29.95.

Spec Screenplay Sales Directory
In Good Company Products
2118 Wilshire Blvd. #934
Santa Monica, CA 90403-5784
310-828-4946
Website: http://gotmilkstuff.com/shop/specscript.html

Copyright Information

It's vital that you protect your material before you start showing it around. Copyright information is available either by regular mail or on the Internet. The fee is $20 per application. My understanding is that you can copyright several pieces of unpublished material under one application. You must send three items: a properly completed application form, a nonrefundable filing fee of $20 for each application and one complete copy of each unpublished work. For each already published work, you must send $20, an application form, and two copies of the material.

Contact the Copyright Office for an application form and for further information.

Copyright Office
Library of Congress
Washington, DC 20559-6000
Website: http://lcweb.loc.gov/copyright

The Writers Guild of America

The Writers Guild not only protects scriptwriters by negotiating contracts and arbitrating their credits, they also are an extraordinary support group. They have an extensive library with essential reference material and film and television scripts of the past and present. Their registration service assists members and non-members in establishing the completion date and identity of their literary property written for theatrical motion pictures, television and radio.

This is not as much protection as registering the copyright with the US Copyright Office, but it does cover a multitude of sins quickly and inexpensively. A copy of the material (no brads, staples, fanfold, covers, etc.) must accompany the fee of $10 for members and $20 for non-members. The Writers Guild will send you detailed information regarding this service if you write, call or fax them. The registration program is available only through the WGA office. Their mailing address is:

> The Writers Guild of America/West
> 7000 West 3rd Street
> Los Angeles CA 90048
> 213-951-4000
> E-mail: Writtenby@wga.org

For programs other than the registration program, the address for WGA/East is:

> Writers Guild of America/East
> 555 West 57th Street #1230
> New York, NY 10019
> 212-767-7800

Through the Human Resources Department at the WGA, there are various programs available to writers in the following categories: female, ethnic minority, physically disabled, 40 years of age or older. For this purpose, a voluntary training program has been established on a company-by-company basis under which novice writers may train with professional writers on episodic TV series. Each series must be in its second or subsequent year of production and under certain terms and qualifications. Write to Georgia J. Mau at WGA/West for further information.

In order to become a member of WGA, an aggregate number of twenty-four (24) units of credit, which are based upon work completed under contract of employment or upon the sale or licensing of previously unpublished and unproduced literary or dramatic material is required. Said employment, sale or licensing must be with a company or other entity that is signatory to the applicable WGA Collective Bargaining Agreement and must be within the jurisdiction of the Guild as provided in its collective bargaining contracts. The twenty-four (24) units must be accumulated within the preceding three (3) years of application. Upon final qualification for membership, a cashier's check or money order, payable to the Writers Guild of America/West, Inc. in the amount of Two Thousand Five Hundred Dollars ($2,500) is due.

Writers residing west of the Mississippi River may apply for membership in the WGA/West, Inc. Writers residing east of the Mississippi River are advised to contact: Writers Guild of America/East.

Units and credits are counted in the following way:

Two units for each complete week of employment within the Guild's jurisdiction on a week-to-week basis.

Three units for story for radio play or television program less than thirty (30) minutes shall be prorated in terms of ten (10) minutes or less.

Four units for story for a short subject theatrical motion picture or any length for a radio play or television program or breakdown for a non-prime time serial thirty (30) minutes through sixty (60) minutes.

Six units for teleplay or radio play less than thirty (30) minutes shall be prorated in five (5) minute increments; Television format for a new serial or series; *Created By* credit given pursuant to the separation of rights provisions of the WGA Theatrical and Television Basic Agreement in addition to other units accrued for the literary material on which the *Created By* credit is based.

Eight units for story for radio play or television program or break-down for a non-prime time serial more than sixty (60) minutes and less than ninety (90) minutes or screenplay for a short subject theatrical motion picture or for a radio play or teleplay thirty (30) minutes through sixty (60) minutes.

Twelve units for story for a radio or television program ninety (90) minutes or longer or story for a feature length theatrical motion picture; or breakdown for a non-prime time serial ninety (90) minutes or longer or a radio play or teleplay more than sixty (60) minutes and less than ninety (90) minutes.

Twenty-four units for screenplay for a feature length theatrical motion picture, radio play or teleplay ninety (90) minutes or longer or a bible for any television serial or prime-time mini-series of at least four (4) hours or long-term story projection which is defined for this purpose as a bible, for a specified term, on an existing, five (5) times per week non-prime time serial as used herein shall be defined as a bible.

A rewrite is entitled to one-half the number of units allotted to its particular category as set forth in the schedule of units.

A polish is entitled to one-quarter the number of units allotted to its particular category as set forth in the schedule of units.

Sale of an option earns one-half the number of units allotted to its particular category as set forth in the schedule of units, subject to a maximum entitlement of four such units *per project* in any one year.

Where writers collaborate on the same project each shall be accorded the appropriate number of units designated in the schedule of units.

In all cases, to qualify for membership, if the writer's employment agreement or purchase agreement is with a company owned in whole or in part by the writer or writer's family, there must be an agreement for financing, production, and/or distribution with a third party signatory producing company or, failing such agreement, the script must be produced and the writer must receive writing credit on screen in the form of *Written By, Teleplay By, Screenplay By* or *Radio Play By.*

The applicant writer is required to apply for membership no later than the 31st day of employment.

In exceptional cases, the Board of Directors, acting upon a recommendation from the Membership and Finance Committee shall have the power and authority to grant membership based upon work done prior to two years before the applicant has filed an application for membership.

All membership applications are to be supported by a copy of executed employment or sales contracts or other acceptable evidence of employment or sales. Dues are based on a percentage of members' earnings.

The schedule of minimum fees is available free from the Guild and is quite lengthy. Fees for an original screenplay (including treatment) range from $35,076 to $65,793. These fees are paid in a system of WGA guideline installments. Rewrites of Screenplay range from $11,510 to $17,546.

The range exists from low end (budgets of $2,500,000 and

under) to high end (budgets of over $2,500,000).

Television minimum fees for week-to-week and term employment minimum (14 out of 14 weeks) are $2,855.

Minimums for television for a teleplay 15 minutes or less are $2,527 and vary by length of script and whether the work includes teleplay or story and teleplay, etc.

These numbers are just to give you a very sketchy idea of compensation. Get a copy of the full schedule from the WGA so you will know what you are aiming for.

The Writers Guild of America/East publishes an indispensable guide for the written form. This guide is called *Professional Writer's Teleplay/Screenplay Format Guide.* available for prices which vary depending on where you live since the postage is included in the price.

If you pick up the guide from the WGA's New York City office, the cost is $3.80. If you have the guide sent within New York City, the cost is $4.58. Outside of New York state, within the United States, you avoid the state tax and the cost is $4.28. The cost from Canada is $4.45 and from other foreign countries, the cost is $5.70.

WGA/East does not accept personal checks from non-members, so send a money order if you're not a member.

The Dramatists Guild

The Dramatists Guild is a collective for playwrights. Not a union in the strict sense of the word, the DG, still manages to protect playwrights by offering collective bargaining agreements and contracts covering those producers and theatre owners as well as guidelines relative to agency agreements and agents.

Active members pay annual dues of $125 and are assessed 2-3% of their first class royalties. When motion picture rights are sold, members pay 2% of the proceeds. Associate Members pay annual dues of $75. Student Members pay annual dues of $35. Subscribing Members pay $50 annually. It is possible for non-members to subscribe to *The Dramatists Guild Quarterly*, the DG literary journal that features articles on current issues in the theatre, discussions with well-known authors on craft, and transcripts of Guild symposia.

Dues entitle members use of the Dramatists Guild's Production Contracts, royalty collection, business advice, members' hotline, free and/or discounted theatre tickets, access to third party Health

Insurance, *The Dramatists Guild Quarterly*, The *Dramatists Guild Annual Resource Directory* and the Guild's *Newsletter* as well as Marketing Information and Symposia (held in major cities across the country) featuring speakers like Comden & Green, Kander & Ebb, John Guare and Marsha Norman. The Guild's Frederick Lowe Room is available to members for readings and auditions for a nominal fee.

The *Resource Directory*, is worth the price of membership alone. Published each August, the directory includes: lists of agents, festivals, conferences, artists' colonies, fellowships, grants, membership and service organizations, residencies and workshops.

All members enjoy discount theatre tickets to certain productions while in New York. The Dramatists Guild Fund, an associate organization, exists to help members in financial need. For further membership information, contact: the membership coordinator:

Doug Green/The Dramatists Guild
1501 Broadway #701
New York, NY 10036
212-398-9366 x13

Alliance of Los Angeles Playwrights

When The Dramatists Guild closed their west coast office, the void for Los Angeles writers for the theatre was filled by the Alliance of Los Angeles Playwrights. Although ALAP is primarily a networking organization, it does offer some legal referrals for members and is in the process of creating a sample contract for 99-seat theatres.

For their $29.95 annual dues, members get a directory of names, contact numbers and credits of members, periodic newsletters, craft and business seminars and the Playwrights Expo, a bi-annual event which gives member playwrights the chance to meet and shmooze with Southland theatre producers.

In October, the ALAP holds a series of readings called *In Our Own Voices*, featuring readings of works-in-progress by members and actors at local coffee houses.

Alliance of Los Angeles Playwrights
Dan Berkowitz/Dick Dotterer
Information: 213-957-4752

ASK Theatre Projects

The Audrey Skirball-Kinis Theatre spends a lot of time and money educating and supporting playwrights. The Literary Manager at ASK Theatre Projects is Mead Hunter who produces three ongoing playwrighting events at the theatre:

The Reading Series — rehearsed manuscript-in-hand play readings staged for the general public. There are 16 readings throughout the year.

Stage One — unrehearsed private readings for the benefit of the playwright.

Common Ground — an outside theatre company receives a stipend to stage full production of a work in progress every June.

The best way for a playwright to access ASK's resources is to send a query letter with ten sample pages of their material.

Greg Gunther administers the Playwright Education and Outreach Program which sends playwrights into the Los Angeles school system once a week to teach playwrighting to high school students.

Contact Mead Hunter or Greg Gunther through the information below.

ASK Theatre Projects
11845 W Olympic Blvd.
Los Angeles, CA 90064
310-478-3200
Website: http://www.askplays.org
E-mail: askplay@primenet.com

Playwrights Kitchen Ensemble

The Playwrights' Kitchen Ensemble is housed at the Coronet Theatre near the Beverly Center. Founded by Dan Lauria (who played the dad on *The Wonder Years*) PKE sponsors a Monday Night Play Reading series featuring star actors reading new scripts.

Since the inauguration of the series in 1990, The Playwrights Kitchen Ensemble has read over 300 new plays. PKE annually considers over 1000 plays for the 48 or so readings held during the year.

In addition to the play reading series, there are two writing fee-based workshops that meet once a week. Actors read 10-25 pages of a work-in-progress so that writers can hear their work aloud. The cost is $50 per month for playwrights and $5 for actors. Each workshop is limited to 18 writers and 18 actors. The Monday Night Play Reading series only presents material written specifically for the stage, but the workshops feature material for stage, film and television. Material for the stage developed at the workshops is considered for the Monday night readings. Director Ted Weiant, actor-director Richard Zavaglia and playwright Joe Cacaci all administer the program. Ted Rawlins, who founded the American Stage Company in Teaneck, New Jersey, has just come on board as the executive director at PKE.

PKE/Playwrights Kitchen Ensemble
Ted Weiant/Coronet Theatre
368 N La Cienega
Los Angeles, CA 90048
310-652-9602

Theatre Sponsored Playwright Developmental Groups

Since the life blood of the theatre is new material and budding playwrights, theatres frequently offer developmental possibilities for new playwrights.

Playwrights Horizons/New York — One of Manhattan's most prestigious Off-Broadway theatres is instrumental in presenting new playwrights on a regular basis. It takes two to four months for them to read your material, but it will be considered.

Playwrights Horizons/Sonya Sobieski
416 W 42nd Street
New York, NY 10036
212-564-1235

Ensemble Studio Theatre — If you're a playwright, EST could be one of your best friends. They produce many new plays, sponsor new play festivals, have week and weekend summer workshops in the Catskills as well as ongoing playwriting groups.

Ensemble Studio Theatre/Eileen Meyers
Literary Department
549 W 52nd Street
New York, NY 10019
212-581-9603

The Public Theatre — New York's most famous off-Broadway theatre has helped develop such plays as *Sticks and Bones, A Chorus Line* and *Hair.* Connected and fearless, The Public also has ongoing playwright groups.

The Public Theatre
425 Lafayette Avenue
New York, NY 10003
212-539-8500

Marjorie Ballentine has merged her successful writing school and laboratory, The Marjorie Ballentine Studio with the Brave New Theatre Company and the American British Acting Company to become the resident theatre company for the 78th Street Theatre Lab.

This ambitious company stages a production each month, so they are constantly looking for new material of every length and genre.

Since Marjorie is known for her Script Interpretation class, she is well qualified to help writers seeking assistance in the develop-mental process. Submit material to:

Evelyn Glover
236 W 78th Street
New York, NY 10024
For information: 212-501-7436
E-mail: stella@idt.net

Mark Taper Forum Developmental Programs

The Mark Taper Forum in Los Angeles sponsors various support groups for playwrights. *The New Works Festival* in November and December features the works of 12-16 new playwrights. Material is presented in rehearsed readings for the benefit of the playwright with feedback from directors, the Dramaturge and other appropriate Taper staff. Submit material between January and April 1.

Blacksmiths are a group of local African-American playwrights who meet for readings and workshops throughout the year. The highlight of the year is the Juneteenth Celebration, a week long showcasing of Blacksmith members' material.

The Asian Theatre Workshop and *The Latino Theatre Initiative* support playwrights of their respective minority communities. *Other Voices* provides a one week forum for disabled writers to hear their works read in their annual showcase, *Chautauqua.*

For consideration for any of the above programs, playwrights should submit 10-12 sample pages plus a description (not synopsis) of their material. Identify the group that interests you. Address queries to

Pier Carlo Talenti/Mark Taper Forum
135 N Grand Ave.
Los Angeles, CA 90012

The New Dramatists

New Dramatists — John Patrick Shanley describes the New Dramatist *the Fort Knox of playwright talent.* Dedicated to finding gifted playwrights and giving them the time, space and tools to develop their craft, ND wants writers to fulfill their potential so they may make lasting contributions to the theatre. This full service, non-profit group serves as a laboratory where writers can develop through a program that includes script-in-hand readings followed by panel discussions. ND also sponsors grants, contests, a biannual newsletter, exchanges with theatres in other countries, the Composer/Librettist studio (a workshop exploring the composer/librettist relationship), a library and free tickets to Broadway and off-Broadway theatre.

Playwrights seeking membership submit two full-length works (no screenplays), a resume and a letter of intent. For applications, write:

New Dramatists
424 W 44th Street
New York, NY 10036
212-757-6960
E-mail: Newdram@aol.com
Website: http://www.itp.tsoa.nyu.edu/~diana/ndintro.html

The International Theatre Institute is an organization started in 1948 by UNESCO committed to fostering theatre communication with 82 centers around the world. ITI provides entree for actors, writers, directors, etc. who are either going abroad or considering it. A quarterly newsletter is yours for a contribution. ITT maintains an extensive research library that is available to anyone doing serious research:

The International Theatre Institute of the United States
Louis A. Rachow (pronounced Rock-Oh)
220 W 42nd Street. #1710
New York, NY 10035
212-254-4141

Louis turned me onto the following publications:

The Original British Theatre Directory
Richmond House Publishing Co. Ltd.
9-11 Richmond Buildings London IV5AF
telephone 44-071-437-9556/telefax 44-071-434-0200

The British Alternative Theatre Directory/Rebecca Books
Ivor House, Suite #2
1 Bridge Street
Cardiff CF12TH Wales
telephone 44-022-237-8452

The Performing Arts Yearbook for Europe
Arts Publishing International, Ltd.
4 Assam St.
London E17QS
telephone 44-071-247-0066/telefax 44-071-247-6868

Price listed on the cover is in pounds sterling with no US equivalent, but Louis says The Performing Arts Yearbook for Europe is roughly $50 and the other books listed are about $30 each.

The Value of Studying

Although studying might provide connections in addition to advice on your craft, some people feel it's not worth the risk:

- *You'd be better off taking a minor in screenwriting and a major in literature or psychology or politics or history or anything because a screenwriting program is essentially just going to teach you the format. A lot of professors are doing this to make a living. My advice to students is to take the part time professors. They are the ones who are working in the field and are able to express what is takes to make it in this town.*

   The value of the film schools is primarily in networking. I entered the business through an internship program.

   Of course, you can work in any menial job at any studio and begin your journey through the system where you meet people and hand your work around. You hopefully meet the right people. You meet people who are all going to be moving up at the same time.

   Anonymous Agent

Even those who think that writing can't be taught agree that if nothing else, being involved in a writing program at least disciplines you, compels you to actually turn out product, and puts you in the company of your peers and good role models. Staff, guest speakers and other writers will be sharing information. You'll learn where things are happening and ways other writers have of coping with some of the same problems you are having.

- *There are the major film schools (UCLA, USC, NYU, AFI, Columbia) and then there's everybody else. Every other school has put in a film program and a screenwriting program and frankly, most of them are very high profit centers for the universities because you get mainly white moneyed people going because it's expensive.*

   Many screenplays from film schools (even the good ones) are bad because the school process becomes a system of homogenization, There was a time when I felt I could pick out not only what school they went to, but which professor they had. A lot of young writers try to second guess the marketplace. Then all you get is a derivative of the last hit that they saw instead of trying to write something original or put their own values on something.

   Not all situations are homogenized, but let's face it, there's only a certain number that come out of the programs that do well. It's a very few. 2% of the

material is unreadable garbage. You get this enormous segment that's got a beginning, a middle, an end, it's in the right format. It's competent. Then you get this 1% that knocks you stupid.
Anonymous Agent

Connected Study

●   *I guess classes can't hurt. I wouldn't say,* This is how you are going to be a success, go to class. *I've had successes with people who are AFI graduates and from UCLA and USC film school and I've had success with people who were plumbers and bus drivers and whatever. I would say, generally, that college educated people have a higher percentage of scores.*
Stu Robinson
Paradigm/Los Angeles

There are valuable screenwriting classes and seminars held across the country, but two schools that immediately get agent attention on a resume are New York University's Tisch School of the Arts Graduate Film Division and the University of Southern California.

●   *NYU - in 1987 there were 497 applicants. In 1992 there were 890 applicants. The number admitted in each of those years was 52.*
USC - in 1988 there were 583 applicants, in 1992, there were 864. In 1988, they admitted 110, 1992 - 188.
Graduates of USC's school of cinema have received 30 Academy Awards.
The Guinness Book of Movie Facts and Feats
Patrick Robertson
Guinness Publishing
Great Britain

UCLA Screenwriting Faculty Chairman in the Department of Film and Television, Richard Walter is also a novelist and successful screenwriter. Many of the agents I interviewed mentioned Mr. Walter by name, so if you are considering university training in screenwriting and were admitted to his program, you would be well served. If you are intent on staying in your own backyard and/or don't want to go the university route, at least get his book: Screenwriting, the art, craft and business of film and television writing.

Lew Hunter is also a well thought of screenwriting teacher who joins colleague Walters at UCLA. Lew says that *one out of two students who write in our three year graduate program become writers who make their living at the keyboard.* What a record! Lew also has a best selling scriptwriting book called *Lew Hunter's Screenwriting 434.*

Sherwood Oaks Experimental College

Having chaired a few seminars for Sherwood Oaks Experimental College in Los Angeles, I would certainly have to include them in my list of connected places to study. SOEC stages year round events, seminars and workshops for screenwriters at very reasonable prices. The range of industry leaders that entrepreneur/teacher/scriptwriter/producer, Gary Shusett manages to attract is mouth watering.

I recently chaired a seminar there where young writers who had sold spec scripts all shared information about how they had entered the system. The classes are structured in such a way that ⅔ of the class is panel discussion and questions from the audience. The remainder of the time is spent in a social setting providing students with the opportunity to speak to the guests in a one-on-one situation.

Sherwood Oaks Experimental College
7095 Hollywood Blvd.
PO Box 876
Hollywood CA 90028
213-851-1769
E-mail: Sherwoodoaks@juno.com

Selling Your Ideas

Not as lucrative, but a real avenue into the business is selling your idea. Screenwriter, Jill Mazursky sold her first idea/script when she was 17. She told her idea to a producer friend. The producer and his partner wanted to use her idea and pay her 10%.

No stranger to deal making, having director Paul Mazursky for a father, Jill managed to go toe-to-toe with a high powered agent and negotiate 25% of the script purchase price for herself and never wrote a line. Since then, Jill has written and sold many scripts, but her idea got her the first deal.

Screenwriter/Producer Steve Kaire is arguably *the best high concept idea man in Hollywood*. He sold seven projects to the major studios including his last screenplay, *Worst Case Scenario*, an eighty million dollar action thriller that's been greenlighted.

His Los Angeles seminar, *Selling Your Ideas to Hollywood* is sold with a money back guarantee. There are not many people who have the courage to make a deal like that, so he must be good.

The one day seminar costs $120 while the two day class is a bargain at $195. You can contact him through the seminar line, his address or via his website.

Steve Kaire
3219 Overland Ave. #6205
Los Angeles, CA 90034
Seminar Line: 310-281-3093
Website: http://www.internexus.net/~mayers/Hwood/

There are many ways to educate yourself for success as a screenwriter. John Mattson was pretty conventional in his approach:

- *A graduate of UCLA Film School, John Mattson worked for three years as a freelance reader and HBO story editor before setting out to write for himself. Last November, his* Milk Money *sold for $1.1 million to Paramount Pictures, marking one of the year's biggest spec sales.*
  Scripter Mattson Signs at UTA
  John Evan Frook
  Daily Variety
  May 12, 1993

In the category of *whatever works for you*, novelist/screenwriter Richard Price (*Sea of Love, The Color of Money, Clockers*) was asked if he ever studied with Syd Field or any of the other screenwriting gurus:

- *All I ever studied was the movie executives. What soothes them, what scares them.*
  The Organizer
  F. X. Sweeney
  Buzz Magazine
  September 1992

If you are going to leave home to study, agents always answer phone calls from any USC, UCLA or AFI teacher who recommends a promising student. The proximity of these schools to the world's movie and television capital ensures participation of the most famous writers, producers and directors as guest teachers and speakers in their extension programs.

- *I'm more likely to look at things from writers from UCLA or USC or NYU film school. I went to film school. I was studying to be a screenwriter and had to write ¾ of a screenplay every quarter at UCLA, so that helped. I'm a frustrated writer and consider myself an editor when I read a script.*
  Howard Sanders
  United Talent Agency/Los Angeles

- *Get into a class at UCLA or USC. Robert McKee's classes are good. Richard Walter at UCLA is a fine teacher of writers. When he calls me about someone, I listen.*
  Rima Greer
  Above the Line Agency/Los Angeles

A connected film school not only puts you in the company of the greats and their material, but has a line to the industry and the ability to get your material read by important agents and producers.

- *What percentage of 1987 screenwriting majors at UCLA had agents? 67...it's now almost 80.*
  Premiere Magazine
  September 1992

Study at Home

It's not necessary to leave home to study. Many hot Hollywood screenwriting teachers take their shows on the road. I am mentioning the names of teachers who have reputations within the business. There are undoubtedly more.

The man who has written the bible for screenwriters is Syd Field. His book, *Screenplay: The Foundations of Screenwriting*, sells almost as well today as it did in 1979 when it was first published. A native of Los Angeles who grew up around the business, Syd began his career as a writer-producer for David L. Wolper Productions, was a free lance screenwriter and became head of the Story Department at Cine Artists. His newest book, *The Screenwriter's Problem Solver* is an interactive book published by Dell. He also has a video available called *Writing the Screenplay: the home course.*

Syd conducts classes in Los Angeles, at various sites around the world and teaches seminars on the Internet on a pay per view basis. Check online at http://www. Buddhascape.com for particulars.

Syd Field
270 N Canon Drive #1355
Beverly Hills, CA 90210
310-271-1839
E-mail: Fieldink@screenwriterscorner.com

Robert McKee, a well regarded screenwriting teacher, not only travels to Dallas, Chicago, Washington, Cleveland, etc., but to London, Brussels and Toronto. No matter where you live, McKee is near. The $450 fee covers classes from 9:30 a.m. to 8:00 p.m. Friday, Saturday and Sunday.

McKee is recommended by people as diverse as director Mark Rydell (*On Golden Pond*), novelist/actor Kirk Douglas, and screenwriter Patricia Resnick (*9-5, A Wedding*). McKee is a writer (*Colombo, Quincy*) and an actor (Broadway and London). I'm told by writers and agents who have attended, that the seminars are worthwhile and exciting.

Robert McKee/Two Arts, Inc.
12021 Wilshire Blvd. Suite 868
Los Angeles, CA 90025
310-312-1002 or 212-463-7889
Website: http://www.mckeestory.com

Michael Hauge is another Los Angeles based high profile story editor and script consultant who takes his show on the road. Author of the best selling book, *Writing Screenplays That Sell,* Michael not only teaches in Los Angeles, but offers his award-winning seminar in Philadelphia, Atlanta, Seattle, Oklahoma City, Austin, Washington, D.C. and numerous other American cities. Michael also teaches in Canada and Europe.

Michael Hauge/Hilltop Productions
PO Box 55728
Sherman Oaks, CA 91413
800-477-1947 or 818-995-4209
E-mail: Hilltopproductions@juno.com

Dave Trottier teaches seminars on all aspects of writing including what seems to me to be the most practical: *17 Ways to Make a Living as a Writer.* The author of the respected format guide, *The Screenwriter's Bible,* Dave teaches across the land, in Los Angeles and by mail. Other information on Dave is found on page 40.

Formatting Software

Dave's guide to formatting is one of the industry standards, but there is software available that takes care of all of that for you. You can buy packages that offer formatting options for plays, television (half-hours, hours, MOWs) and for theatrical films. One of the best resources for software and scriptwriter related computer goodies is The Writers' Computer Store in California. Their main store is in Santa Monica. They have a branch in Sausalito which is also the home of their huge mail order business. TWCS also sells hardware. Call their 800 number or check out their website for a complete list of their wares.

The Writers' Computer Store 11317 Santa Monica Boulevard Los Angeles, CA 90025 310-479-7774	The Writers' Computer Store 2631 Bridgeway Avenue Sausalito, CA 94965 415-332-70050
800-272-8977/fax 800-486-4006/Website: http://writerscomputer.com	

Although we think of the big money and attention being focused on screenwriters, the truth is that playwrights today are high on the wish list of many agents.

One agent I interviewed said that the playwright is the golden goose and his eggs just keep making money every time a theatre company performs the material.

High on the list of schools known as major sources for play-wrights are Yale, Columbia, Carnegie Mellon and NYU.

There are important writing programs of one kind or another at the Universities of Iowa, Utah and Missouri, as well as Syracuse University, Carnegie Tech and University of California, Irvine.

• *Minneapolis has a playwrights group (Midwest Playwrights Labs) and Chicago has a really good theatre community. If you are near a university town, you're lucky, because you can tap into film through the university. If you aren't, you may have to make your own support group. People who want to form a support group should put an ad in the paper as well as places like art film houses in their community. Then have meetings and try to cull out the people who say they are writers, but are actually not. A lot of really important writers' groups grew out of somebody's living room.*

Robin Moran Miller
New York

Gotham Writers' Workshop

Writers David Grae and Jeff Fligelman started the Gotham Writers' Workshop as a no-nonsense writing school in 1993 with a staff of seven working writers. Today there are 42 staff members, so their no-nonsense approach stressing structure, craft and support obviously filled a niche in the Manhattan writing scene.

GWW has beginning and advanced classes in writing fiction, filmscripts, plays, non-fiction, poetry, situation comedy, comedy, script reading and film analysis. Classes of 14 or less meet weekly for three hours for ten weeks. The cost is $395. Returning students get a discounted rate of $345. One day intensive workshops cost $145 with repeat students paying $125. Minimum age is 18.

Gotham Writers' Workshop has four Manhattan campuses and a series of online workshops as well. Their website lists all details.

Gotham Writers' Workshop
1841 Broadway #809
New York, NY 10023
212-974-8377 which is 212-WRITERS
E-mail: Gotham@write.org
Website: http://www.write.org

Access to Hollywood/5 Minute Film School

Two websites were started by executives from Turner Network and Aaron Spelling's production company to marry those with access to true stories, life rights, comic books, books, game ideas, etc., to people in the marketplace who might be able to turn that information into financial gain for both parties: http://www.accesstohollywood.com and http://www.5minutefilmschool.com.

So You Can Make Money When You Make Money

I'm told by scriptwriter, Sharon Cobb, that one of the most valuable classes she ever took was a class that taught her how to second guess her agent called: *Making Your Deal.* The class is taught randomly at UCLA by high powered entertainment attorneys, Patty Felker and Philip Rosen. Cobb says she learned the hard way that there is no protection like self protection. The class taught her strategies even her agents didn't know. Some version of this class is a must for any scriptwriter who ever plans to make real money.

Information Information Information

Wherever you are, it is imperative that you begin to familiarize yourself with the names and credits of producers, directors, writers, actors and all the other people that you either work with or will work with in the business. Identifying trends in script buying can also save frustration. If drama is in and you are a comedy writer, you'll realize the rejection is not personal, you're just not where the business is right now. The pendulum will be coming your way again in the future.

The Hollywood Creative Directory

The Hollywood Creative Directory is known as the film and television industry bible. Published three times a year, this collection of contact information for producers, studio and network executives, production companies, studios and networks will answer most any question you have about who's where. Listings include not only names, addresses and phone numbers, but credits, deals and E-mail addresses. The *HCD* costs $49.95, but is well worth the money if you're looking for production company information. The same information is available from *HCD* on the Internet for a yearly, monthly or per hit fee. They'll even give you a free taste. I'd certainly go look if I were you. The information is updated daily.

HCD also publishes a complete guide to agents & managers, *Hollywood Agents & Managers Directory*. It's published twice a year and costs $49.95 per copy. The information is also available on the Internet and is updated daily. You can have a free taste here, too. Check it out. Same contacts and information for both.

> *Hollywood Creative Directory/Hollywood Agents & Managers Directory*
> 3000 W Olympic Blvd. # 2525
> Santa Monica, CA 90404
> Website: http://www.hollyvision.com
> E-mail: hcd@hollyvision.com

Lone Eagle's Industry Guides

Lone Eagle Publishing also publishes guides for the film industry. A couple of their books *are: Film Directors: A Complete Guide,* which lists directors and film listings along with contact information and costs $65 and the *Film Writers Guide* which sells for $60 and lists screenwriters, film titles and listings of unproduced screenplays.

LEP also has guides for producers, actors, composers, distributors, stunts, television writers and on and on. *Eaglei: The Entertainment Industry Reference Guide* on the Internet has a particularly interesting feature: you can call up the name of some film professional, get that person's credits and cross-referenced information linking all the people that person has worked with. Lone Eagle also tracks trends in script purchases. Their website also features a limited amount of free looks! $199 per year, $19.99 per month.

> Lone Eagle Publishing Company
> 2337 Roscomare Road, # 9
> Los Angeles, CA 90077-1851
> 310-471-8066/fax 310-471-4969
> 800-FILMBKS
> Website: http//www.loneeagle.com

Internet Movie Database

The Internet Movie Database is an international organization whose objective is to provide useful and up to date movie information free on-line. There are plot summaries, running times, production companies, distributors, release dates, sequel/remake information, reviews, links to official studio pages, box office grosses, credits of every profession in the industry plus bios of everyone you can think of. Their website: http://us.imdb.com pretty much looks like the key to the bank.

Book Proposal Pointers

Agent, Sheree Bykofsky maintains an informative website for authors. Sheree's webpage details the book-writing process from idea to publication, setting forth guidelines for book proposals and the kind of material that interests her.

The address is: http://www.users.interport.net/~sheree. Sheree is profiled along with her agency on page 162.

The Trades

For film and television writers, I recommend subscriptions to one or both of the daily Los Angeles showbiz newspapers as well as *Written by...*, the monthly magazine of The Writers Guild West.

Daily Variety	*The Hollywood Reporter*
5700 Wilshire Blvd.	5055 Wilshire Blvd.
Los Angeles, CA 90036	Los Angeles, CA 90036
213-857-6600	213-525-2000

Written by...
7000 Third Street
Los Angeles, CA 90048-2456
213-951-4000

Books listing credits of directors, actors and producers should be part of your reference collection. I strongly suggest you begin assembling a library stocked with books that give you an idea of what the business is really like instead of just dwelling in your fantasy life.

It's fruitful to examine the lifestyle inherent in your goal before you invest a large part of your life to attaining it. The idea of being a successful television writer can be more fulfilling than the reality. It doesn't matter if you have all the money in the world if you have no time, mate or friends to spend it with.

Biographies of successful people provide role models in your quest for achievement and may even inform your goals. Big success requires big sacrifices. Don't find out later that the cost was too high. Denial is said to be even more potent than cocaine; neither drug enhances your marketability.

Here is a list of books that will give your library a good start:

Adventures in the Screen Trade/William Goldman
*The Complete Directory to Primetime /
    Network TV Shows*/Tim Brooks-Earle Marsh
The Devil's Candy/Julie Salamon
Dramatists Sourcebook/Theatre Communications Group
The Directors Guild of America Directory of Members
The Film Encyclopedia/Ephraim Katz
The Filmgoer's Companion/Leslie Halliwell
Final Cut/Steven Bach
Halliwell's Film Guide/Leslie Halliwell
Hollywood Agents & Managers Directory/Hollywood Creative Directory
Hollywood Creative Directory/Hollywood Creative Directory
Hype & Glory/William Goldman
Making a Good Script Great/Linda Seger
Making Movies/Sidney Lumet
Indecent Exposure/David McClintock
Insider's Guide to Book Editors, Publishers and Literary Agents/Jeff Herman
The Last Great Ride/Brandon Tartikoff
Lew Hunter' Screenwriting 434/Lew Hunter
The New Screenwriter Looks at the New Screenwriter/William Froug
NY Times Directory of Film/(Arno Press)
NY Times Directory of Theatre/(Arno Press)
Ovitz/Robert Slater
Playwright's Companion/Mollie Ann Meserve
Rebel Without a Crew/Robert Rodriguez
Reel Power/Mark Litwak
Saturday Night Live/Doug Hall/Jeff Weingrad

Screen World /John Willis
Screenwriter's Workbook/Syd Field
The Screenwriter Looks at the Screenwriter/William Froug
Screenwriting/Richard Walter
Screenwriting Tricks of the Trade/William Froug
The Season/William Goldman
Selling a Screenplay/Syd Field
Spec Screenplay Sales Directory/Howard Meibach
Theatre World/John Willis
Tinker in Television/Grant Tinker & Bud Rukeyser
TV Movies/Leonard Maltin
You'll Never Eat Lunch in this Town Again/Julia Phillips
Wake Me When It's Funny/Garry Marshall
Who's Who in the Motion Picture Industry/Rodman Gregg
Who's Who in Television/Rodman Gregg
Who's Who in American Film Now/James Monaco
Wired/Bob Woodward
The Writers Guild of America Membership Directory
Writing Screenplays That Sell/Michael Hauge

    The Playwright's Companion lists 194 pages of theatres and productions companies.
    Both The Directors Guild and The Writers Guild membership directories are free to members, but are available for a fee to non members through the guilds and some bookstores.

Directors Guild of America West 7920 Sunset Blvd. Los Angeles, CA 90046 310-289-2000	Directors Guild of America 520 North Michigan Ave. Chicago, IL 60611 312-644-5050
Directors Guild of America 110 West 57th St. New York, NY 10019 212-581-0370 Website: http://www.dga.org	

Writers Guild/West	Writers Guild/East
7000 Third Street	555 West 57th St. #1230
W Hollywood, CA 90048	New York, NY 10019
213-951-4000	212-767-7800
Website: http://www.wga.org	

Wrap Up

Ways into the system
✓ industry job
✓ classes with connected instructors
✓ writing groups
✓ acting classes
✓ directing classes

Film support
✓ Independent Features Project
✓ Scriptwriters Network/Los Angeles
✓ Freelance Screenwriter's Forum
✓ The Writer's Network
✓ The Writers Guild of America

Theatre support
✓ Playwrights Horizons
✓ The Public Theatre
✓ Ensemble Studio Theatre
✓ The New Dramatists
✓ The Dramatists Guild
✓ Alliance of Los Angeles Playwrights

Formal study/benefits
✓ exposed to role models
✓ discipline
✓ networking
✓ learn form and structure

Formal study/ detriments
- ✓ can lead to homogenization of product
- ✓ can make your vision too narrow
- ✓ real life sometimes thought to be more conducive to good writing

Keep informed
- ✓ reference library
- ✓ read the trades
- ✓ DGA Membership Listing
- ✓ WGA Membership Listing
- ✓ Websites

6 Agents/Attorneys/Managers

This part of the book is geared to helping you get attention for your material, and before you proceed, I urge you again to make sure your script or book is ready: correctly formatted, polished, copyedited and rewritten to showcase your material in the best possible light.

Once you show your material to someone important who actually reads it, you have made your impression. You are only new once. If someone reads you and you're not ready, it's worse than not having been read. But, if you and your material are ready, it's time to enter the marketplace.

Most writers possess neither the contacts, information, nor the appetite for representing themselves over the long haul, so it's wise to enter the industry with representation.

Whether you choose to be represented by an agent, attorney, manager or all three, making the choice and getting appropriate representation can become a career in itself. Although you may be able to get your script to a producer on your own, unrepresented material faces a rocky road.

What does an agent, attorney or manager do? Where do I find one? What do I need? How can I get someone to talk to me? What would I say to one of these people? Are there rules of behavior? How can I tell when someone is credible? When is the right time to look for representation? What if everyone wants to sign me, how can I make an appropriate choice? What if no one wants to sign me, do I have to go back to Iowa? What will I tell my family?

Tell your family that you are writing and learning the business. Tell them that when you have representation you will let them know, but that whether or not you have an agent has nothing to do with the fact that you are pursuing your dream. Being a writer is about writing, not about being employed. Tell them that writing is making you happy and that making money will be icing on the cake.

Civilians (those who have never pursued a job in show business) and would-be writers who are still in school, can't possibly empathize. They have no idea what any artist goes through in pursuit of employment and/or representation. They're not going to understand anything except your name up on the screen in big letters where it says, Written by.

In its simplest incarnation, the agent/attorney/manager, acting on your behalf, sets in motion a series of events that result in your having a shot at a job. You and your representative conceive a plan for your career. He then, gets you in the door for meetings, interviews and pitch sessions. He sends your work around and gets people to read it. He adds credibility to your cause by his interest in you.

This book primarily deals with agents, per se, but agents, attorneys and/or managers are all technically agents when they are sending your work around and getting you meetings.

• *The networks will not read projects submitted by an unrepresented writer under any circumstances because of the potential for legal action. Most production companies will require a waiver to be signed by the writer who submits on his own, protecting the company from legal action. These waivers are rarely in the best financial interest of the writer. The writer's agent is, therefore, an all important person in my ability to find writers. It is hard to discover a writer if he is not represented by an agent.*

Ken Raskoff/MOW Producer
Ken Raskoff Productions/ABC Films

Getting representation takes on enormous significance in the quest for a writer's credibility. Not being able to get an agent hurts our feelings, makes us hostile and undermines self confidence.

The dictionary, which knows very little about show business, has many definitions for the word *agent*. By combining a couple I've come up with: *A force acting in place of another, effecting a certain result by driving, inciting, or setting in motion; a go between.*

It seems you can't do business without an agent, and unless you are already making money, it's impossible to get an agent to talk to you, take a meeting or in any other way validate your existence.

Even though the quest for an agent can become a full time job in itself, untried people still manage to get an agent and enter the business hourly. These new people may be related to others in the business or otherwise connected giving them entree. Those without this benefit need to be driven, clever, ingenious and of course, very talented. Many are all of the above.

Most writers, actors and directors have no idea how agents train for their jobs and therefore no basis on which to evaluate an agent intelligently. Do agents attend Agent University or something? Actually, some of them do. Those universities are the training programs (mail rooms) of the conglomerate initial agencies: CAA (Creative Artists Agency), ICM (International Creative Management), WMA (William Morris Agency) and UTA (United Talent Agency).

Whether or not the agent has such formal training, the agent I want has been getting to know the business, reading every screenplay, television script, play, novel; the written word in any form that might interest a buyer or teach an eager mind. He's watched the development of writers, actors, directors, and producers by attending every show in town, seeing every film and at least sampling every television show. He's apprenticed under some connected role model at another agency or at a studio. He's been meeting people on all levels of the business, networking, staying visible, and communicating. He's met producers, directors and vice presidents of development and he's cultivated relationships with them.

He only represents those writers whose work he personally knows so when he tells a prospective buyer that he's found a brilliant new writer who is perfect for an upcoming project or who has written the next *Sling Blade* or the new *X-Files*, the buyers will pay attention. Just like a writer, an agent builds his credibility slowly, one step at a time.

The relationships agents build take time. To get people out and introduce them and get their material read, takes a lot of time and effort. To follow up on it takes more time. It's a large investment. An agent who has done his homework is probably not going to be interested in you until you have done yours.

Why would an agent talk to you? Have you spent years perfecting your work, reading, writing, writing, writing, watching films, television, reading classic screenplays, devouring television scripts, learning who you are, focusing your goals? Do you read the trades? Do you know who the buyers are who might be interested in what you specifically have to sell? Have you digested the written form of whichever kind of script you want to sell? Do you have the vocabulary with which to discuss the business with your prospective business partner?

No? Well, get to it.

• *My reputation is as good as the writers I send from my office. My reputation relies upon my clients, so I have to be careful about what I send out.*

Ken Sherman
Ken Sherman & Associates/Los Angeles

Besides getting the writer's work read, the agent must be prepared to negotiate a brilliant contract when the material sells. That entails knowing all the contracts and all of the rules and regulations of The Writers and Dramatists Guilds, as well as having an understanding of the marketplace and knowing what others at similar career levels are getting for similar jobs. He must then have the courage, style, and judgment to stand up to the buyers in asking for what is fair without giving in to the temptation to sell the writer down the river financially in favor of his future relationship with the buyers or without becoming too grandiose and turning everyone off.

A writer who is a member of The Writers Guild can represent himself anytime he wants if he can get someone interested in his material. An agent conducting business for a WGA member must have a license from the state, experience as an agent and have signed an agreement with the WGA. That agreement is called a franchise. Just because an agent is franchised by the Guild is no guarantee that the agent is ethical, knowledgeable or effective. He probably is, but since this is an important decision, check him out.

Some high-level writers have a manager, a lawyer and an agent and some writers are represented only by an attorney or a manager.

Sometimes writers employ an attorney or a manager for negotiation and sometimes for the express purpose of connecting them to an agent. Last year I had a call from two writers in Chicago. They had sent their material to a hot Beverly Hills entertainment attorney who passed the material onto CAA, ICM and Endeavor. All three agencies wanted to represent them. Their only dilemma at that point was choosing from an embarrassment of riches.

Finding and evaluating entertainment lawyers requires diligent research. An excellent source of information regarding names of entertainment attorneys who have participated in screenplay sales is the *Spec Screenplay Sales Directory* (contact information on page 50). You might also check with friends, the library reference desk, in news stories in the trades, the Internet and in the Yellow Pages. Make your decision based on who they represent and what agencies they have relationships with.

A manager who believes in your work can also enhance your chances of having your material move up the food chain. Not only can a manager introduce you to an agent who might be interested, but routinely, managers shop material. Although they are not allowed legally to negotiate, there is no law against managers shopping product. Since managers generally carry a much smaller client list, personal attention is supposedly a key factor in the relationship. I say *supposedly* since my adventures with managers did not include that component.

The downside of working with a manager is that there is no universal contract protecting the writer from exploitation as there is in the agreement forged with the WGA and agents. Managers may charge whatever they can get and sign you for as long as you will agree to. Agents are bound to charge no more than 10% and may only sign you for 3 years at a time.

More high profile agents are leaving the star/conglomerate agencies to become managers. Joan Hyler (WMA), Barry Mendel (UTA), Gavin Polone (UTA) and Warren Zide (ICM) are but a few of that elite list.

A word of caution regarding managers and attorneys: although most managers and attorneys are there to make sure their clients get the very best deals, many of them are looking to become producers and are feathering their own nests at the expense of their clients' careers. Be alert to the ultimate goals of your business partners.

Although this is a book that deals mainly with writers and agents, I decided this time to interview a manager. Since I ordinarily give managers a bad time believing that they are basically just agents with smaller lists, I thought I would give a manager a shot at telling me why someone should have a manager.

• *If you are at a small agency, you shouldn't need to have a manager. If you are at the big agency, if you want to get in the game, you gotta pay to play. And if you are making a lot of money, I'm a write-off. You can save a little money by dumping the manager, but how many jobs are you losing? Many people don't look that far into the future, they only deal with what is happening right now.*
Jon Brown
The Brown Group/Los Angeles

Jon agrees with me that a manager is just an agent with a smaller list and I agree with him that if you are at one of the big agencies, having a manager might be well worth the money.

For a comprehensive list of managers, try *The Hollywood Agents and Managers Directory* (contact information page 70). This directory lists names, addresses and details the category of clients. *The Spec Screenplay Sales Directory* (contact information page 50) also lists names of managers involved in screenplay sales.

Wrap Up

Agent
✓ a force acting in place of another, effecting a certain result by driving, inciting, or setting in motion; a go between

Agent's job
✓ to become connected to the buyers
✓ to get the writers' work read, arrange meetings, and interviews
✓ to negotiate salary and billing
✓ to have credibility, taste and courage

Attorneys and Managers
✓ can be avenues of opportunity
✓ are not governed by WGA writer-protective contracts
✓ may well have their own agenda
✓ are mainly agents with smaller lists

7   What Everybody Wants

Before a smart business person confronts the marketplace with a new product, he takes the pulse of the buyer to determine how his offering will fare. If he is looking for an agent, it makes sense to find out what is on the agent's wishlist. What is he looking for? Do you have to be a WGA member to arouse his interest? Does your personality enter into the equation? Is it enough to be industrious? Is he going to read several of your scripts to decide whether or not he thinks you can write and/or sell?

•   *The ideal writer is the one that has a great concept, a great story and can execute it. Usually, you get one of those things.*
Candy Monteiro/Fredda Rose
Monteiro Rose/Los Angeles

•   *Most of what we see is on the Bell Curve, written by intelligent people and it's all about C- to C+. In the C to C+ range, we try to help them. We may send them off and tell them to come back with another script. There are very few where it's clear they should be in another field. The other ones who jump off the page, where it's clearly special that it's superstardom, that's rare.*
Elliot Stahler
Kaplan Stahler Agency/Los Angeles

•   *You can tell if somebody is funny in three pages. You recognize it when you see it. It's just sincere and genuine.*
Bob Hohman
Hohman Maybank Lieb/Los Angeles

•   *What people want to see is a script they haven't seen before. If you are new in town and your script has been covered by every studio, it's worthless to your agent.*
Rima Greer
Above the Line Agency/Los Angeles

•   *Some people believe their representative is going to do everything for them and that they are just going to sit back. You have to work together and brain-storm.*

It's really a synergy. When I start working with a new writer, I ask him to think of which publishers or producers he would like to work with and I call those people first. The writer is out there in the marketplace, meeting people. He knows titles. When he is writing, he should know how many books have been written on that subject and which publishers are doing them. Same with screenplays.

It's not just here it is. It's give and take. As much as they rely on me, I rely on them, too. I think their input is valuable. They know things because they have created the product. They might feel a certain producer is open to this kind of material. I may not know that. I can't know everything. I know a lot of things, but I don't know everything. So working together is best.

Miriam Stern
Miriam Stern, Esquire/New York

• *We like our clients to have as small a resume as possible with one entry every several years because that means that people want you back. If you spend one year on this show and one year on that show and the next year on show #3, something is wrong. We like to have a small resume where you start as a term writer and then you're a story editor and then you're an executive story editor, then you're a producer, then you're a supervising producer and then you're an executive producer.*

The keys to this business are continuity and consistency and you don't get that from jumping around. I want to be able to show the network that the writer has moved up in class, and that says something. That says much more than if he's had 20 entries in 5 years. If you've done that many shows, nobody thought you were good enough to ask you to stay around. When somebody comes to me with a resume of 10 shows in 10 years, I don't respond to that.

Elliot Stahler
Kaplan Stahler Agency/Los Angeles

• *We like to sign people with experience who have been around, but there's always a little bit of room to develop something. No agent can take on a slew of new people because you can't make a living out of it. We don't get paid by the hour. Our time is speculative so every agent has to make a judgement call about how many new people he or she can take on in any given year.*

Marc Pariser
Metropolitan Talent Agency/Los Angeles

• *There's a difference between writing and trying to write. It's just elegant.*
Bob Hohman
Hohman Maybank Lieb/Los Angeles

• *There's no mystery about writing. You can read one page and know. You know if you are in good hands by how somebody writes. Good writers have an ear for how people use language. With most new writers, all the characters sound alike. You can tell by the density of pages sometimes. If the descriptions go on forever instead of one line or if a writer needs a half page of prose to describe the scene, generally speaking, you are in trouble. Not to mention that it can be really boring.*

Lynn Pleshette
Pleshette/Millner Agency/Los Angeles

• *I won't look at treatments. We won't look at outlines. If we look and when we look, it's really at finished material. You almost never sell an outline or a treatment unless you are selling a big name writer. There's no money in just selling an idea and it doesn't help anybody's career.*

Marty Shapiro
Shapiro-Lichtman/Los Angeles

• *Oh, I probably look for the same things that producers are looking for; good writing, a good story, well developed characters, something that feels real, something that feels unusual and not too familiar.*

Jim Preminger
Jim Preminger Agency/Los Angeles

• *Whether it's a great script or not is secondary. The first evaluation is the writing. How good is the person? It's really a subjective thing. I can say they're not good and they can go across the street and someone else can say they're brilliant.*

Marty Shapiro
Shapiro-Lichtman/Los Angeles

• *I look for originality, passion, an individual voice, as well as someone who is a craftsman and is not afraid to be different.*

Ken Sherman
Ken Sherman Agency/Los Angeles

• *A great screenplay - 118 pages or less in correct format, with paragraphs no more than 4 lines long with castable parts with a story I've never heard before.*

Rima Greer
Above the Line Agency/Los Angeles

• *We try to answer query letters within two to three days. I'm always looking for new material. If I weren't, I would be out of business. The competition is very fierce. If you don't answer query letters quickly, the good ones are gone. I have 20 to 30 new novels to be read. It's part of this business. If you aren't looking at the new writers, pretty soon, if you live that long, your writers are deceased and they're not writing anymore.*

Susan Schulman
Susan Schulman Literary Agency/New York

• *I read it on two levels. I read it in terms of my pure emotional reaction to it, but at the same time I have to read it with the overlay of its practicality and reality to the market. That doesn't mean that if I'm absolutely captivated or blown away, even though it may not appear to be commercial, that doesn't mean that I'm going to be scared off and I give you as examples:* Driving Miss Daisy, Chariots of Fire, Fried Green Tomatoes, *none of these are what you would call slam-dunk commercial vehicles. If you have a passion for something, that can be fun, too. I may not expect to sell it, but if I think it's going to be a great calling card of this person's ability, it can lead to other employment. We've had that happen a number of times where the original script that got me turned on is still on the shelf, but in the meantime, it has resulted in 10-11 other jobs as a result of somebody reading the script.*

Stu Robinson
Paradigm/Los Angeles

• *It's an important thing to say that tastes change. My taste has certainly changed. I'm no longer interested in representing the traditional straight human relationships family portrait story unless it's told from a very wry humorous point of view. I want something that has a more modern tone to it.*

Susan Schulman
Susan Schulman Literary Agency/New York

• *Most good literary agents will request the script before even sitting down with the writer. I try to do that. I prefer reading just because I don't want any prejudices about really liking the person. I want to see the material. I might be charmed as can be, talking with you, but then I read the material and then I think, oh, I'm not the agent for this person, how am I going to say that? It doesn't mean you can't write, it means that I don't respond in a personal, gut manner.*

Ken Sherman
Ken Sherman Agency/Los Angeles

- *Money is not one of the top five considerations ... more important is that they are realistic about where they are in the continuum of their career and they can't be insane. All anyone really wants is that they feel they are not going to be in the same place in their career in six months as they are now.*
  Bob Hohman
  Hohman Maybank Lieb/Los Angeles

- *One of the reasons why we have successfully mined theatre is that the training playwrights get is character first. All you have is the stage and the people. We can all fix a story or come up with a twist on a story or fix the plot, but if the characters are not there, you don't have anything. Great writing is character.*
  Jonathan Westover
  The Gage Group/Los Angeles

- *I look for an adult who is psychologically sound that you can spend 10 hours a day with.*
  Bob Hohman
  Hohman Maybank Lieb/Los Angeles

- *I want to know what kinds of personal and professional maturity they demonstrate.*
  Elliot Stahler
  Kaplan Stahler Agency/Los Angeles

- *If you have a difficult personality and they want you, they'll take you. The choices do get dimmer and slimmer, however. Charm will help you, but ultimately, it's in the script.*
  Lynn Pleshette
  Pleshette/Millner Agency/Los Angeles

- *We find that we are attracted to writers that we like as individuals. I think writers select agents frequently based on the agents' personality.*
  Jim Preminger
  Jim Preminger Agency/Los Angeles

- *I evaluate off the work, but I won't take someone who behaves antisocially. When one of my clients goes in, they represent my agency. They represent me, it's my name that goes in on that letterhead. It has to be someone I feel I can work with. I am not looking for the one shot, it has to be someone for the long haul.*

Ken Sherman
Ken Sherman Agency/Los Angeles

- *When you are working with new talent, you have to trust your gut, not only that it's worth the gamble, but that it's a decent human being that'll appreciate you and remember you. The hardest job is to get the first deal. The second deal is a piece of cake.*

Miriam Stern
Miriam Stern, Esquire/New York

If you have your life in a fairly balanced state; have a cozy place to live, have several scripts in your bag, have at least a nodding acquaintance with the economic perils of life as a scriptwriter, have some of the traits described by agents as being attractive, and are involved with other writers, it's time for you to begin serious research to determine the attributes that you require for an agent to be on your wish list.

Unfortunately, agents don't send out resumes in search of clients. Even if they are looking for clients (and they are all looking for that one client who will make them wealthy and powerful beyond their dreams), agents don't send out a list of their training, accomplishments, and/or a personality profile. Beyond their list of clients (which is not, by the way, posted on their door), there is no obvious gauge of their worth; it is up to you to conduct a study of your future business partners.

You have already taken your first step; you bought this book giving you the benefit of my interviews with a cross-section of agents. I've asked about their background, looked at their client lists, queried clients, and in general conversed with anyone and everyone in the business who might have something informed to say about literary agents. I've also read everything I could get my hands on regarding agents and the way the business is conducted.

You have probably already begun having agent-conversations with every writer you come in contact with. If you are just beginning in the business and your writer contacts are limited to your peers, they will probably be just as uninformed as you. Never mind, ask anyway. You never know where information lurks.

- *Ask any other screenwriter you can meet, any writing professors at universities, anyone you know. One of the jobs of writing professors is to refer their students to agents. Because the best agencies are constantly seeking to renew themselves by scouting new talent, they stay in touch with the universities. Agents attend screenings from time to time to see new writers and directors who come out of film school.*

Jim Preminger
Jim Preminger Agency/Los Angeles

Agent Attributes

Even though Mark Litwak's informative book *Reel Power* is no longer hot off the presses, I endorse it for information about *how it really is* to survive in the film and television businesses and for insightful reporting about what it takes to be an agent:

• *First, an agent must have the stamina to handle a heavy workload and be able to endure the frenetic pace in which business is conducted.* It's like working in the commodities pit, *says William Morris agent Joan Hyler.* It's hectic, *says agent Lisa Demberg,* because you can't do your job unless you're always on the phone, always talking to someone, or socializing with someone or trying to do business, or following up on the projects you've discussed.

Great agents, *says agent-turned-executive Stephanie Brody,* have enthusiasm and tireless energy. And they must be efficient. The agent is juggling 30 phone calls a day. He has to send out material, and follow up. You have to be extremely well-organized.

Second, agents must be able to cope with the vicissitudes of the business. In a certain sense it's like Dialing for Dollars, *says William Morris agent Bobbi Thompson.* Each call may be the big money. You never know. It's all a roulette wheel.

Third, an agent must be an effective salesman.

Fourth, agents must be able to discern talent.

Many top agents are very aggressive in their pursuit of deals, some would say ruthless. Says a former CAA agent, In order to be an extraordinarily successful agent you can't have any qualms about lying, cheating, stealing and being totally into yourself.

Mark Litwak
Reel Power
William Morrow, NY

I was particularly struck by what Joan Hyler (who is now a hot manager), said about agenting being like working in the commodities pit.

Frequently there is no tangible reason why the commodities market goes up or down, just as there is frequently no tangible reason why one property sells and another one doesn't. It really is *Dialing for Dollars*. Is it the same way when we choose an agent? Is it all just kismet?

Maybe, but just in case planning, intelligence and knowledge can inform your luck, let's consider a few things that affect the hierarchy of representation.

The ratio of agents to writers is more crucial to successful representation than the size of the office. One person cannot effectively represent 100 people. It's like going to the store and buying everything you see. You can't possibly use everything, you're just taking it out of circulation.

Many agents believe a good ratio is one agent to 20 to 25 clients. An agency with four agents can do well by 100 or even 140 clients, but that really is the limit. Look closely at any lists that are extravagantly over this size. It's easy to get lost on a large list.

• *We have managed to keep the size of the client list relatively small so that we can give a great deal of attention. I think for us, a ratio of 20 clients to one agent is actually a lot. Although I know that there are plenty of literary agents who represent 60-70 clients, I find for the kind of quality work that we do, that 20 each is a lot. We currently do have about 20 to 1, but we'd prefer less.*

Jim Preminger
Jim Preminger Agency/Los Angeles

The next important aspect to consider in terms of an agency is how much access it has. The dictionary defines access as *ability to approach* or *admittance*. Because the conglomerate agencies have so many star writers on their lists, they have plenty of *ability to approach*. If the studios, networks and producers do not return phone calls, they might find the agency retaliating by withholding the important actors that add credibility to the writer's projects. Some agencies who threaten withholding big star writers, actors and directors are actually able to bully the television networks into a prized time slot for their clients' shows. The trick, of course, is to be the client important enough for the agency to wield that power.

CAA's real talent is not the deals they swings for superstar writers, it's *attracting* those successful writers.

Those agencies that get *A* for access — The William Morris

Agency (WMA), International Creative Management (ICM), Creative Artists Agency (CAA), The Agency for the Performing Arts (APA) United Talent Agency (UTA) and Endeavor do not usually offer career-building services. These large corporations are there to cash in once credibility has already been established. Although it is true that star representation enhances some careers, it is not true in all cases.

In making your agent selections, make sure you are seeking an agent you have the credits to attract. Billy Bob Thornton's agent (WMA) is probably not going to be interested. Make sure other clients on the agent's list are your peers. It's all very well and good to think big, but you must walk before you can run.

Don't expect an agent who has spent years building his credibility to be interested in someone who just got off the bus. You must effectively agent yourself until you are at a point that a credible agent will give you a reading.

Stature should be high on your wish list when you are evaluating agents. You don't have to be CAA to have stature. The dictionary defines it as *level of achievement*. So, Stu Robinson and Maggie Field surely have more stature than some lowly agent at William Morris, but possibly not as much access and muscle — although once you have strong clients, you can beef up pretty fast.

- *An agent is only as strong as the clients he or she represents.*
  Elliot Webb
  Broder•Kurland•Webb•Uffner/Los Angeles

It's all very well to have stamina, discern talent, have a short list, be a great salesman, have access and stature, but the attribute that can make or break the decision is personality. Will you be able to stand talking to this person?

- *There are some agents about whom you would say, this person is never going to be able to help me because I would never want this person going into a studio representing me. And yet, there are some major agents in town you wouldn't want to have a cup of coffee with. Every agent works in his own way.*
  Ken Sherman
  Ken Sherman Agency/Los Angeles

A friend of mine left her agent because she wanted a better

negotiator. She switched agencies and got a hefty raise. Unfortunately, she lost rapport and communication in the process and ended up leaving that agent as soon as her contract came up for renewal.

Some things are more important than others. Writing is a such a solitary occupation that it's worthwhile to have someone you can bounce things off of, so don't sell rapport short.

Just as some agents evaluate your unseen material by whether or not you have studied at UCLA, NYU or USC, finding out an agent's background and training can give you initial insights into who he/she is and what you might expect from him. Getting in on the ground floor with an agent ambitious enough to survive the grueling training at the large conglomerates may be an important way into the system for you.

Absorbing articles on this subject are: *Slaves of Wilshire Boulevard* by Andy Marx in the November/December 1991 issue of *Buzz* magazine; *The Players* by Lynn Hirshberg, *Vanity Fair*, January 1993; and *Is This the Next Mike Ovitz?* by Johanna Schneller, *GQ*, May 1992.

The articles are not only chilling reading, but they give a feeling for the vulnerability of beginning agents and insights into how to approach the literary power brokers of tomorrow. Check your library to see if they archive those magazines. They are also available from the magazines Back Issue department for $7 a copy.

I asked agents to switch places with the writers and tell me what they thought writers should be looking for in an agent:

- *Honesty. The agent works for you. You don't want an agent who is conning you. You want someone who is honest. A lot of agents aren't. A lot of agents are. I don't want to ever get in a position where I have to figure out what I said yesterday. If you tell the truth, you don't have to do that.*
  Marty Shapiro
  Shapiro-Lichtman/Los Angeles

- *I think that you want to feel that there is someone who is not just selling you on himself or herself to sign you and to keep you off the market, but that you have someone who is generally going to take an interest in you and your work for a long time. I would also pick someone I could stay with, not someone I can see, going into the relationship, that I'm going to outgrow in two years' time.*
  Jim Preminger
  The Preminger Agency/Los Angeles

• *I think first of all you have to evaluate if the agent understands the work. Is he simpatico in practical or abstract ways? You don't have to be crazy about your agent, after all, this is business; more important, does the agent understand your writing? Does he understand you? Does he understand you as a person? Is this someone you can feel comfortable calling? Who you will (hopefully) feel comfortable talking to on a regular basis?*

Ken Sherman
Ken Sherman Agency/Los Angeles

• *Evaluate the agent for rapport. Are they comfortable talking to the agent? Be sure they are going with someone who has the time for them. Someone that doesn't have a lot of other new people at the same time because you can only walk in with a certain number of new people. You have to make that decision partly based on the accomplishments of the agency with other people in the past who have been in similar situations. If someone has the kind of track record where they have taken other brand new people and been with them when their careers have been made, then that becomes a plus.*

Marty Shapiro
Shapiro-Lichtman/Los Angeles

As to be expected, birthing a new career takes time and extraordinary energy from the agent just as it does from the writer. It's not just that the agent must find a buyer willing to take a chance on a newcomer, the industry has to have a place to absorb the new writer into the system in a protected manner while he is digesting all the new things about his career that affect his writing.

Assuming that all the other unestablished writers are at least as good as you, separate yourself from the pack by virtue of those traits that impress agents almost as much as your work: your emotional maturity, professionalism, dedication and willingness to be visible in the community.

• *What they have to be terribly concerned with is that they don't get snowed and go with someone who is just giving them a line. Of course, they may never get to the point of having to do that because it is difficult at best for them to get in that door.*

Marty Shapiro
Shapiro-Lichtman/Los Angeles

- *My idea of success is sustenance. It's making it last and challenging yourself. You can have all the short term success in the world. You need a plan and you need a partner. My role is varied with each client. I'm not best friends with my clients, I'm very friendly with all of them, but we don't go on vacation. My relationship with some of them is quite formal and professional.*

  Bob Hohman
  Hohman Maybank Lieb/Los Angeles

- *If an agent turns you down, don't be depressed. It means that that agent would not have been able to sell the project anyway because you can't sell a script unless you have a passion for it. Once you get a passion for a script, you don't put it down. You don't put it down until it's sold. You should only want an agent who is passionate about your work. If you have passion, you can't stop.*

  Raphael Berko
  Media Artist Group/Los Angeles

- *Choose the agent who has the highest enthusiasm for you. A company with five people is probably going to be stronger than a company with one person. But a company with 50 people is not necessarily stronger than a company with five people. The real question is,* Is your agent going to be saying your name every single day? *If the enthusiasm level is there, you are better off with the not-quite-so-important agent. If you are a brand new writer, you are probably better off with The Gersh Agency than with William Morris.*

  Rima Greer
  Above the Line Agency/Los Angeles

Two components to be evaluated in agent selection as you travel up the food chain are taste and intelligence. Once you are considering an agent with packaging potential, you want to make sure that your agent not only has the kind of talent on his list that you would be happy to work with, but that the agents' track record in combining ingredients speaks for itself.

Every year, the television schedule features new shows with actors, writers and directors with impressive track records, yet the shows fail. The same good news/bad news holds true with feature films. Films starring top actors, written by prized writers and directed by A-list directors somehow disappoint. That kind of production is frequently the result of packaging by a powerful conglomerate agency.

In order to get Actor A, the buyer must take Director B and

Scriptwriter C. In fact, if you are writer D, you might not even hear that you were requested, because Writer C makes more money and your agency would rather make a larger commission.

If you are choosing an agent/agency because of their packaging ability, make sure you look at the end result of their packaging and evaluate whether the agent/agency has a taste quotient that can result in a synergistic outcome.

Be Patient. Read the agent quotes and statistics carefully before you make judgments about which agent you might seek or even your readiness to attract an agent. Since the information is enhanced by an overview, make sure you have one. Then, go back and read the agent listing section of the book again, taking notes. You'll learn their lineage, education, credits (clients), the size of their list and get some idea of their style.

If an agent interests you, check the index to see if the agent is quoted elsewhere in the book. Those quotes can give you a further clue as to how the agent conducts business, views the world and how compatible you two might be.

If all the names on the agent's list are stars and you are just beginning, that means this agent is too far along for you. If you read his dossier and don't recognize any of the clients' names, they may well be respected working writers whose names you don't happen to know. Buy a copy of the WGA directory and look up that client's credits. Ask questions.

Perhaps it's an up and coming writer who has not yet sold. Maybe the agent is just starting and is building his list. If you are a beginning writer, perhaps you and the agent can build credibility together. It's worth a shot.

If you are a member of the Writers Guild, you have access to the Agency/Client lists. Once you have decided on three or four agents, if you are in New York or Los Angeles go by the WGA and spend an afternoon leafing through the listings of agencies. You can see that CAA has 500 clients and that Broder•Kurland•Webb•Uffner represents The Charles Brothers and James Burrows.

You can access similar information (though organized by writer and not by agency) by obtaining a copy of The Writers Guild of America membership directory available free to members or for $20.00 to non-members. Address your check to the WGA and note the word *Directory* on your envelope.

WGA members are listed with representation and key credits. You will begin to get an overview of the agents and also become more knowledgeable about your fellow writers. Look for those agents you have noted. See who their clients are. You'll see famous writers with famous agents, but also some well known clients represented by agents you might not have considered.

If you are a writer of stature, you will be looking for an agent that lists some of your peers. Some fine agencies have opened in the last two or three years whose names may not be as well-known as older agencies, but who nonetheless are quite important. Usually they are agencies started by agents who trained at larger offices, learned the business, groomed some clients, and left the agencies (frequently with some of the agency's choicest clients).

As you look at these lists, you are probably having fantasies about the large corporate agencies. Before you form your final opinion, read Chapter 9 on conglomerate/star agencies. There are many pros and cons to star representation at various levels of one's career.

While you are salivating, remember that most stars come to star agencies after a struggling independent agent helped the writer achieve enough stature and access of his own so that the conglomerate agent felt his interest was financially justified.

A friend of mine made her decision to choose an agent another way. Walking past an open door she overheard a phone conversation: *If my client's check is not on my desk by 5 p.m. this afternoon, I'm going to come over there and burn your office down*, and knew she had found her agent.

In making agent selections, be sure you are seeking an agent you have the credits to attract. Are the other clients on the list your peers? It might be nice to be on the list with William Goldman, but realistically, such stars command larger fees and more devoted attention from their agents than you would. If you are successful in acquiring such an agent, your competition will only make you feel dissatisfied with your results. Remember, one step at a time.

Any Agent Better than No Agent?

If no credible agent will give you the time of day, is it better to have just anybody? Opinions vary, some subscribe to the theory that although your ego may be fed — *I have an agent* — it may only take you out of the marketplace.

• *A hard question to answer. I'll confine the* any agent *to a* real *person that the buying community recognizes as a valid agent. Not someone who has an office on Moorpark and charges to read. Even if you are a beginner, you could call the Writers Guild and ask what they know about this particular agent. Or if you know anybody in the business that you can call and say,* Do you know anything about this person? *And if they say,* He's a nice person/she's a nice lady, but she doesn't have much clout, *then you'll have to decide.*

It all depends on how desperate you are. If it was me personally, if I had faith in my own ability, I'd wait until there was somebody with more credibility, someone that the community recognizes as a valid agent who has been able to sustain and earn a living for whatever, 10-20 years. That should say something for them.

Stu Robinson
Paradigm/Los Angeles

• *If you have no one else wanting you to sign, carefully evaluate the situation. Does this person seem to be in a situation where he or she can help you? Look around the office. See what some of the names are on the scripts. Check out the writers a bit with the work or with other writer friends. You can say to the agent,* Do I know any of your writers? This is exciting to me, who would be I be with? *It's all in how you present yourself.*

Ken Sherman
Ken Sherman Agency/Los Angeles

• *Just to get your foot in the door, somebody's got to know somebody somewhere. Even if you are doing the peddling. First of all, most studios won't look at a script without an agent's submission because the town is so litigious. Logistically, it pays to have somebody, a show business lawyer, somebody to represent you.*

Lynn Pleshette
Pleshette/Millner Agency/Los Angeles

• *Well,* hold out *for what? They* could hold out *indefinitely. What are they going to do while they are holding out? All they can do is to continue to write. The writer's interest is in trying to sell something so that he can find someone who is willing to work with him. The writer won't find entree in the marketplace because the studios and the production companies won't talk to him without an agent, so any agent is better than no agent.*

Marty Shapiro
Shapiro-Lichtman/Los Angeles

- *What do you have to lose? You can't accomplish anything without an agent because no one will look at your material.*

  Debbee Klein
  Paradigm/Los Angeles

- *Any agent who is signatory to the Writers Guild is better than no agent. Keep writing and keep after the agent. And don't send your own material around to studios and/or producers. Everyone wants to see new material they've never seen before.*

  Rima Greer
  Above-the-line Agency/Los Angeles

If you are in the position of choosing, the question to answer is: who will provide the best opportunity for you to be gainfully employed in the business and beyond that to build a real career?

When you have finished this book, you should have some idea of which agents appeal to you. Some names will keep coming up. Make a list. Even if you know you are only interested in Gary Salt or Joyce Ketay, target at least five names. You can't intelligently make a choice unless you have something to compare. You may not be in a situation where more than one agent will see you, but if you are, you can only choose Agent A after you have compared him to Agent B and Agent C.

Ask advice from any show biz insiders (other writers, producers, development executives) with whom you have formed relationships. Explain that you are agent shopping and that you would like advice about the names on your list.

Ask for any names they might like to add. Listen to their opinion but remember, producers and network honchos have a far different relationship with an agent than you will have. Make your own decision.

Wrap Up

The ideal client
✓ has talent
✓ displays a singular personality
✓ exhibits professionalism
✓ maintains mental health
✓ is a WGA member

✓ writes well
✓ is realistic about his career

The ideal agent
✓ is aggressive
✓ has stature
✓ has access
✓ is enthusiastic about your work
✓ shares your vision regarding your career
✓ has an optimum ratio of writers to agents
✓ has integrity
✓ communicates with you
✓ gives you guidance
✓ has the ability to tastefully combine ingredients

Research
✓ carefully read the information in this book
✓ check WGA Agent/Client Lists
✓ check The WGA Membership Directory
✓ consult your friends in show business
✓ don't underestimate word of mouth
✓ check to see what they have packaged
✓ *Spec Screenplay Sales Directory*

8 Query Letter & Meetings

You've finally settled on a list of two or three agents that appeal to you. Since you don't have a connected industry job and you don't know anyone who knows anyone to give you entree to an agent, it's time for your secret weapon: the query letter.

Although many agents do not accept unsolicited scripts, most will respond to query letters if you include a self-addressed-stamped-envelop. If your letter is interesting or clever enough or incredibly well written, they might ask to see your manuscript. If they don't ask to read something, it's probable that you are not ready yet.

Although hand-written notes are nice, one agent told me that if he receives a hand-written letter, he is afraid he will receive a hand-written script.

• *The approach is all important. I'll say,* I'm not going to look for anybody else right now, *then the letter or communique is so well done or so well written that we'll say,* let's take a look *either because the writing is so good in the presentation or because they are so clever in their approach. It also depends on what their piece of material is. Invariably, they will say, I've just written this thing about* — *and then put in a one paragraph synopsis and you realize that none of this sounds as though it's anything, whereas someone coming out of UCLA will say,* I just wrote three *Seinfelds* or I have a sample script for *ER* or *X-Files or whatever or they are in a Masters program at UCLA and you might say,* Hey, let's take a look at it.

I would generally ask, How many agents have you gone to before you came to me? *If they have been to agents, then we may try to qualify it and say,* well, we'll look at it, but not in competition with anybody else. If we like it, we want to be able to sign you.

Marty Shapiro
Shapiro-Lichtman/Los Angeles

• *Although 90% of the writers we see are through referral and we are inundated with query letters, it never hurts to try. A clever note or a clever package gets our attention.*

Debbee Klein
Paradigm/Los Angeles

- *When you write a query letter, take the time to find out who you are writing to. If you are writing a letter to* Dear Sir or Madam, *you haven't taken the time to find out enough about the company you are hoping will represent you. Why should that person take two hours of their time to read your script? Names are important and very easy to get. Simply call the agency and ask for the name of the person you should write to.*

  Barbara Alexander
  Media Artists Group/Los Angeles

- *The shorter, the sweeter, the more successful. And make it easy on the agent. If you want a reply, send a card with a SASE with the agency's return address written on it so the agent doesn't have to write that in.*

  Candy Monteiro/Fredda Rose
  Monteiro Rose/Los Angeles

- *I got a letter from someone who wanted me to read his script. It was totally formal:* Pursuant to my conversation with your assistant *and so on* I've written an outrageous, zany comedy. *We looked at this and we said* how can we believe he wrote an outrageous, zany comedy? *There is no interest on my part to read it. He didn't make me laugh. I have no ideas from this letter that would make me think the script is going to work. So, think about what you are doing. Position yourself in a way that reflects your work.*

  Ken Greenblatt
  J. Michael Bloom Agency/Los Angeles

- *Calling an agent who doesn't have time for you is wasting everybody's energy. Somewhere at some agency, there is some guy who doesn't have any clients. An agent at a mid-level place or a young agent at a big conglomerate like ICM is a prime agent to target. There are people there who would take a* pocket *client.*

  Daniel Ostroff
  Daniel Ostroff Agency/Los Angeles

I talked to a writer just the other day who told me he had sent his material to CAA and received a letter in reply asking to be kept abreast of new material. It was signed and there was a phone number. The writer assumed it was some low level person who didn't count. That low level person is only beginning, but most likely he will not be on the bottom rung of the ladder long.

This is the kind of situation that can result in your becoming a pocket client. You are not signed, but the agent watches your progress and ultimately sends out a script or two to see how they are received. If the script stirs interest, you and the agent are both further along in the relationship and you will probably become a signed client.

Don't put yourself off thinking you have no entree. If you have a feature script, there is always someone who will give it a look. Particularly at big conglomerates. What do you care if it is someone in the mail room who is writing back to you? People in the mail room are Harvard law school graduates who will be moving up. And they are hungry.

• *We don't accept any unsolicited material. If you send us an unsolicited script, it'll go into the recycling bin, which in our case is not the garbage can, it's actually a recycling bin. It will only be sent back if there is a self-addressed-stamped-envelope. It's okay to send a short treatment or a synopsis though I probably won't read that either.*

The thing I will read is a letter. If in that letter you have a one or two paragraph synopsis of the story, that's good, so I know what it is that you are trying to send me. If the subject matter really interests me, I might read a treatment if it's enclosed or I might contact you to send me one. Anything beyond that will not be read and will not be returned.

Stuart Jacobs
CNA/Los Angeles

• *Anything over the transom, not requested, we won't read. We will call them to come get it, we don't like to dump it. We do take query letters.*

Jonathan Westover
The Gage Group/Los Angeles

• *Always try to get an introduction or a name of somebody in your inquiry letter. Don't fabricate it, it's too small a town. The key that is going to get attention is good writing. That's the truth. I wish I could show you some of the things we get in the wrong format. You know immediately if it's a first script and no one's bothered to do his homework.*

Barbara Alexander
Media Artists Group/Los Angeles

• *For legal reasons, we look at no unsolicited material. We respond to query letters as long as they come with self-addressed stamped envelopes. Nine times out of ten, we're not going to take material that comes from a query letter, but occasionally I do. I have two scripts now that first came to my attention through a query letter. The query letter outlined a script I was interested in reading, but that's unusual.*

Gary Salt
Paul Kohner, Inc./Los Angeles

• *They can send a mailing out to agents, not a manuscript, but a description of the material and a brief resume. [They should say] whether they have written for cable, magazine articles, school plays, student films or a graduate film.*

Lynn Pleshette
Pleshette/Miller Agency/Los Angeles

• *There are a lot a query letters that I do like, but I don't make the phone call. I have a file of maybe 100 letters about scripts that I actually like, but if we called every single one of them, we'd have no room on our floors or time to do our jobs. Who knows when we will get to them? But there are certain letters that stand out, that make us say,* There's something cool here.

Anonymous Agent

• *There has to be something in the letter, not just a synopsis of the script or a tag line, but something about them, either an educational background or a career background. Something that says,* okay, this person knows how to write and has something to say.

Jonathan Westover
The Gage Group/Los Angeles

• *If people are just going to write letters, a letter is a letter, I get hundreds of letters. The only reason I called the one team I have signed from a query letter was because the letter they sent put me on the floor, it was so funny. It was as funny as anything you've seen on television and when I read it, I laughed so hard that I said,* these guys are worth talking to. *That's why I met with them.*

Stuart Jacobs
CNA/Los Angeles

• *I respond to the idea, to how well the letter is written, the letter itself. I think if they can't write a letter, they can't write a script.*

Lynn Pleshette
Pleshette/Millner Agency/Los Angeles

Whether you live in the large production centers or not, the query letter is an essential component to your acceptance into the system. When you consider how carefully agents read your letter, you will unquestionably want to take just that much care in how you write it. The letter should be brief, articulate and informative. Tell them who you are, list your most important credit (if you have one), give a three or four line synopsis of your story or idea (look to see how TV Guide does it) and ask if they would be interested in reading it. The more you tell, the more they have to reject. Be brilliant and/or witty but above all, be brief.

If you have entree to meet with several agents, by all means do so.

- *It's not that easy to get an appointment with an agent and get read, but if a writer has entree, I think he should meet with several agents.*

I tell clients that I am signing, You should go and you should meet with these other people because they may be better for you, they may service you in a way that I hadn't thought of. You guys may click in a way that we're not going to. *I think it's really about forming relationships that are going to last where both the agent and the client feel that their needs are being met.*

Certainly, I would advise anyone to shop around so that you will be happy signing with me. I don't want them to have to worry that in 3 or 4 or 5 months, they'll think, Gee, that other agent seemed so great, I wish I had at least taken a meeting.
Stuart Jacobs
CNA/Los Angeles

The Meeting

Once you have interested an agent and he has read some of your material, the next hurdle is the meeting. For starters, be on time and look terrific. This is a job interview, after all. Choose clothing that makes you feel good and look successful and that suggests you take pride in yourself. Bright colors not only make people remember you, but they usually make you feel good, too. Remember, in today's world, packaging is at least as important as content.

- *I read every letter that comes in to me. If there is a SASE, I will respond with a form letter. Of the hundreds and hundreds of letters I have received, I think I have responded twice, and from one of them, I signed a writing team. These writers came in unshaven and in shorts and weird shirts and I fell in love with those guys, but that is who they are.*

If somebody comes in and they haven't showered in three days and they are cantankerous and you just don't want to be in the room with them, then, yes, I would have felt better about them if they had showered and shaved. If it's your personality, if you only wear t-shirts and Reeboks, then be who you are. When my writers go into meetings with people, I want them to be who they are, they are selling their mind to people and it's really about that rather than an Armani suit. If someone is comfortable wearing a suit and tie, I'd love to see them in a suit and tie for the meetings.

Stuart Jacobs
CNA/Los Angeles

Go in and act like yourself. Be natural and forthright. Don't badmouth any other agents. If you are leaving another agency, don't get into details about why you are leaving. If the agent asks why you left, just say it wasn't working out. Agents are all members of the same fraternity. Unless this agent is stealing you away from someone else, he will be at least a little anxious about why you are leaving. If you badmouth another agent, the agent you are meeting with is wondering — subconsciously, at least — when you will badmouth him.

Don't talk too much. Give yourself a chance to get comfortable. Adjust to the environment. Notice the surroundings. Comment on them. Talk about the weather. Talk about the stock market, the basketball game, or the last play you saw. That's a great topic, it gives you each a chance to check out the other's taste.

If you do discuss a play or a film, say what you think. If you hated it, be tactful (the writer may be his client), just say it didn't work for you. Remember, this is a first date. You are both trying to figure out if you are interested in each other.

Don't be afraid to ask questions, but use common sense. Phrase questions in a positive vein. Discuss producers that you know and have worked for. If you admire one of his clients, say so.

Don't be afraid to tell the agent what your plans are. Ask him if they seem realistic. Are you on the same wavelength? How does he see your career progressing? Don't just send out, make sure you are also receiving.

Find out how the office works. If you are being interviewed by the owner and there are other agents, ask the owner if he will be representing you personally. Many owners are not involved in agenting on a day-to-day basis.

Find out office policy about returning phone calls. Are you welcome to call? Does the agent want feedback after meetings? What's the protocol for dropping by? Will they consistently read your work? Will they consult with you before turning down work? Explore your feelings about these issues before the meeting.

If you need to be able to speak to your agent regularly, address that issue. If these conversations turn the agent off, better to find out now. This is the time to assess the chemistry between the two of you.

During the meeting, be alert for subtle things that define a person, how he treats his employees, whether he really listens. Notice his body language and how he is with people on the phone. How you feel when he's speaking to you. What's the subtext?

Be the One to End the Meeting

When the meeting is over, be the one to end it. No one can be fascinating forever so get the hell out of there before the agent finds that out. Schedule a trip to your dentist immediately following the meeting to give you the urgency needed to depart.

If the agent tells you at this point that he would like you for a client and you don't feel the need to think it over, swell. More than likely, he will need to discuss the matter with the rest of the office so don't be downhearted if things seem a little vague. Let him know you were pleased with the meeting. Even if it was not your finest moment — or his — be gracious. After all, you both did your best. Tell him you've enjoyed meeting him, but that you have another appointment. Let him wonder where. Leave.

As soon as possible, write down all your perceptions and feelings about the meeting and put them away for 24 hours. Then write your feelings down again and compare them. When I was interviewing agents for this book, I found that I would have signed with almost all of them on the spot. They are all salesmen and they were charming. By the next day I was more objective about it all. By then, the hyperbole seemed to have drifted out of my head and I was able to hear more clearly what had gone on.

If the agent says he will call you and doesn't, leave it. There are others on your list. If he forgot you, do you want him as your agent? If he is rejecting you, don't insist he do it to your face.

If he does call, be circumspect in your decision. You are choosing an agent. The qualities you look for in a pal are not necessarily the qualities you desire in an agent. There are very successful writers who deal with brusque, self-centered agents that have masterminded brilliant careers.

Many artists feel anxious about choosing an agent. They feel their whole career is on the line. It's not. The agent is your business partner. Your writing is the basis of your career, not your agent.

Wrap Up

The query letter
- ✓ must be interesting, clever, brief and innovative
- ✓ needs to demonstrate you've done your homework and understand how the business works
- ✓ needs to include self-addressed-stamped-envelope

Tools to set up meetings
- ✓ referrals
- ✓ credits
- ✓ awards
- ✓ resume
- ✓ great writing

The meeting
- ✓ be punctual
- ✓ be yourself
- ✓ dress well
- ✓ focus on what you want
- ✓ act intelligently
- ✓ ask for what you want
- ✓ end the meeting

9 Conglomerate/Star Agencies

If you are really hot and ICM and CAA are vying to buy your dinner, perhaps you want to consider life at the top with one of the big conglomerates. If you have that choice, is it a good idea?

When my writer friend, Mary began to make money ($150,000 a year), she left the small independent agent who had nurtured her and succumbed to the seductions of one of the star agencies.

Though happy with her perceived change in status, she found she had less money to pay her bills since the agent was not vigilant in collecting her checks in a timely manner. When she called to inquire, the agent was irritated and said: *I wish you were more successful and made more money so you wouldn't be calling me about money all the time.*

Mary called up her old agent, admitted she had made a big mistake and begged to return home. She's even more successful now due to her excellent writing and the efforts and courage of her prestigious independent agent.

- *A lot of the people that I am representing were at bigger places (CAA, William Morris, etc.). Let's say that your agent left the business and you have been at a nice small place for a long time where you have had lots of attention. All of a sudden, you are faced with a decision, you weren't unhappy with your representation, but that person no longer exists.*

  The dog and pony show that these big places do is (and I was at a big agency and I used to do it), Here we are, we are all powerful and all connected and look at all the information we have *(and they pull out reams of paper)* and we represent all these movie stars and we'll package you with our people and we'll use our clout to get you this and that.

  For 75% of the list, that's heinous bullshit, because it's impossible to spread that wealth around. It's clout because it's only used on a few people, that's why they call it clout. It's impossible to service 150 directors well. CAA has a gigantic directors list and I would say they do an incredible job for about 25% of that list. The rest of them, I hope it works out.

  The point is that with some people, they wake up one day and say, Gee, I'm here at this big agency and I keep getting shuffled from one agent to another. How do I access that *clout? And they decide they need a little more personal representation. Large agencies give very personal representation to about*

25% of their clients. The rest of them are dangling.

A lot of the people that I've gotten into business with aren't seduced by the clout thing. I've been here at the party long enough, I can get anybody on the phone and frankly, if a client of mine is a long shot on a project, he has a much better chance with me because I'm only calling about him, I'm not calling about 10 people with bigger names or 10 equally long shot names.

Most people in the business are not operating at the highest levels. They're having good careers and making a good living off it. What you need to make sure is that you are maintaining that level and that you have someone who is keeping you fresh and keeping you out there. It takes very personal focused representation.

I don't represent Bernardo Bertulucci and I don't represent Sydney Pollock. While I would love to represent both of them, I probably never will. I'm very realistic about who I am as an agent. I represent a very nice high end writer and director base, but they are all people that I feel some sort of parity with as people. I'm very proud of and very comfortable with the people I represent and I think we deal with each other as equals. I always approach it that I'm able to give them the time that they deserve or I wouldn't have taken them on.

Bob Hohman
Hohman Maybank Leib/Los Angeles

• *We're a small agency that's been able to take people all the way. We always have people at every level from the lowest level, from the writer looking for his first job to people who are writing their own series.*

Elliot Stahler
Kaplan Stahler Agency/Los Angeles

• *There are certain kinds of clients who want to be with us. The thing that separates the wheat from the chaff is that we are with a very realistic group of people. We have very few virgins, we've all been around for a while. We are in the business with a lot of adults who know what representation is all about. We have a relatively small practice. We are not in the volume business. We don't take people on just for money. It wouldn't be worth it. We have to have a real affinity for the person's work.*

Bob Hohman
Hohman Maybank Leib/Los Angeles

Patricia McQueeney echos the words of Hohman and Stahler. McQueeney not only runs a one-woman office, she runs a one-client office managing the interests of her client of 27 years, Harrison Ford. As Ms. McQueeney says:

- *We all know where the jobs are every day, we know what's out there and any agent worth his or her salt knows exactly what's going on at any given moment. It's ridiculous to think one agent can do better than another.*
Your Last Film Bombed? Simple: Get a New Agent
Bernard Weinraub
The New York Times
May 10, 1997

- *Obviously I've chosen to spend my life in a small setting, part of that is based on the fact that I'm most comfortable in a smaller setting, so if a writer chooses to go with us, they probably choose us because they think they won't get lost here. It's a matter of individual choice, some writers like the razzle dazzle of the larger agency with just the sheer amount of activity and the access to whatever those resources are.*
Jim Preminger
Jim Preminger Agency/Los Angeles

- *I'm real opinionated about the agency business. I know a lot about it, it's the only thing I've ever done...I'm very happy being in a small agency environment. The primary difference between a big agency and a small agency is that it's impossible for a big agency not to have its own agenda. Some portion of the clients end up serving that agenda whether that is in their best interests or not. Small agencies are generally about the clients' interests and desires. It's far more client driven. The big agency has a big overhead, whereas we have a very contained, intelligently drawn overhead which is fairly easy to meet. We are recession proof whereas a big agency isn't.*
My partners and I feel that we have enough successful clients and that there is always enough prosperity that if you say, You know, I want to take off a year and write a book, *we're able to say* good for you *assuming that you have the financial wherewithal to do that. It really is a marriage relationship where it is, hopefully, two adults trying to behave like adults with each other. If you want to do something that isn't financially remunerative, then that's your decision. It's far more about your desire than it's about us needing to use your talents.*
Bob Hohman
Hohman Maybank Leib/Los Angeles

I guess we've all heard the joke about the writer who killed four people, stole a baby, bombed a building, then ran across the street into The William Morris Agency, and was never seen again. It's the quintessential story about the wisdom of being signed by a big conglomerate agency.

The question of whether the large star-level conglomerate agency is the best place to be is confusing. There is a case to be made for both choices. In the end, as in all other important decisions (who to marry, which doctor or lawyer to hire, whether or not to have elective surgery, etc.), you can only collect data and then, using your research and instincts, decide.

Research does lead to the conclusion that the star agencies (CAA, ICM, WMA, UTA, Endeavor) have the most power, information and the best likelihood of getting you in for meetings and ultimately, jobs, if (and these are the operative words here) someone there who is powerful and/or hungry believes in you. It's a fact that the conglomerates have more power and information.

The questions are: *What will they do with it?* and, *Do power and information compensate for lack of personal attention?*

Power Sources

The power of the large agencies comes from the star writers, directors and actors. When you have Joe Eszterhas, Diane English, Neil Simon, Steven Bochco, David Milch and Chris Carter on your list (plus hundreds of other big names) you have the attention of the buyers. The Catch 22 is, if you are Eszterhas or English, you are the power and you really don't need those agencies and if you're not one of those folk, you are not going to get the same kind of attention.

No matter where you are though, it's up to you to generate the juice. The director of a current blockbuster confided to me that although his agents at CAA made sure that everyone in town knew about him when he first joined the agency, his inability to make a decision about the next project after his first few moments of heat, resulted in him being almost unemployable for a time. His agents didn't drop him, but he wasn't saleable.

Only by generating his own product, writing his own script and getting it to a producer that he had worked for before, was he able to get back into the game And with that kind of drive and determination, he could have been represented by almost any agent, although I'm sure that having CAA for an agent improved his price.

- *When I was in a one-room office on 57th Street in New York, I was as powerful as anyone, if I believed in someone. I could get them in anyplace, because I wouldn't take no for an answer. I believe if someone works out of a phone booth on Hollywood and Vine, if they believe in you, they can get you in as quickly as the strongest agent in town.*

John Kimble
William Morris Agency/Los Angeles

One of John's colleagues at William Morris, Gene Parseghian confessed that there are days he wishes he still had a small office with three or four people and 20 clients, tops.

As mentioned elsewhere in the book, conglomerates are not equipped to handle clients who are not making a lot of money. They have a big overhead. Although most of them take one or two young writers, directors and actors a year to develop into the system, they are usually not career builders.

• *Until a year ago, the agency world was like the Old West,* says Joe Roth, chairman of Walt Disney Studios. *CAA's dominance made for a moral order. There was no expectation that you could steal clients away since people were afraid to leave. When Ronnie [Meyer] and Mike [Ovitz] left, however, chaos became the norm.*

The New World Order
Elaine Dutka
The Los Angeles Times
June 23, 1996

Tracking the machinations of the power struggles among the conglomerates is fascinating.

• *Three agencies dominate the movie business: Creative Artists, International Creative Management and William Morris. The smaller United Talent also has a strong client list that includes stars (Jim Carrey and Sandra Bullock) and some top television actors and writer producers. A fifth agency, Endeavor, is also emerging as a power.*

Your Last Film Bombed? Simple: Get a New Agent
Bernard Weinraub
The New York Times
May 10, 1997

You would probably be thrilled to have your name alongside the stars on any of the conglomerate agencies, but there are name writers at many agencies in town, other than the conglomerates. You'll see some listed in this book. For a fuller list, check *The WGA Directory* or their agency lists.

If one of the star/conglomerate agencies beckons, you can be sure they will do it with great style: limos, fancy restaurants and other appealing lures.

Obviously, independent agents are not amused. In speaking with them, I kept hearing, *I got this person started. Just when it was all paying-off, CAA or ICM came with the limos, the flowers. The client left. Why?*

I'm reminded of something Elliot Stahler said when I asked about writers changing agents: *Some clients demonstrate a certain amount of immaturity through their susceptibility to other agents telling them what they will do for them, etc.*

He's right, of course. It is immature. It's hard to be balanced in the face of luxury. But, when all the wine is drunk, the dinner at Maple Drive is over and the limos have gone home, you're going to have to make your decision based on what is important to you. Do you want a family member and the personal attention that involves, or do you want a corporation?

You may not care what producers think, but I did ask some producers their thoughts on the matter. Several told me they hate to deal with some of the conglomerates because they routinely gets calls dictating just who the producer is going to use on a packaged project.

Unless the producer uses Client A, the agent will withhold Client B. On the one hand, if you are Client A, you might be thrilled. If, on the other hand, you are Client B, you might miss a job that you never knew you had. It's something to think about.

So there you are. My final vote is for a prestigious, successful, tasteful mid-size agency. Of course, no one has plied me with limos and flowers yet, either.

Wrap Up

Conglomerates
✓ have more information
✓ have a lot of muscle
✓ have access to more perks

✓ say they can package effectively
✓ provide less support in times of duress
✓ give advice that is corporate, less personal
✓ have a big overhead
✓ may lose interest when you are not in demand

Independents
✓ can have just as much access
✓ are making calls for less people
✓ have lower overhead
✓ are more likely to stand by you through thick *and* thin
✓ depending on their client list, might also package
✓ are able to give more individual attention

10 Divorce

It's difficult to decide where to place information about relationships that don't work out. When I first started writing about agents, I began the book talking about this painful subject and vigilant folk pointed out that you have to have an agent before you can leave them.

That is true, but some people reading this book may already have an agent and are contemplating leaving. Even if you've never had an agent, you might find a discussion of relationship difficulties enlightening. The writer may be leaving just because he's not selling any material and that may not be the agent's fault.

If your agent won't return your calls, if he's been dishonest or is not getting your material around, you have good reason to leave him.

In the rules of The Writers Guild, if a writer has had no work in 90 days, he can void his contract with an agent by sending a letter to the agent plus copies to the Guild dissolving the partnership citing Article 7. Maybe you and your agent have different ideas regarding your potential. This is something that should have been ironed out before the contract was signed, but sometimes that conversation comes later in the relationship.

Sometimes careers change and writers feel they can be better serviced by agents with a different set of contacts.

Perhaps your level of achievement in the business has risen. You have now, through brilliance or possibly a lucky break, become a writer of greater stature than your agent. (Very possible if fortune has just smiled on you.)

The bottom line is that writer/agent relationships are just like any other relationship: as long as it's mutually rewarding, everyone is happy, when it's not, things must change.

Writers and agents seek each other because they see money-making potential. 35 perfectly credible agents may pass on you and then agent number 36 will fall in love, send your material to the right place with the right director, and you are suddenly a star.

It can happen the other way, too, of course. One minute you're hot and the next moment you're not. You didn't necessarily do anything so differently to get un-hot (frequently getting hot works the same way).

- *The business is high stakes. It's easy for another agent to whisper in a client's ear,* I could do better for you. *It was done as far back as the apocryphal story about Swifty Lazar telling Humphrey Bogart,* I could get you four deals in a day *and when he did, he got Bogart as a client. Even then, there was a tremendous amount of competition to represent talented people because that's where the strength is.*

Elliot Webb
Broder•Kurland•Webb•Uffner/Los Angeles

At a smaller agency, being *warm* or even *cold* won't necessarily make you persona non grata, but at the big agencies, it might be difficult for you to get your agent on the phone. They are not in the business to handle less profitable jobs, so they either drop you or their lack of interest finally tells you that you're no longer on their level.

Representing a client is expensive and time consuming necessitating answering phone calls, being constantly available, reading material, contacting buyers, staying in touch, tracking and sending out material. If you're not making money over a period of time, it's a vote of confidence for a smaller agency (in particular) to keep trying.

Agents sometimes end up being rude to you because they can't afford to take the time to talk to someone they can't sell anymore. This is the moment when you might be sorry you left that small agent who worked so hard to get you started and engineered the big break for you. Will he want to see you now? He might. He might not. It depends on how you handled it when leaving.

I asked agents if they ever dumped clients and if so, why?

Why Agents Drop Clients

- *Drop clients? When it's a mutual thing. We try for a period of time and if we haven't been able to do it. We have a responsibility to the writer and if you feel that you'd like to get someone else, we'd certainly understand. We wouldn't throw somebody out.*

We have dropped people when they have been abusive. We are in a highly charged business and we really don't have to tolerate that.

Marty Shapiro
Shapiro-Lichtman/Los Angeles

- *I would only get rid of a client for two reasons: if they don't keep writing*

(18 months without a new script) or if they are unpleasant to deal with. Life is too short.

Rima Greer
Above the Line Agency/Los Angeles

• *There are some agents that clean house at the beginning of the year. If the client hasn't made x amount of money in a year or two, they automatically sever the relationship. I tend to think if I liked a writer once, that it's going to work eventually.*

Barbara Alexander
Media Artists Group/Los Angeles

Maybe you want to leave your agent because the magic has gone out of your marriage just as the magic can go out of a traditional marriage if both partners don't put energy into it. And just as in marriage, it's always a better deal to try to rekindle the relationship, if possible. You were in love once, what went wrong? If you are both willing to save the relationship, that process will take a lot less energy and resourcefulness than the just learning to get to know each other period involved in any new relationship.

• *The first thing a writer thinks of that needs to be changed when he is not doing well is his agent. Rather than look on the outside, you have to look inward: examine what you have been doing — the quality of your work. Are you a good communicator with the producers you have been working with and with your agent? Have you burned bridges? Is your work as good as it should be? All these things should be examined before you change agents. There are good agents and bad agents, but you carry your problems from one place to another.*

Fredda Rose/Candy Monteiro
Monteiro Rose/Los Angeles

If something is bothering you, speak up. This comes easily to very few people. We all want to be liked and it's hard to confront the situation. If you are unhappy and feel you will never sell anything again, call your agent and tell him you are concerned. He knows as well as you that you are not selling. Ask him if there is anything you can do. Ask if he has heard any negative feedback.

Whatever you do, don't just start interviewing other agents. You owe it to yourself and to your agent to talk before you get so angry that it is impossible for you to continue the relationship. If you have a conversation early on, perhaps both of you can find some way to remedy the situation. If not, at least he will have some idea of where you are coming from later when you are ready to leave.

• *We don't want clients not communicating, sitting at home, stewing and brewing. I don't mind if a client calls once every two weeks and says,* hey, what can I do?

Stu Robinson
Paradigm/ Los Angeles

• *You should be able to talk to each other and understand where you are each coming from. There may come a time where you are at a crossroads where the agent's experience and belief is that this is not the right thing for your client to be doing. If both the client and agent have differing thoughts about direction, then you have to go your separate ways because the client isn't going to be happy until he finds out if his ideas are correct.*

Candy Monteiro/Fredda Rose
Monteiro Rose/Los Angeles

Looking/Telling/Ethics

Before you start looking for a new agent, you must make a decision about telling the agent you are going to leave. Most writers are hesitant not only because they are embarrassed and guilty, but also because they feel the agent might stop submitting their material. The writer would be left unrepresented while he is shopping. First of all, I doubt the agent would want to forego the commissions due on any new jobs. Every agent I questioned said he would never leave a writer without representation while he was shopping. Secondly, if he wants to keep you, this is his chance to demonstrate you are making a mistake and he really is the best agent in the world, after all.

Another plus for telling your agent that you are shopping is you don't have to worry about word getting back to him prematurely that you are doing research or actually interviewing. Not only that, any agents you contact during your search will note you are a person of integrity.

If it is too late for a talk or you talked and it didn't help, at least leave with a little class. Even though it might be uncomfortable, get on with it. There is no need for long recriminations. No excuses. Not *My wife thinks* or *My manager thinks.* No, it's *I've decided that I am going to make a change. I appreciate all the work you have done for me. I will miss seeing you, but it just seems like the time to make a change. For whatever reason, it's just not working. I hope we'll see each other again.*

You don't need to be phony. If you don't appreciate what the agent has done and don't think he's done any work, just skip it. Talk about the fact that you think the relationship is not, or is no longer, mutually rewarding. Be honest and leave both of you with some dignity. You may see this person again. With some distance between you, you might even remember why you signed with him in the first place. Don't close doors.

If you are leaving because your fortunes have risen, it is even harder. The agent will really be upset to see you and your money leave. Also, your new-found success has probably come from his efforts as well as yours. But if you are really hot and feel only WMA or ICM can handle you, leave you must. Tell your agent you wish it were another way but the vicissitudes of the business indicate that at a certain career level, CAA and their peers have more information, clout, and other stars to bargain with, and you want to go for it.

If you handle it well and if your agent is smart, he will leave the door open. This has happened to him before and it will happen to him again. That doesn't make it hurt less, but this is business, he will probably just shake his head and tell his friends you have gone crazy. *This isn't the same Mary I always knew. It's gone to her head.*

The agent has to find some way to handle it just as you would if he were firing you. It will not be easy for you to begin a new business relationship, but you are hot right now and the world is rosy.

Wrap Up

Grounds for divorce
✓ dishonesty
✓ writer abuse
✓ agent not reading your work
✓ agent not getting your work read
✓ sudden career change
✓ lack of communication
✓ differing goals

✓ personality differences

Ethical, smart, professional and personal behavior
✓ speak to agent before shopping
✓ leave doors open

11 Relationships

All your good work has paid off and you have now been proposed to and you have accepted. You and your agent are going to sign the piece of paper — you now have representation.

The next stop is your new partner's office to sign contracts and meet and fix in your mind all the auxiliary people who will be working for you. If there are too many to remember on a first meeting, make notes as soon as you leave the office as to who is who and where they sit. Until you become more familiar with them, you can consult the map before each subsequent visit.

Now the real work begins. If this agent is a replacement for an old partnership, perhaps you are leaving your old agent because you felt he didn't work hard enough. Maybe your expectations were out of line. Maybe you were lazy. Maybe you didn't keep his enthusiasm high enough. Maybe he was a goof-off. It doesn't matter now. What matters now is how well you and your new agent are going to function together.

The agent only gets 10% of the money so you can't really expect him to do 100% of the work. The concept of 90%-10% is intriguing. How many of us have resented our agents when we have been requested for a job and all the agent had to do was negotiate? In fact, if all our jobs were requests, would we just have a lawyer negotiate and do away with the agent altogether? Or is the support and feedback worth something?

Maybe our whole thought process about agents is incorrect. In our hearts, we really think the agent is going to get us a job. Based upon my research and my years in the business, I finally really know that the agent does not get me work. He gets my appointments, but my work gets me work. Not only by my ability to function well in my profession, but also by my successful (or not) adjustment to the vicissitudes of my own life.

The times I have not worked as steadily have been directly connected to my rise and fall as a person. Life processes must be endured. We can change agents and mates and clothes sizes, but we can't alter reality, we must experience it. Those realities are reflected in our work and enrich us as artists.

As in all relationships, each party assumes certain responsibilities. And as in all relationships, things go much smoother when both parties are putting energy into the union and have mutual expectations.

Be pragmatic regarding what you have a right to demand of an agent, what you can realistically expect of an agent and what your contribution is to the mix. A novice writer's expectations of his agent should be far different than expectations of the writer who is paying a major portion of the agent's rent.

In the interest of keeping you from feeling paranoid about your agreement with your agent, I asked several agents what they felt were reasonable expectations in the writer/agent relationship.

Reasonable Writer Expectations

• *You have a right to expect the best professional judgement I can give you. The best professional opinions that I can give you with respect to your work. That within the limits of normal business practice and within the normal limits of working days that the agency is looking out for your interests, promoting your work, subject to a general consensus between writer and agent that the work is promotable.*
Gary Salt
Paul Kohner, Inc./Los Angeles

• *Writers have a right to expect that their agents return their phone calls, tell them the truth and work hard on their behalf.*
Maggie Field
Field-Cheh Agency, Inc./Los Angeles

• *Frequent, honest open communication. Support for their dreams. If you are not in sync with each other about what the goals are, why bother? Also, it's a writer's prerogative to expect a great deal of patience. If it doesn't happen with the first round of submissions, some agents think it's over. Your agent should be your best professional friend.*
Candy Monteiro/Fredda Rose
Monteiro Rose/Los Angeles

• *You have a right to expect your agent to work for his 10%. You should be able to speak to him every week. Just hello and an update is fine and the agent should attend your tapings.*
Debbee Klein
Paradigm/Los Angeles

• *As a client you have a right to expect an honest, open relationship. With a brand new writer, there's not a lot you can do, but the agent should be sending out your material and trying to introduce you to the community as a new talent so that people get to know you.*

Marty Shapiro
Shapiro-Lichtman/Los Angeles

• *The agent is your link to the outside world. It's helpful if your agent is thinking of you enough to pick up the phone and call you, even if I just say,* there's nothing happening right now, it's a very dry time of the year, but never fear because in 6 weeks or 13 weeks, staffing will begin.

Rima Greer
Above the Line/Los Angeles

• *The agent is not an editor, but if he has been doing the job for any length of time, he or she does have the advantage of having read more material than any writer will ever read...ever. I've probably read more material and consumed more material, books of any fashion than any five writers will ever do. Right or wrong, when represented by an agent, you are banking on their experience and their opinion. It doesn't mean that it's gospel, it just means it's the best they can give you at this time. They can be wrong and sometimes they are wrong, but more often than not, they ought to be right and so, long term, you want to feel that the agent is a sounding board for you and a better professional sounding board than your relatives or your friends or your wife or your kids or your next door neighbor.*

Gary Salt
Paul Kohner, Inc./Los Angeles

• *The writer has a right to expect the agent to be honest about the work: we look at every script we get from our clients, as though it were a piece of gold. We are our clients' biggest fans. Nobody wants it to be better than we do, so it's very difficult for us to criticize it, if it's not good, but in order to service the client, we have to.*

Fredda Rose/Candy Monteiro
Monteiro Rose/Los Angeles

• *What we try to do is to successfully maximize a client's career over a long period of time which will help him or her become both financially and creatively secure. Being financially secure provides a certain power, the power to say no to a project or having a range of work options to choose from. An agent's power is in his ability to*

say no *or* yes *on behalf of his client.*
>   Elliot Webb
>   Broder. Kurland.Webb.Uffner/Los Angeles

●   *I can't speak for all agents at all agencies, but for me personally, I talk to every single one of my clients every day. With actors you are filling jobs, with writers, you are creating jobs. At least a writer can go home and write a spec.*
>   Rima Greer
>   Above the Line/Los Angeles

●   *Communication. I constantly hear horror stories from would-be clients discussing their old agents. Either the agent won't return the phone calls or the new spec script sits unread for three months. That to me is absurd. Clients have the right to hear the good news as well as the bad in terms of why it got rejected. Is there a consensus? Is there a flaw in the script that none of us saw or is it something in the marketplace?*
>   Jonathan Westover
>   The Gage Group/Los Angeles

●   *It's most important that you'll be told the truth about what's going on. People should remember that unlike lawyers who get their $300 per hour whether their advice is right or stinks, the agent doesn't get anything unless he's successful. People should bear that in mind. That doesn't mean that you can't ever say anything because the guy hasn't made any money off you. I think if I were a client I would say,* Look, I'm entitled to honest direct communication, I'm entitled to having my phone call returned. And I'm entitled to occasional evaluation periods as to, Are we doing the right thing? What can we do to change it? *Stuff to me that is common sense.*
>   Stu Robinson
>   Paradigm/Los Angeles

●   *The writer should be able to ask where his material is at all times and within 24 hours have an answer. If you call me today, I'll be able to give you a list tomorrow of where your stuff has been. If the agent can't answer that, get a new agent.*
       Your agent should be able to get you meetings. If your agent isn't getting you one meeting a month, get a new agent.
>   Rima Greer
>   Above the Line/Los Angeles

- *Show their work. Answer their phone calls within a day. Give them good advice. Not lie to them. Read their work. An agent has to be careful how he responds. A person's work is very personal to them.*

Lynn Pleshette
Pleshette/Millner Agency/Los Angeles

- *It's not a given that just because you sent me a script that I am going to do it. If you send me a script that is absolute rubbish and I say it's rubbish and I try to convince you it's rubbish and that it needs work, I'll either win that argument or I won't. You'll either see my point or you won't. You'll either agree to do some work on it or you won't. What happens if you insist that you're the writer and I'm the agent and I've gotta send this out?* Well, the answer is, I don't gotta send this out.

It happens sooner or later. It happens with good writers, indifferent writers, old writers, young writers. It happens that people take a fancy to a certain script, a certain story and just go and do it and insist that this is going to be a good thing, a turn around thing, this is going to be a breakthrough movie. But, what they don't take advantage of is the agent's overview. While the writer is off isolated for three months writing the script, the agent is getting up every morning, every day, every afternoon, every evening, plowing through the town, going through buyers, plowing through scripts, rights, trade papers and everything else and has at least a reasonable feel for what's out there.

Gary Salt
Paul Kohner, Inc./Los Angeles

- *To accurately assess where the client is in the continuum of their career. To honestly tell the person where they are. To evaluate whether the person heard you. To figure out how to get from where you are to where you want to go. To keep the client growing. If you don't do 1-2-3, it won't work. You need a plan.*

Bob Hohman
Hohman/Maybank/Lieb/Los Angeles

- *If the writer says,* I'm gonna write a script. I'm thinking of a subject. *Tell me what it is. Because if you're telling me that you're going to write a story inspired by latest headlines, I'm going to tell you that in about two weeks, CBS is going to put it on the air and ABC is going to put it on the month after that, so go on to another subject because it's already lost to you. So the first thing you can expect from the agent is a certain knowledge of the market.*

He ought to be able to tell you (within reasonable limits) what's going on out there. Not so much trends, there is always the flavor of the month, but long term,

what's around the networks, what's around the studios, where they're going to go. If you're going to engage in specing out something that can take you weeks and months of time and effort for no money, you don't want to find out later on that somebody's already doing it. So it seems to me that if I were someone's client, the first thing I would want from him is, I want to pick your brain every once in a while. I want access, I want to know what you know about the market. *That may have a tremendous effect on my story selection. I believe that the biggest mistake that the writer makes is story selection. Not about the quality of the work. It's about picking something that's isn't going to sell or is already being done. You should expect to be able to pick the agent's brain about material.*
Gary Salt
Paul Kohner, Inc./Los Angeles

• *The power in Hollywood is money. It's true. Every powerful person in Hollywood is wealthy. There is a certain power in the ability not to be needy.*
Elliot Webb
Broder•Kurland•Webb•Uffner/Los Angeles

I also asked what was too much to expect:

• *Too much is calling three times a week to ask the same question. I'd call the agent every two to two and a half weeks just to say* Hello, here I am. What? Tell me something, anything?
Stu Robinson
Paradigm/Los Angeles

• *I deeply resent being made to feel responsible for their rent. That's the bane of my existence. Sometimes you are successful at getting them work and sometimes you are not, but you are not their mommy and you're not their daddy. It is a free lance market, after all and there are no guarantees.*
Lynn Pleshette
Pleshette/Millner/Los Angeles

What Agents Expect

Of course, it goes both ways, agents have expectations, too:

• *We expect a partnership. Some agents sign a client and then expect the client to go out and get a job so the agent can commission it. Sometimes clients expect*

agents to work hard and they wait until the agent calls them with a job.
We expect our clients to do as much work as we do and vice-versa.
Cultivating relationships in the industry. Meeting with people, pitching ideas,
continuing the relationships they do have, following up on that and even calling us to
make sure we follow up on specific things.

We are meticulous about following up on things, but we do have a lot of
clients. It doesn't hurt if a client just calls me up and comfortably reminds me, Have
we heard on this? *or* Have we followed up on this?

Maybe I was planning on calling next week, but maybe it's a good idea
that I call this week anyway. I like that kind of rapport with a client. I think it is as
much their responsibility as mine. It's a two way street.

Sharing information is also very important. If they hear something, a job,
an assignment, whatever, we expect them to come to us immediately so we can work
on that and the reverse is true. If we work on a project and we either remember or
have written down that our client has a relationship that's one, two, or three years
old, we may say You make the call to this friend *and we'll hit them from both*
sides and see if we can coordinate this. You get a lot further using a partnership.

Stuart Jacobs
CNA/Los Angeles

•   *That the client is continually turning out spec material, otherwise he's no use*
to himself or to me.

Marty Shapiro
Shapiro-Lichtman/Los Angeles

•   *We expect* full time *writers. We're* full time *agents. We're not interested*
in dilettantes. If they are going to be writers, they should write. We understand that
in the beginning of their career, they may have to wait tables — they have to eat, but
we are not interested in people who do something else and *also write. Writer-dentist*
doesn't work for us.

Fredda Rose/Candy Monteiro
Monteiro Rose/Los Angeles

•   *If you are my client, I expect you to continually write new material. I expect*
you not *to embarrass me when you go to meetings. Not that this happens that often,*
but it does happen. You've got to be prepared for your meetings. You've got to be on
time for your meetings, generally have good attitude.

Rima Greer
Above the Line/Los Angeles

- *To listen to what the agent has to say because the agent is out in the marketplace and knows what is going on. Some people are hell bound to write scripts about things that will not sell, we'll tell them up front not to write about that, but they must and they do and they don't sell. For instance, we had a client who wanted to get into half-hour prime time. We told him for four years that if he wanted to do that, he would have to write sample scripts. He never wrote one and could never figure out why we were not getting him work in this genre.*

    Fredda Rose/Candy Monteiro
    Monteiro Rose/Los Angeles

- *Someone that has taken the time to know his/her craft and is able to utilize it in a way that works best for what he wants to do.*

    Barbara Alexander
    Media Artists Group/Los Angeles

- *That the clients do professional work in a timely manner and not call me every day. That's not a good way for me to spend my time. My worst days are the days when I have more calls from clients than buyers. How can I sell your script if I am on the phone with you?*

    Maggie Field
    Field-Chech Agency, Inc./Los Angeles

Synergy is one of my favorite words. The thought that in some instances two plus two can equal five because two components complement each other elegantly, appeals to my notion that anything is possible. The possibilities that exist when an agent and client are both motivated above and beyond the call of duty is actually a necessity if you want to be one of the 5% to 10% of the WGA that works regularly.

- *A lot of talent doesn't understand their relative importance to the business. We believe that this is a business like any other business and that our job is to focus and manage the career, to explain the business to the talent. Yes, we recognize you have talent. Now, what do you want do with that?*

    Elliot Stahler
    Kaplan Stahler Agency/Los Angeles

- *We service our clients in many different ways. It varies enormously from client to client. One thing we encourage our clients to do whether they're established or not, is to write speculatively. We find that whether they are in the feature film business or the television business, that speculative writing is the most powerful tool to expand a client's contacts, enhance employment possibilities and generally open new doors.*

Also if a writer is trying to up-grade a career, let's say he's working on television shows that are not particularly prestigious, but wants to work on the A shows. If he's making good money, he may want to write a spec script for one of the high quality shows; sometimes that can be the means to moving onto one of those shows. Or if someone has been working in the half-hour field and wants to work in the hour field and vice versa, they can write a spec script for the genre they want to move into.

Also, spec features, I'm sure you have read in the trades (as we have here) of the big sales that have occurred over the last few years of original screenplays written speculatively by writers of all levels of experience. Our agency sold one of those scripts just a few weeks ago by a young woman who was referred to us by one of our clients. This is a script that she researched and wrote while one of our agents worked quite closely with her in the development of the screenplay. That agent together with the writer developed a strategy for going out in the town with it and in a three day period got serious interest by a number of major producers and a studio snapped it up for a huge price on the third day. There's nothing as exciting as doing a significant piece of business for either a newcomer or someone who has struggled to get to a new place in their career.

Jim Preminger
Jim Preminger Agency/Los Angeles

• *A good agent can plan a career for a writer. I can plan out five years of a career for a writer. The show is clearly a stepping stone from staff to story to exec story position on the next show. A good agent thinks* What can I get for my client from this show?

Elliot Stahler
Kaplan Stahler Agency/Los Angeles

• *I insist (though I am not always listened to) that everybody give me an original screenplay at least every two years because there's a real danger of going from assignment to assignment. The development business has never been great, but right now it is pretty bad.*

You can price yourself out of the market. We all have clinkers. Everybody has good work and bad work. On occasion, you'll get paid a lot of money to write a script for hire and it won't be what you want.

I think being a writer for hire is a very difficult business to stay in because writers are very badly abused in the business in the sense that the motion picture business is very much a movie star driven business and the next most important person is the director. Writers seem to be viewed as interchangeable.

If a big star comes onto your project and the star has worked with some other writer or script doctor, the star might want that writer to come in and do a polish on your script and perhaps this person is a fine writer and will do a good job, but that becomes the movie star's project. Writers are generally not as well respected as other pieces of talent. I encourage people to get out of that low-man-on-the-totem-pole position by becoming writer-producers.

Bob Hohman
Hohman/Maybank/Lieb/Los Angeles

• *I think that there is variation between agencies and the amount of the editorial or creative work that writers are given. Also within our agency, there's some variation. Some writers don't want a great deal of input from us. But I do find that most writers that write speculatively are quite interested in our notes and welcome any constructive suggestions or criticism that we might make.*

Jim Preminger
Jim Preminger Agency/Los Angeles

• *We do a lot of in-house development here. We take pride in the fact that we actually read the stuff and can analyze it and do a good job. We do read and we do give notes. Each client is different in how much they want to hear. From the three of us, Martin (Gage), Wanda (Moore) and I, from our different background and different age groups, we have a pretty amazing collective eye here.*

Jonathan Westover
The Gage Group/Los Angeles

• *We have been known to go through three or four drafts with a writer before we go out with a script; in other words, a writer will write a first draft screenplay, give it to us for our comments and we make suggestions and they'll go back and rewrite it based upon those comments. Sometimes that takes two, three, four passes before the writer and we are mutually satisfied that it is in shape to go out.*

Jim Preminger
Jim Preminger Agency/Los Angeles

• *I got into business once with someone that I knew was talented. I had seen some of their work earlier on and that work had not been followed up with work of the same or better caliber. I sat down with them and said,* you're leaving a big agency now. Let me ask you, have people at the agency been talking to you about your work? *The writer said,* No. *I said,* Well, you know, it's not very good. I know a lot about you and you are a lot better than that and you need to write about things that you really care about. *Well, the writer heard me and has blossomed into an incredibly successful writer.*

Bob Hohman
Hohman/Maybank/Lieb/Los Angeles

• *Part of our job is to give writers a little bit of an edge or a different way of thinking. I'll suggest a show.* Why do you hate it? Do you think you can make it better? Write me an Emmy Award winning episode of a show.

Elliot Stahler
Kaplan Stahler Agency/Los Angeles

Above and beyond forging a successful relationship with your agent, continually writing and networking with your fellow writers, agents tell me that it's important to get out and meet people by going to parties, taking classes, having lunches and generally making yourself visible.

• *One of the biggest mistakes writers make is thinking they have finished their job when they give their script to their agent. Then, they just sit back and expect the phone to ring. This is a business of contacts and relationships. Writers have to be in the sales process as well.*

Fredda Rose
Monteiro Rose/Los Angeles

• *Reinvent yourself. The easiest way to reinvent yourself is to have a script of your own that you have the control over and you can decide what happens with it. I think it's important for artists to reinvent themselves every 3 to 5 years anyway.*

Dean Pitchford is someone who has reinvented himself. Dean is an Academy Award winning lyricist for Fame. *In 1984 he wrote a hugely successful screenplay,* Footloose, *followed by other successful screenplays, and in 1990, he decided that he was going to become a director. He entered the Discovery Program and out of 600 people, he was one of 5 people who were picked. He did a movie that turned out terrifically. Then he got another film at HBO called* Blood Brothers.

Bob Hohman
Hohman/Maybank/Lieb/Los Angeles

- *Work on ideas, write spec scripts. We're in a community where everybody knows everybody, so when a writer is playing tennis with somebody and tells him about an idea, he may call and say,* So and so said to send my script over. *That's very helpful. The squeaky wheel sometimes gets more attention. It's an industry town. You need to do anything you can to make things happen.*
  Lynn Pleshette
  Pleshette/Millner Agency/Los Angeles

Wrap Up

Writer expects
✓ communication
✓ honesty
✓ market overview
✓ feedback
✓ taste/judgement
✓ agent to read and show work
✓ agent to be able to track material
✓ career guidance

Agent expects
✓ professional behavior
✓ you to continually write
✓ that you won't embarrass him at meetings

Synergistic relationship
✓ writer networks
✓ writer continually reinvents himself
✓ agent acts as editor
✓ agent helps in developmental process

12 Researching the Agents

There are various categories of agencies; big, small, conglomerate, beginning, the-next-big-thing and/or just getting by. Since agency/client relationships are so personal, any classifications I might make would only be subjective, so I'm presenting you the facts as best I can, based upon my research and personal experience both in interviewing these agents and my years in the business.

There are new agencies with terrific agents building their lists who, like you, will be the stars of tomorrow. You could become a star with the right one man/woman office and you could die on the vine at CAA. There are no guarantees, no matter whom you choose. The most important office in town might sign you even without a single credit if your material excites them. But mostly, they want you when you are further along. Whomever you choose, if you are to have a career of longevity, you can never surrender your own vigilance in the process of your career.

If you read carefully, you will be able to make a wise decision using client lists, the agents' own words, and the listing of each agency. It's unwise to write off anybody. In this business, you just don't know. One's own tastes and needs color the picture. I could have an agent I love and you might hate him.

There are nice agents who are good agents and there are nice agents who are bad agents. There are agents who are not nice who are good agents and so on. Just because I may think some agent is a jerk doesn't mean he is. And even if he is, that might make him a good agent, who knows? If I badmouth someone, no matter how I write it, it always ends up looking petty.

If you read all the listings, you will have an overview. If I think someone is full of it, read carefully, you'll figure it out. I've endeavored to present the facts plus whatever might have struck me about the agent; this one is a pilot and that one is a computer freak.

Some agents have survived for years without ever really representing their clients. They wait for the phone to ring. Some agents talk a better game than they play. I believe it is better to have no agent than an agent who is going to lie to you.

We all know the stereotypes about agents, *They lie, that's their job.* Well, some agents lie, but most agents don't. Most agents are hard working, professional regular people who (like you) want to make it in show business. They too, want to be respected for their work, go to the Academy Awards and get great tables at Spago. And they, like you, are willing to put up with the toughest, most heartbreaking business in the world because they are mavericks who love the adventure and can't think of a single thing that interests them more.

I know many who read this book are just starting out and will be scanning the list for people who seem to be building their lists. There are many of those agents who have great potential. There are some who don't.

In the past, my practice has been to personally interview every agent listed in the book, other than CAA, ICM and WMA. That's still mostly true, though in the interests of time, there are a few agents that I interviewed on the phone.

Most of the time, I went to the office because that was the most convenient for the agent and seeing the office helped me make judgments about the agency. I didn't always meet everyone in every agency or all the partners, but I did meet with a partner or an agent who was acting as a spokesman for the company. I could be wrong in my judgments, but at least they are not based on hearsay.

I went through a real crisis about whom to include. Anybody who would talk to me? Only those agents that I could actually in good conscience recommend? It seems inappropriate for me to try to play God about who is worthy and who is not. On the other hand, I don't want my readers to think I would recommend everyone who is in the book. That automatically makes anyone not in the book suspect. Also, there are people who for whatever reason won't talk to me, or I just couldn't get to. I finally decided to include everyone I researched.

Agents reflect a major portion of the business. If you are currently employed in the business in any conspicuous way, people are usually nice to you and validate your existence. If you are not, the lack of respect can be appalling.

Keep your wits about you and you'll gain perspective when these same people fawn all over you once you actually do some visible work. Maybe their fawning is not just an exercise in fakery. It is true that successful people are usually sending off better vibes, although some are still stinkers.

Whether you're gainfully employed in the business or not, endeavor to keep your sense of humor handy, it will help you survive.

Some agents would not let me name any of their clients and others didn't mind if I named clients, they just didn't want to be responsible for singling any one out. As a whole, just assume that I looked up the client list plus credits and listed a few that I thought were representative of the list.

If you find an agency that seems to appeal to you, check the index in the back of the book to see if that agent has any quotes and if so, check them out. This will give you more insight.

When you query agents, be discriminating. Don't blanket the town with letters. Target the agent that seems right for you and ration yourself. It's a better use of your energy and more likely to pay off.

Agents are already inundated with query letters and while they are all looking for the next hot writer, there are only so many hours in a day, so don't waste their time or yours. If you are just starting, don't expect ICM to come knocking at your door. Choose someone who is at the same level as you are and grow together.

If you have just gotten a job on your own, you will probably have some referrals already. Check them out and see who appeals to you. A job is not automatic entree. As you have probably noted throughout the book, most agents are not interested in a one shot deal. In my experience researching agents for writers, directors and actors, I keep learning that agents are interested in a body of work.

They want to see a progression of you and your product. They want to know that they are not squandering their hard won contacts on someone who doesn't have the ability to go the distance. They won't be able to buy a cottage in the south of France on their commissions for one job. Neither will you.

Like attracts like. You will ultimately get just what you want in an agent. I believe you can get a terrific agent. I believe you can be a terrific client. There are no shortcuts. And today is not the last day of your life. In her book, *My Lives,* Roseanne quotes a line from Sun Tzu's, *The Art of War,* which she says everyone in Hollywood has read. It says: *The one who cares most wins.*

Again: Check all addresses before mailing. Every effort has been made to provide accurate and current addresses and phone numbers, but agents move and computers goof. Call the office and verify the address. They won't know it's you.

Kevin Bacon/Referrals

As you read the agency listings, you will see that many of the agents, though they will read query letters, are not open to being contacted by new people who have no one to recommend them. Before you wring your hands and gnash your teeth, remember The Kevin Bacon Game. It's the same concept as the play/movie *Six Degrees of Separation* which contends that anyone in the world can find an association with anyone else in the world through six associations, only in the Kevin game, it only takes three.

It goes like this. *Your mother shops at the same grocery store that Kevin Bacon does*...or in my own case, I have worked with Tom Hanks who knows Kevin Bacon, so, ostensibly, if I had a script I wanted to get to Kevin, I ought to be able to get it to him through Tom.

This all goes by way of saying that if you track all the odds and ends of your life, you should be able to produce *somebody who knows somebody who knows somebody* and come up with an authentic (however tenuous), connection to someone who can make a call for you so that you are not just querying/calling cold.

I've listed several data bases in Chapter 5 that track everyone who ever worked on a particular movie. Scrutinize names, perhaps some grip or production assistant crossed your path once or is the friend of your friend.

Dan Lauria, who originated PKE (Chapter 5 again) wanted to get Peter Falk to participate in a playreading for his group. He didn't know anyone who knew Peter Falk, so he bought a map of the Hollywood stars, put the script in Falk's mailbox with a note saying who he was and what he wanted and Falk responded.

Falk not only participated in that reading, he has become a fan of the group and made himself available for other projects.

If you can't come up with a connection, you'll write the best darn query letter in the world and knock some agent right on his butt, but if you can score at *the Kevin Game,* it *would* be best.

❖ Remember

✓ Your first agent is yourself. You must be your own agent until you attract someone who will care and has more access than you. It's better to keep on being your own agent than to have an agent without access or passion.

✓ Make yourself read all the listings before you make a decision. Then, cull your list down to five. If none of the five are interested, then you can go back and choose some more. If you find an agent who interests you, look in the index and see if he is quoted. If he is, this will give you more information.

✓ Mass mailings are usually a waste of money. There is no use sending WMA or ICM a letter without entree. It's pointless to query someone you have never heard of. If you have no information about the agent, how do you know you want him? Take the long view. Look for an agent you would want to be with for years. Be selective.

✓ Don't blow your chances of being taken seriously by pursuing an agent before you are ready.

✓ Although rules were made to be broken, presuming on an agent's time by showing up at his office without an appointment or calling and asking to speak to the agent as though you are an old friend, will ultimately backfire. Observe good manners and be sensitive to other people's space and time.

✓ Getting the right agent is not the answer to all your prayers — but, it's a start!

Agency Listings

❖ Above the Line Agency

9200 Sunset Blvd. #401
just W of Doheny
Los Angeles, CA 90069
310-859-6115

On September 1, 1994, Rima Greer pulled off a tremendous achievement. She not only opened her own literary office representing writers, directors and a few actors, but managed to leave mentor/boss Joan Scott at Writers & Artists in a good mood.

A secretary for the Writers Guild before moving to William Morris and then on to Writers & Artists for 12 years where she became president of the literary department, Rima's agency is fast becoming at the top of everyone's wish list. She recently made a million dollar sale for clients David Engelbach and John Wolff's script, *Blades*.

The rest of the list is equally impressive sporting names like Monte Merrick (*Memphis Belle*), Gregory Widen (*The Prophecy, Backdraft, The Highlander*), Greg Taylor and Jim Strain (*Jumanji*), John Hopkins (*Dunston Checks In*), Andrea Davis (untitled *New Year's Eve Romantic Comedy*), Ryan Rowe (*Charlie's Angels*), Chris Matheson (*Bill & Ted's Excellent Adventure, Mr. Wrong*) and *Niki Marvin* who produced *The Shawshank Redemption* and is currently writing *A Dry Spell* for Tom Cruise.

Rima tells me she speaks to every one of her clients daily. About 75% of the list are writers who direct.

She's not taking on anyone new for the present, preferring to concentrate on her current clients. You'll see quotes from Rima throughout the book. I like her a lot.

Agents
Rima Greer
Client List
19
Clients
Monte Merrick, Gregory Widen, Greg Taylor, Jim Strain, John Hopkins, Ryan Rowe, John Wolff and David Englebach, Chris Matheson, Niki Marvin, Andrea Davis and others

❖ Acme Talent & Literary

6310 San Vicente Blvd. #520
near Crescent Heights
Los Angeles, CA 90048
213-954-2263

Lisa Lindo Lieblein and husband Adam, opened their Los Angeles based office in 1993. When they booked 8 people onto Broadway and 2 into soaps from Los Angeles, they figured they needed a New York office to service those clients, so in January of 1997 they opened one.

Lisa began her career working for the legendary Norman Lear at Act III and was trained as an agent at The Susan Smith Agency before agenting at Triad and ICM, so it's clear that Lisa knows how to do things right. None of that, however, prepared me for what I consider to be the most creative accomplishment in her background, creating The Fifth Network.

The Network was a group of working industry folk who wanted to make a difference. A core-group of 600 met once a month for a sit-down dinner for several years discussing how they could influence the business in a positive way. The group no longer meets, but the thought, energy and organizational skills required to bring off such a feat, makes me certain that anything Lisa sets out to do will become reality.

Husband, Adam Lieblein is no slouch either. He started as a PA in commercial production, becoming a production coordinator, a production manager and finally a producer for Bob Giraldi, Koppos, Propaganda and other big commercial production companies.

Between them, Lisa and Adam were brilliantly equipped to start either their own production company or talent agency. With no project that interested them to produce, the merger between Triad and William Morris afforded them the opportunity to open their own agency with an enviable client list of Triad orphans.

They started the business with actors for film, television and commercials, bringing over Steve Simon from William Morris to start a kids department. In 1996, they absorbed Writers & Artists' commercial department. In 1997, Marlene Sutton left Sutton, Barth and Vennari to join Acme making the commercial department in Los Angeles one of the most important in town. This agency also handles voice-overs.

❖ Acme Talent & Literary

625 Broadway 8th floor
between Bleeker & Houston
New York, NY 10012
212-328-0388

Lisa's says her 12 feature film and long-form writers are all currently employed, so obviously if you get on Lisa's list, you are in good hands. She shepherds her writers on both coasts.

Because they are inundated with so many requests, Acme only sees clients referred to them through the industry. They did, however, sell a script that came to them through a blind submission, so lightning does still strike. You may send a query letter, but please don't send unsolicited manuscripts to this office.

Clients include Ed Savio of Savio and Mackie (*Swiss Family Rubinstein, Idiots in the Machine*) and Gary Horn (*Crooked*).

The agency represents writers, comedians, actors, young adults, teenagers and children. Lisa represents the literary clients.

Agents
Lisa Lindo Lieblein
Client List
12
Clients
Ed Savio, Gary Horn and others

❖ Bret Adams

448 W 44th Street
btwn 9th & 10th Avenues
New York, NY 10036
212-765-5630

If it's a job in the theater, Bret Adams has probably done it. He has been an actor, a publicist, a producer, a manager of ACT, and a binoculars renter at the theater. The number of things that Bret has managed to figure out a way to make money from in the business is a testimony to his creativity. All that resourcefulness began paying off for others when he started his own agency in 1971.

Bruce Ostler began his career in the business as Bret's assistant in 1989 and later, left to be a literary agent for Fifi Oscard. In 1996, he returned home to Bret and now heads the literary department. Writers from his list include Jack Heifner (*Vanities*), Keith Glover (*Thunder Knocking On the Door, In Walks Ed*), Jon Marans (*Old Wicked Songs*), John Dempsey and Dana Rowe (*The Fix, Zombie's Prom*), Gip Hoppe (*Jackie*), Mary Zimmerman and Ron Nyswander.

This agency handles playwrights, scriptwriters, directors, variety artists, composers/songwriters, musical artists, below-the-line personnel, dancers, choreographers, designers, musical directors, and actors of all ages for theatre, film and television. They are particularly strong in the area of musical theater.

Query letters should include a brief synopsis of the material. As with most agencies, this office does not return unsolicited manuscripts. Most of their clients come to them through referral.

Agents
Bruce Ostler
Client List
20
Clients
Jack Heifner, Keith Glover, Jon Marans, John Dempsey, Dana Rowe, Gip Hoppe, Mary Zimmerman, Ron Nyswander and others

❖ The Agency

1800 Avenue of the Stars #400
S of Little Santa Monica
Los Angeles, CA 90067
310-551-3000

The Agency has been strengthening its position for years as a mini-conglomerate. In 1992, when InterTalent disbanded and Triad merged with William Morris, The Agency became an even stronger contender as one of the lucky beneficiaries of talent and agents who traded affiliations at that time.

Agency principal, Jerome Zeitman worked in production at both Wolper Productions and Columbia Pictures before he became an agent at William Morris. Moving onto MCA, Zeitman was one of the early architects of the concept of packaging.

Though The Agency represents actors, authors, children, directors, scriptwriters, producers, teenagers, young adults and below-the-line personnel, its basic strength lies in the list of writers and directors. Writers' representatives are Dino Carlaftes, Nick Mechanic, Jason Neswick, Vincent Gerardis, Michael Van Dyke and Walt Spadone.

Clients include Christopher Pike(the *Spooksville* books), Elliot Stern (*Act of Treason*), Jeff Gottleib (*After the Rains*), Greg Martin (*Archangel*) and Drew Gitlin and Mike Cheda (*The Chill Factor*).

Agents
Dino Carlaftes, Nick Mechanic, Vincent Gerardis, Jason Neswick, Walt Spadone and Michael Van Dyke.
Client List
150
Clients
Christopher Pike, Elliot Stern, Jeff Gottleib, Greg Martin, Drew Gitlin, Mike Cheda and others

❖ APA/Agency for the Performing Arts

9000 Sunset Blvd. #900
btwn San Vicente & Doheny
Los Angeles, CA 90069
310-273-0744

The most personal of all the conglomerates, APA gives clients the opportunity to be represented by a full service agency and still have their hand held at the same time. Although not as strong as CAA, ICM and WMA in some areas, APA has long been known as the place for emerging comics. APA's comedy development showcases held two to three times a year are hot tickets with studio, network and casting executives. They are led by senior vice-president of personal appearances, Danny Robinson. Danny's is speciality is spotting promising comics and bringing them to the attention of the rest of the staff, so if you're a stand-up looking to cross-over, APA might be the perfect agency for you.

Senior vice-president, Lee Dinstman leads the literary division, which was strengthened when APA lured Justin Dardis from the Susan Smith Agency and made him a vice-president.

Additional literary agents in Los Angeles office are Bryant Mulligan, Brant Rose, Art Rutter (The Artists Group, The Agency, Harry Gold and Associates) David Saunders, Adam Shulman and Scott Seidel (Broder ·Kurland·Webb·Uffner). Leo Bookman heads up the New York literary division.

Representative clients from APA's combined LA/NY lists are David Newman (*The Life, Bonnie and Clyde, Superman*), writer-director Nick Cassavetes (*Unhook the Stars*), Harry Dunn (*In Living Color*), Michelle Jones (*In Living Color*), Evan Sayit (*Arsenio Hall*), Adam Lapidus (*The Simpsons, Who's the Boss*), Lew Green (*The Wire, Premonition*) and Miguel Arteta who wrote and directed *Star Maps*.

APA represents scriptwriters, authors, playwrights, directors, producers, composers/songwriters, dancers, actors and musicians for theatre, film, television, concerts, personal appearances, college tours, etc. They also represent newscasters. APA also has an office in Nashville that specializes in personal appearances.

APA recently acquired the New York based music talent agency, International Talent Group to add to it's already hot personal

❖ APA/Agency for the Performing Arts

888 Seventh Avenue
at 59th Street
New York, NY 10016
212-582-1500

appearance profile.

Connected enough to get you in, the staff/client ratio gives you a much better chance for personal attention to career development than any of the other conglomerates.

Because they need to try harder, APA does. They develop talent, check out the town and return phone calls.

Agents

Los Angeles: Lee Dintsman, Justin Dardis, Bryant Mulligan, Brant Rose, Art Rutter, David Saunders, Adam Shulman, Scott Seidel
New York: Leo Bookman

Client List

not as large as the other conglomerates

Clients

David Newman, Miguel Arteta, Nick Cassavetes, Harry Dunn, Michelle Jones, Evan Sayit, Adam Lapidus and Lew Green

❖ Aimee Entertainment

15000 Ventura Blvd. # 340
btwn Kester & Noble/S side of street
Sherman Oaks, CA 91403
818-788-9115

Yes, there really are good things in the Valley and Helen Barkan is one of them. An agent for 26 years, Helen began her career at the George Hunt Agency where she first met Joyce Aimee. While Helen went on to the William Schuller Agency, Joyce opened her own agency specializing in personal appearances. The friendship turned into a partnership when the ladies decided to pool their resources forming an office that could represent both actors and entertainers.

Joyce still handles personal appearances and Helen is the godmother to all the actors. I ran into one of Helen's clients one day who said that Helen was the nicest lady she had ever met.

As this book goes to press, a new literary department is being created. All the papers were not signed, so Helen didn't want me to mention any names. If you want to query this agency, call and check to see who is head of the literary department. Since they are just starting this department, they might be open to new clients.

Agents
Helen Barkan
Client List
Forming
Clients
Forming

❖ Amsel, Eisenstadt & Frazier, Inc.

6310 San Vicente Blvd. #407
at Crescent Heights/S of Wilshire
Los Angeles, CA 90048
213-939-1188

Fred Amsel was an ex-actor and personal manager who worked at Kumen-Olenick and Progressive Artists before creating his own agency in 1975. In 1992, Fred retired and his colleagues, Mike Eisenstadt and John Frazier, who started in the agency business with Fred, bought the business and their names were added to the masthead.

Since that time, AEF has continued to evolve, adding new divisions, so that now the agency reps writers, directors, producers, actors, comedians and sports personalities.

The literary department at this agency is run by Sara Margoshes (Writers & Artists). Margoshes has experience in film development, film marketing and film and television production. She has two degrees from USC school of Cinema-Television and an MFA from the Peter Stark Motion Picture Producing Program. She has worked in market research at both production companies and studios. While an agency trainee, Sara sold her first spec script, *Juice,* which was produced independently and distributed by a major studio.

Sara's client list of screenwriters, directors and producers for feature and television is small. She is only open to new clients who are established writers who are unhappy with their current representation.

Only query here. If you send unrequested material or don't include a self-addressed-stamped-envelope with your material, this office makes a deposit in your name to the recycling program. An agency release form is required with all requested submissions.

Agents
Sara Margoshes
Client List
Confidential
Clients
Confidential

❖ Marcia Amsterdam Agency

41 W 82nd Street 9A
just off Central Park West
New York, NY 10024
212-873-4945

Marcia Amsterdam started in the business as a book editor. When one of her writers landed a film deal, she represented them and started her own agency. This was back in 1969. Today, her list of clients numbers about 30 and she rarely adds to that list although she does read brief query letters.

Query letters should include a brief paragraph with the main concept, not all the details. What she and other agents are always looking for is a slightly offbeat voice that says something *interesting, particularly in a humorous way*. Ms. Amsterdam handles scripts for film and television, no playwrights. She is not interested in pilots. One of her clients is Robert Leininger (*Killing Suki Flood*).

Agents
Marcia Amsterdam
Client List
30
Clients
Robert Leininger and others

The Artists Agency

10000 Santa Monica Blvd. #305
at Century Park East
Los Angeles, CA 90067
310-277-7779

This elegant agency was created in 1971 when ICM expatriates Sandy Bresler, Jim Cota, Mike Livingston and Don Wolff created what has endured as one of the class agencies in town representing high end talent in every area. Originally called The Sandy Bresler Agency and Bresler, Wolff, Cota, and Livingston, the partners settled on the current moniker in 1980.

Bresler left years ago preferring a smaller office, but the other three partners continue, joined by new partners Mickey Freiberg, Dick Shepherd and Merrily Kane. They, along with Bettye McCartt (Agency for Artists, McCartt Oreck Barrett) and Mike Wise all represent literary clients at this agency.

Jimmy Cota was gracious enough to still speak to me even though he said the onslaught of mail he received from *The Los Angeles Agent Book* was somewhat more than he might have wanted to handle. With this in mind, please do not send unsolicited material to this agency or any other without sending a query letter first. The material won't be read and probably won't be returned.

Agents
Mickey Freiberg, Merrily Kane, Dick Shepherd, Bettye McCartt and Mike Wise
Client List
100
Clients
Confidential

❖ Artist's Agency, Inc.

230 W 55th Street #29 D
btwn 7th and 8th Avenues
New York, NY 10019
212-245-6960

Jonathan Russo was an advertising account executive at
BBD&O, Foot Cone & Belding and the Interpublic Group of
companies handling accounts like Pepsi-Cola and Western Electric
before deciding to exploit his creative entrepreneurial talents more fully
by becoming an agent.

And he didn't just become an agent. He waltzed into the
William Morris Agency and totally circumvented their famous mailroom
and started his WMA life as a full fledged agent handling cable,
syndication and network packaging in the New York office.

Partner Barry Weiner, also an alumnus of WMA, was a vice-
president of syndication at Viacom and an expert in the daytime television business before he and Jonathan joined to start Artists Agency,
Inc. in 1982.

They started their business concentrating on writers for daytime
and syndication. Today their client list is filled with important names in
soap opera, syndication, primetime, features and books.

AAI's soap opera list is led by James Reilly, head writer on the
#1 daytime show, *Days of Our Lives.* Others writers include Bob Vila (*Bob
Vila's Home Again*), Robin Leach, Gordon Elliott, Paul Rauch, Megan
McTavish and Boyd Matson.

In addition to the major talents in film and television represented here, Lydia Wills heads the successful book department
representing authors like Elizabeth Wurtzel (*Prozac Nation, Bitch*).

When Jonathan and Barry decided to expand in 1985, there was
already an agency in Los Angeles with a similar name so their west coast
office is called Favored Artists. That office handles nighttime and
features and is headed by Scott Henderson. Since agencies are listed in
this book alphabetically, you'll find Favored Artists on page 178.

New writers come to this office mainly by referral, but the right
query letter always gets a response.

Agents
Jonathan Russo, Barry Weiner and Lydia Wills
Client List
50
Clients
Bob Vila, James Reilly, Robin Leach, Paul Rauch, Gordon Elliott,
Elizabeth Wurtzel, Megan McTavish, Boyd Matson and others

❖ Becsey·Wisdom·Kalajian

9229 Sunset Blvd. #710
W of Doheny
Los Angeles, CA 90069
310-550-0535

Laurence Becsey managed to take his law degree, skip the mailroom and start as an agent at WMA 22 years ago. Along the way, Becsey and partner Richard Berman bought The William Schuller Agency and changed the name to Talent Management International. When they merged with Jerome Zeitman in the '80s, the name became The Agency.

In 1990, Becsey left to open the Laurence S . Becsey Agency where he was joined by colleagues Victoria Wisdom (ICM, Tom Chasin) and Jerry Kalajian (APA).

When Wisdom and Kalajian became partners in 1993, their names joined the masthead. BWK represents scriptwriters, authors, directors, producers, showrunners, line producers and assorted hyphenates.

I gleaned the following names from their impressive list: Tom Holland (*Thinner, The Langoliers*), Jeremy Kagan *(Color of Justice, Roswell, Journey of Natty Gann)* Ken Cameron (*Oldest Living Confederate Tells All, Miracle of Midnight*), Neal Israel (*Bachelor Party*), Peter Doyle (*The Thomas Crown Affair, Fortress II*), Susan Sandler (*Crossing Delancey*), Debbie Amelon (*Exit to Eden*), showrunners like Paul Haggis (*Eazy Streets, Due South, Michael Hayes*), Bob Papazian and Jim Hirsch (*Nash Bridges*) and authors, Carol Shields who won a Pulitzer for her novel *The Stone Diaries*, W. P. Kinsella (*Shoeless Joe/Field of Dreams*) and Marele Day *(The Lambs of God).*

As you can see from the client list, this agency is not for beginners. They will read query letters, but accept no unsolicited material. Becsey is impressed by people with *fire in their eyes* and if you ever have the chance to take a meeting with him, you'd better have a a new script in your hand and a director in mind..

Agents

Laurence S. Becsey, Victoria Wisdom and Jerry Kalajian

Client List

80

Clients

Tom Holland, Jeremy Kagan, Ken Cameron, Neal Israel, Peter Doyle, Susan Sandler, Debbie Amelon, Paul Haggis, Bob Papazian, Jim Hirsch, Carol Shields, W. P. Kinsella, Marele Day and others

❖ Berman, Boals and Flynn, Inc.

225 Lafayette Street #1207
S of Houston/E of Broadway
New York, NY 10012
212-966-0339

Judy Boals, the literary force at this blossoming agency, started in the business as an actor. At an audition, she heard an older actor say to someone, *If you don't love acting more than anything in the world, don't do it.* Judy realized that, in fact, acting was not the most important thing in the world to her so she began career shopping.

Her next job, working part-time at the Dramatists Guild processing royalty statements and assisting in the legal department introduced her to literary giant, Lois Berman, who offered Judy another part-time job. That part-time bookkeeping job led to the discovery of what Judy does love more than anything else in the world: representing gifted writers and seeing that their voices are heard.

Judy worked for Berman for six years in varying capacities finally becoming her colleague, and with the birth of Berman, Boals and Flynn in 1994, she is her partner. Today Berman is a silent partner and consultant, leaving the day-to-day work to Judy and partner, Jim Flynn.

Jim Flynn entered the business answering phones for Susan Smith at her agency in 1990. His first agenting job was at The New York Agency which later merged with and became Alliance.

Though Jim heads the theatrical arm of the business with Judy shepherding the writers, he still represents the literary clients he brought with him. Former actor/restaurant manager, Charles Grayauski heads the emerging commercial division at BB&F.

Boals and Flynn say they have strong opinions about what they like and what voices they want to help. They boast a prestigious list of playwrights including Lee Blessing, Sam Shepherd, Oyamo, Will Sheffer, John Kline and Brian Crowley. They do not handle screenwriters per se, only those clients whose material crosses over from the theater to the screen.

Although this office looks at all query letters, they rarely call anyone from them. There are good quotes from Judy and Jim elsewhere in the book.

Agents
Judy Boals and Jim Flynn
Client List
30
Clients
Lee Blessing, Sam Shepherd, John Kline, Oyamo, Will Sheffer, Brian
Crowley and others

❖ The Bethel Agencies

360 W 53rd Street, #BA
just E of 9th Avenue
New York NY 10019
212-664-0455

Lewis Chambers worked in Admissions at Roosevelt Hospital before fate intervened, introducing him to the world of photographers and their agents. When he opened his own agency three years later, he began making deals even before he had time to name his agency. Concluding negotiation on a deal, when pressed for a name, he decided on the spot to name his agency for a small town just south of his home town of Randolph, Vermont.

This was back in December, 1967. The Bethel Agency initially represented only photojournalists. Within six months they began representing writers and among other prestigious works, sold *Auditioning for the Musical Theater* as well as one of the best books an actor could ever buy — Michael Shurtleff's *Audition.*

On the agency's 15th birthday in 1982, Lewis expanded the agency's client list to include actors. Today Lewis represents actors, playwrights, novelists and writers of non-fiction. Some of his current clients include Edgar nominee (the prize for mystery writers), Dean Feldmeyer (*Viper Quarry, Pitchfork Hallow*), Fred Silver (*Auditioning for the Musical Theatre*) and Jeffrey Tennyson (*Hamburger Heaven*).

Agent Norma Liebert and Lewis have formed another agency that specializes in children's books using both of their first names as their moniker, The Norma-Lewis Agency. Lewis umbrellas both businesses under the same roof. That's why it's called The Bethel Agenc*ies.*

Agents
Lewis Chambers
Clients List
20
Clients
Michael Shurtleff, Dean Feldmeyer, Fred Silver, Jeffrey Tennyson and others

❖ J. Michael Bloom & Associates

9255 Sunset Blvd. #710
W of Doheny
Los Angeles CA 90069
310-275-6800

J. Michael Bloom entered the business as an actor, but quickly changed sides of the desk to become one of the most successful agents in the business. After making his fortune via commercials in New York, Michael sought to expand his realm by not only adding a Los Angeles office, but creating an important theatrical division representing some of the finest actors in the business: Alec Baldwin and Fred Hoskins to name but two.

Ken Greenblatt (Media Artists) heads the arm of the television literary department at JMB while colleague Nicholas Staff (Acme) takes care of the clients writing for film.

Greenblatt was a consultant on Wall Street and the general manager for a Los Angeles company of *A Chorus Line* before turning his humanity, business savvy and show biz history towards a career agenting.

Ken's television writers include all areas including game shows, animation and MTV. I chose a few of Ken's clients to give you an idea of who is on the J. Michael Bloom list: Jim Lincoln and Dan Studney (co-executive producers *Honey, I Shrunk the Kids*), Joe Slowensky (*CBS Miracle in the Woods*) and Shelly Goldstein (producer *Game World*).

Agents
Ken Greenblatt and Nicolas Staff
Client List
20
Clients
Jim Lincoln, Dan Studney, Joe Slowensky, Shelly Goldstein and others

❖ The Brandt Company

12700 Ventura Blvd. #340
across from Jerry's Deli/E of Coldwater
Studio City, CA 91604
818-783-7747

Geoffrey Brandt manages as a sole proprietor with the power client list of a large conglomerate. With names like William Wisher (*Die Hard with a Vengeance, Broken Arrow, Judge Dredd, Terminator 2*) and one of my favorite directors, multiple Emmy winner, Lamont Johnson (*Last Great American Hero, My Sweet Charlie, The Execution of Private Slovak*, etc.), one gets the idea that this guy knows what he is doing.

From a show biz family (relatives founded The American Film Institute, the National Association of Theater Owners, the Brandt Theaters, etc.), Geoffrey must have found it just a hop, skip and a jump from working as the Associate Artistic Director of the New Jersey Shakespeare Festival to being a talent agent at William Morris and creating the directors' division at APA.

In 1989, Brandt formed this company with a very small list of important writers, directors, editors, costume designers and producers. A charming and articulate man, Geoffrey displays humanity, taste, class and clout.

Other writers on his list include Michael Backes (*Rising Son, Congo*) and Stuart Birnbaum (*Summer School*).

Agents
Geoffrey Brandt
Client List
22
Clients
Michael Backes, Stuart Birnbaum, William Wisher and others

❖ The Broder.Kurland.Webb.Uffner Agency

9242 Beverly Blvd. # 200
at Maple Drive
Beverly Hills, CA 90210
310-281-3400

At Broder·Kurland·Webb·Uffner, gazing at the waiting room
walls covered with Writers and Directors Guild Awards and Emmy
nominations and awards for people like Donald Bellisario (*Quantum
Leap*) James Burrows (*Cheers*) and Les and Glen Charles (creators of
Cheers), I'm hard put to think of anyone with more impressive clients.
Who could possibly be left for CAA? BKWU's list also includes
directors, cinematographers, editors, costume designers and more.

Bob Broder was an agent at IFA and Norman Kurland worked
for Leonard Hanzer (Major Talent) before they joined forces to
represent writers and directors in 1978 (Broder Kurland). I interviewed
the third partner to join the operation, Elliot Webb, whose degrees in
marketing and finance are a perfect background for an agent. Although
his first job was finding employment for high priced accounting and
financial personnel, it was a side-line venture selling sweat shirts to
Madison Square Garden and negotiating with The William Morris
Agency that led Webb to the WMA mailroom in 1972.

Creative enough to circumvent actually delivering mail by
driving executives to the airport and any other excuse he could think of,
Elliot became secretary to various agents and as he describes it, *I was the
secretary to the agent who handled the horse, Secretariat. My career was nowhere
when I left for California with an entree to IFA.* IFA soon merged with CMA
to form ICM, where Elliot spent 10 years, eventually running the
television literary department.

Broder and Kurland urged Webb to join their partnership for
years before he finally succumbed in 1983. Former ICM colleague, Beth
Uffner, was not only head of development at MTM, but ran her own
successful agency before becoming the fourth partner in 1989.

Elliot is happy to point out that although most of their clients
have been with them for many years, the life blood of the agency is
acquiring new young talent. Although they look at query letters, the
main avenue for new people is a referral from someone already in the
business, so be creative and find someone connected to this agency

before querying.

Agents

Bob Broder, Norman Kurland, Elliot Webb, Beth Uffner,
Ted Chervin, Pat Faulstich, Greg Fields, Emile Gladstone,
Terry Norton-Wright, Chris Silbermann, Paul Allan Smith,
Rhonda Gomez-Quinones, Bruce Kaufman, Ian Greenstein,
Tammy Stockfish and Gayla Nethercott

Client List

Confidential

Clients

Confidential

❖ The Brown Group

9300 Wilshire Blvd. #508
just W of Doheny
Beverly Hills, CA 90212
310-247-2755

Manager, Jon Brown comes from a rich literary lineage. His
father, Ned Brown was head of MCA's literary division, his mother
turned most of the experiences of Jon's early life into 23 children's
books: *Company's Coming for Dinner, Ice Cream for Breakfast*, etc., and Jon's
sister was an agent before she became a published author.

He was an agent on his own for 12 years before joining APA for
five years. In December of 1992 when both his bosses died within
weeks of each other, Jon decided it was time for a change. He left APA,
started this management company and seems to be doing very well with
his short list of three estates, one author, four directors and six writers.

Jon is also a producer and spends as much time producing as he
does repping his clients. Of ten projects in four years, he has set up nine
and gotten one made.

He may add actors to his list at some point. Some of his writer
clients include Susan Gauthier (*Anastasia*), John Maas (*Betty Book, Ann
Boleyn*), Richard Maxwell (*The Serpent and the Rainbow*), writer-directors,
Gary Tieche (*Nevada*) and Fred Walton (*When a Stranger Calls, When a
Stranger Calls Back*) as well as book writer Wilber Smith (*The Birds of Prey*)
and the estate of Paul Gallico.

Jon is not in the TV writer business and only represents writers
of features, novels and mini-series.

Manager
Jon Brown
Client List
12
Clients
Susan Gauthier, John Maas, Richard Maxwell, Gary Tieche,
Fred Walton, Wilber Smith, the estate of Paul Gallico and others

❖ Sheree Bykofsky Assoc. Inc.

11 E 47th Street
just E of 5th Avenue
New York, NY 10017
212-308-1253

Sheree Bykofsky completed her masters at Columbia and was on her way to becoming a professor when, she heard of a job in publishing as a managing editor. Actually, she ended up being the whole publishing house: *I did everything that Random House does, except that I was doing it all by myself: production, negotiating, contracts, sales, marketing and dealing with the warehouse.*

After five years, Sheree had acquired many skills, but was so burned out that when she heard of a job in book packaging, she jumped at it. As executive editor at Stonesong, Sheree's job was to think of ideas for books, hire writers to write them and place the books with publishers. She not only hired writers, but wrote some of the books herself. Since many of the writers were unrepresented, Sheree decided to capitalize on her relationships with publishing houses and open her own agency representing authors.

In one month, she placed 20 books, so I'd say she made a good choice. Her forte is trade books. Authors include Beth Allen (*Life's Little Temptations*), Ken and Lois Anderson (*The Encyclopedic Dictionary of Food and Nutrition*), Gene Brown (*Movie Time: A Chronological History of the Movies and the Movie Industry*) and Don Gabor (*Big Things Happen When You Do the Little Things Right*) .

Sheree's website: http://www.users.interport.net/~sheree details her areas of interest. Her next frontier is scriptwriters, but she would prefer clients with some kind of track record.

Agent
Sheree Bykofsky
Client List
50
Clients
Carnie Wilson, John Link, MD, Jennifer Busye Sander, Gene Brown, Don Garbor, Martin Edelston, Jamie Miller and others

❖ William Carroll Agency

139 N San Fernando Road # A
Buena Vista exit of Ventura Fwy
above and behind the record store
Burbank, CA 91502
818-848-9948

Two of the nicest ladies I have ever met opened this office in 1976 and named it after their children: Frances Girard's son, William, and Hope Blackwood's daughter, Carroll. Hope died in 1990 of cancer and Frances has now retired. The business is now owned by long time colleague Gina Eggert.

Since Gina has taken over the agency, she has expanded their horizons and added two literary agents, Patricia DeNiro (Bobby Ball Agency) and Greg Thomas (D & H Talent). Patricia and Greg represent a list of about 20 scriptwriters and authors.

The agency now represents writers and actors of all ages for theater, film and television. The agency has also begun to package.

Agents
Patricia DeNiro and Greg Thomas
Client List
20
Clients
Confidential

❖ CNA & Associates

1925 Century Park East #750
S of Little Santa Monica
Los Angeles, CA 90067
310-556-4343

A child actor in an earlier life, Christopher Nassif also has a background in production, casting and news. He graduated from USC in broadcast journalism and opened his own talent agency a year later representing mostly actors. Today, the agency has expanded its horizons to include composers/songwriters, writers, directors, below-the-line personnel, sports personalities, print commercials and young adults.

The literary department is in the capable hands of Stuart Jacobs who left The Irv Schechter Company in 1991 to organize this thriving, respected literary department. Originally an actor, Stuart assisted Don Buchwald in New York before leaving snow and sleet for sun and sand.

Stuart's list includes writers for film, television and theatre. Among his clients are Peter Gallay (*Empty Nest*), Jamie Tatham (*Full House*), E. Paul Edwards (*My Cuba*), Brendan Burnes (*VTV*), Kevin Bernhardt (*Veronica*), Eric and Russell Taras (*Mr. Moron*), and Jackie Kinkade and Courtney Silberberg (*Cavers*).

There are insightful quotes from Stuart throughout the book. Stuart only sees new clients through referral.

Agents
Stuart Jacobs
Client List
25-30
Clients
Peter Gallay, Jamie Tatham, E. Paul Edwards, Brendan Burnes, Kevin Bernhardt, Eric and Russell Taras, Jackie Kinkade, Courtney Silberberg and others

❖ Coast to Coast Talent

4942 Vineland Avenue #200
N of Camarillo & Riverside
North Hollywood CA 91601
818-762-6278

Political Science major, Elyah (rhymes with heal 'ya) Doryon graduated from college and entered show business in 1989. Elyah says he had no idea how hard it would be, but pluck, determination and drive and the aid of brother Jeremiah have held both in good stead, for today Coast to Coast is thriving and many many notches ahead of where it was when the Doryon's entered the agency business.

The literary department of this agency has grown enormously since it was started by Vanessa Howle (AFH Talent, The Robb Group) in 1993. Today, the literary clients are in the capable hands of Ann McDermott. Although her original show biz goal was to become a producer, her job as an assistant at the Irvin Arthur Agency introduced her to the world of agenting and she was hooked.

Ann's list tops out at 24 writers, writer-producers and writer-directors, though she prefers to limit the number to 20. Ann wants her scriptwriters versatile; able to handle comedy, action, romantic comedy, sci-fi, etc. Ann also handles novelists and has specifically targeted the development of young adult novels with the intention of packaging them into family entertainment films.

Most clients come to this agency by industry referral, though Ann reads all queries. She reads on Friday, so I'd make sure my letter arrived on a Friday so it would be on the top of the stack.

Agents
Elyah Doryon, Jeremiah Doryon and Ann Mc Dermott
Client List
24
Clients
Confidential

❖ Contemporary Artists

1427 Third Street Promenade, Suite 205
at Broadway
Santa Monica, CA 90401
310-395-1800

After the demise of MCA in 1963, Ron Leif opened his own office. Known at one time as Contemporary Korman, this prestigious agency has an important list of writers, directors, producers and actors.

Larry Metzger heads the literary department as this agency. For whatever reason, he declined to talk to me, but I was told that the literary department at this agency mainly services those writers and actors who are already clients, so I would think twice about wasting postage querying this agency.

I have no background on Larry, but my reference sources indicate that Larry has been with Contemporary since 1994.

Agents
Larry Metzger
Client List
Confidential
Clients
Confidential

❖ The Coppage Company

11501 Chandler Blvd.
at Tujunga
North Hollywood, CA 91601
818-980-1106

It's easy to see how Judy Coppage, the personification of charisma, became a vice-president of production and development at Hanna Barbera Studios before anyone even knew what that meant. And it's easy to see how she was one of the first women to break through into the executive area in show business.

One of those fortunate people who knew from the get-go that she was destined for Hollywood, she left home in Seattle for UCLA and as quickly as possible, earned two degrees and hit the ground running. An executive at Paramount as well as HB, it didn't take long for Judy to see that as a woman in corporate show biz there were plenty of limitations, and that she could parlay her entrepreneurial skills and her love of writers into a much more satisfying life on her own. Judy started her own business in 1984 and loves what she does. Because she truly believes that the script is what it is all about, she is fearless in helping and selling her writers. Although she is famous for jump-starting careers, it's clear to me that anything this woman set her mind to, she would be famous for.

Besides being a successful representative for film and television writers like Larry Bishop, Scott Davis Jones (*Mavis Keates*) and Harry and Renee Longstreet (*With a Vengeance*), Judy is successful selling books as well. Two of her most visible success stories are Roderick Thorpe (*Die Hard*), Brian Garfield (*Death Wish, Hopscotch*) and Larry Bishop.

Fiercely committed to the clients she already has, Judy only accepts industry referrals. She is assisted by Tim Reilly.

Agents
Judy Coppage
Client List
24
Clients
Scott Davis Jones, Harry and Renee Longstreet, Roderick Thorpe, Larry Bishop, Brian Garfield and others

❖ Coralie Jr. Theatrical Agency

4789 Vineland Avenue # 100
btwn Magnolia & Moorpark
North Hollywood, CA 91602
818-766-9501

Coralie Jr. (yep folks, that's her real name) has been repping horses, orangutans and actors for over 20 years. She booked the monkeys for *Every Which Way but Loose*, the drunken horse in *Cat Ballou* and one of the leads (Angelo Rossito) in *Mad Max Beyond Thunderdome*. Boy, talk about one-stop shopping. Coralie has had more employees, but feels she and fellow agent, Mario Solis *do a better job than when they had six more helpers.*

Her first role as an actress was when she was two days old. She also worked in the old *Our Gang* comedies. Coralie says she's *not like any other agency.* That's surely true. She books commercials, variety acts, musicians, writers, animals and about 150 actors who just act (as opposed to those who juggle as well). And now she has a literary department, too.

Mario shepherds the literary list of about 25 writers for film and television. Two names from their list are Lynn McMillan and Joe Stefano.

Agents
Mario Solis
Client List
25
Clients
Lynn McMillan, Joe Stefano and others

❖ CAA/Creative Artists Agency

9830 Wilshire Blvd.
at Little Santa Monica
Beverly Hills CA 90212
310-288-4545

In 1975, William Morris agents, Mike Ovitz, Ron Meyer, Will Haber, Rowland Perkins and Michael Rosenfield defected and created a totally new prototype for a Hollywood agency. CAA quickly became respected, feared and undeniably #1 among a field of powerful star-laden agencies. By the end of 1995, however, none of the founding five remained and there were fears that CAA would not survive.

Through the kind of courage, team spirit, hard work, aggressiveness and determination that built the agency initially, CAA has regained its equilibrium and today stands, if not unquestionably as #1, certainly as one of the #1s in town.

The agency management is split among Richard Lovett, Lee Gabler and Rick Nicita. CAA is said to have 120 agents and 1200 clients. Gee, that's 10 clients to each agent. Doesn't sound bad to me or evidently to clients like William Goldman, Barry Levinson, Melissa Mathison, John Waters, Joshua Brand, John Falsey or 1194 other lucky clients who have CAA in their corner.

Agents who represent writers at this agency include Brian Siberell, David Styne and Justin Connolly. For a more complete list, consult *The Hollywood Agents & Managers Directory*.

Agents
Todd Smith, David O'Connor, David Tenzer, Tina Nides, Adam Krentzman, Glenn Bickel, Sonya Rosenfield, Jack Rapke, Brian Siberell, Rick Kurtzman, Ken Stovitz, Scott Landis, David Styne, Justin Connolly and 116 more

Client List
1200

Clients
Marshall Brickman, William Goldman, Barry Levinson, Dick Wolf, Melissa Mathison, Ruth Prawer Jhabvala, Bo Goldman, George Stevens, Jr., John Waters, Joshua Brand, John Falsey, Jerry Seinfeld, David Letterman, Neil Simon, Oliver Stone, Ron Howard and others

❖ Dade/Shultz Associates

12302 Sarah Street
near Whitsett
Studio City, CA 91604
818-760-3100

Dade/Shultz Associates was originally Dade/Rosen in 1962 when Ernie Dade and Mike Rosen formed their agency with Kathy Schultz as their secretary. Kathy has been Ernie's partner ever since Mike left the agency in the early 80s.

DS has recently added a literary department headed by Ernie. A couple of clients from his short list are Michael Druxman *(Cheyenne Warrior)* Joe Sprosty, Steve Baer and Lisa Gordon Tanner.

Ernie has a colorful life in addition to being an agent as he's a also teacher of ESP. If Ernie won't take you as a client, perhaps you'll be able to take his class and learn via extrasensory perception what the next hot trend is in scriptwriting.

Ernie says he is open to query letters with a *brief* synopsis of your material for features only.

Agents
Ernie Dade
Client List
5
Clients
Michael Druxman, Lisa Gordon Tanner, Joe Sprosty, Steve Baer and others

❖ DGRW/Douglas, Gorman, Rothacker & Wilhelm, Inc.

1501 Broadway, #703
btwn 43rd & 44th Streets
New York, NY 10036
212-382-2000

Barry Douglas (ICM, The Barry Douglas Agency), Fred Gorman (Bret Adams), Flo Rothacker (Ann Wright) and Jim Wilhelm (Lionel Larner, Eric Ross, The Barry Douglas Agency) created this effective, congenial agency in 1988. Barry and Fred died in 1996, but all the partners worked diligently to make sure that the agency survived the sad changes. Today DGRW is as strong as ever, and continuing to diversify and expand their client list.

Long been known as one of New York's most prestigious agencies representing actors, the literary department is described by the head of the literary department, Beth Schacter, as *a cottage industry in a larger agency.*

It turns out that Beth is well-suited to be caretaker for the cottage. Her first job after leaving Kenyon College was protecting, helping and nurturing new writers at New Dramatists. After her stint at ND, she moved to Williamstown producing, assisting and generally shepherding writers, directors and plays.

Instead of returning to graduate school and moving toward her goal of directing, casting director/mentor Pat McCorkle suggested DGRW as the best place for Beth's background and sensibilities.

Beth has a list of 10 writers, including screenwriters, playwrights and independent filmmakers. Clients from the list include David Gold, Brett C. Leonard, Neil Alumkal, Sander Hicks, Barbara Weichmann (*Feeding the Moonfish!*) and Cheryl Royce (*My Son, Susie*). Beth shares clients, Laurie Hutzler and Kelly Masterson with her Los Angeles counterpart, Jeff Melnick of Gold/Marshak/Liedtke.

Beth reads no unsolicited scripts, but does read every query letter and every 10 page writing sample. She says that it is necessary for her to read every sample *because it's important for me to know what I'm saying no to.*

Beth is not looking to expand, but *There is an exception to that rule. I welcome someone who can make me change my mind. I'm a one-man-band, so I have to be careful, but the idea that a small agency can package is very attractive. I think little agencies should do it. They have the clients to do it, they know their clients and they should.*

Agents
Beth Schacter
Client List
10
Clients
Brett C. Leonard, Neil Alumkal, Kelly Masterson, Ernie Joselovitz, Laurie Hutzler, David Gold, Sander Hicks, Barbara Weichmann and Cheryl Royce

❖ Douroux & Co.

445 S Beverly Drive #310
4 blocks S of Wilshire
Beverly Hills, CA 90212
310-552-0900

In March of 1977, Michael Douroux escaped from IBM and entered show business to work as an executive in business affairs for Norman Lear. A Los Angeles native and USC graduate, Michael always wanted to be involved in the industry and after a chance meeting produced a showbiz job offer, Michael took it.

When Stu Robinson and Bernie Weintraub (Robinson Weintraub, now Paradigm) offered Michael a chance to add to his negotiating skills and business affairs acumen and become a literary agent, Michael's wish to become more creatively involved was fulfilled.

By 1983, Michael was ready to open his own agency with partner Candace Lake. Lake & Douroux lasted until 1991 when Michael founded Douroux & Co. to represent directors and writers. An alternative to conglomerate representation, Michael's idea is to provide career management with very hands on involvement. Booking jobs doesn't excite him; sculpting a career does. Michael has some practical quotes elsewhere in the book, so be sure to check them out.

A couple of Michael's 12 writer clients include Edward Allen Bernero (*Brooklyn South*) and Bill Froehlich (*The Outer Limits*).

Agents
Michael E. Douroux
Client List
12
Clients
Edward Allen Bernero, Bill Froehlich and others

❖ Duva - Flack Associates, Inc.

200 W 57th Street #1008
just W of 7th Avenue
New York, NY 10019
212-957-9600

Originally an actor, Robert Duva began pestering his agent at Talent Associates to become her assistant instead of her client. He soon became her colleague and then worked with Mort Schwartz, Robby Lantz and The Gersh Agency New York.

Elin Flack's show-biz baptism was as a secretary for Lionel Larner. She became an agent at LL and then worked for Don Buchwald and Robert Abrams Associates before joining J. Michael Bloom in 1981.

Elin and Bob had known of each other as competitors for 15 years when a friend who knew that each of them was pondering new paths suggested they meet. Although both were skeptical, they meshed immediately and in October of 1993, when other agencies were merging or closing, these two tasteful, connected agents decided to join forces and open an agency representing writers, actors, directors, designers and director/choreographers

Writer clients at DF include Bill C. Davis (*Mass Appeal, Avow, Dancing in the End Zone*), Mark Hampton (*Full Gallop*), Anna Deavere Smith (*Twilight: Los Angeles, 1992, Fires in the Mirrors*) and Kenny Solms (*Carol Burnett Show, The Smothers Brothers Comedy Hour*).

Even though their client list in every discipline is stellar, they do still take the time to start young artists or jump-start careers that are stalled.

Richard Fisher and Steven Stone are Elin and Bob's colleagues.

Agents
Robert Duva, Elin Flack, Richard Fisher and Steven Stone
Clients
12 writers
Client List
Bill C. Davis, Mark Hampton, Anna Deavere Smith, Kenny Solms and others

❖ Endeavor

9701 Wilshire Blvd. 10th floor
just E of Little Santa Monica Blvd.
Beverly Hills, CA 90212
310-248-2000/310-248-2020

The writer-director oriented powerhouse known as Endeavor joined the Los Angeles agency scene in 1995 when key ICM agents David Greenblatt, Tom Strickler, Rick Rosen and Ariel Emanuel defected and set up business on their own. Previously partnered at equally hot and connected InterTalent, these upwardly mobile agents had been acquired by ICM in an (evidently) ill-fated merger in 1992.

Frequently mentioned in the same sentence with CAA, ICM, WMA and UTA, Endeavor continues to acquire star writers, directors and agents.

Other agents at this agency include Steve Rabineau (ICM, WMA, Gersh), Leanne Fader (J. Michael Bloom), David Lonner (CAA), Doug Robinson (CAA), Adam Venit (CAA), Marty Adelstein, Sandy Epstein, Ari Greenburg and Jason Spitz (ICM).

Clients include Scott Alexander and Larry Karaszewski (*The People vs. Larry Flynt*), Howard Gordon (*The X-Files*), Glen Morgan and James Wong (*The X-Files*), David E. Kelly (*Picket Fences*), Jeffrey Lane (*Ink, Mad About You*), Lionel Chetwynd (*Kissinger and Nixon: Peace at Hand*), David Mandel (*Seinfeld*), Jerry Belson (*Tracy Takes On*), Peter Hyams (*The Relic, Timecop, Narrow Margin, 210, Outland*), Charles H. Eglee and Channing Gibson (*Murder One* - pilot episode) and Bonnie and Terry Turner (*3rd Rock from the Sun*). This information is based on research not interview.

Agents
Marty Adelstein, Ariel Emanuel, Sandy Epstein, Leanne Fader, David Greenblatt, Ari Greenburg, David Lonner, Philip Raskind, Doug Robinson, Rick Rosen, Jason Spitz, Tom Strickler, Steve Rabineau and Adam Venit

Client List
150

Clients
Howard Gordon, Scott Alexander, Larry Karaszewski, Glen Morgan, James Wong, Bonnie and Terry Turner and others

❖ Epstein/Wyckoff & Associates

280 S Beverly Dr. #400
S of Wilshire Blvd.
Beverly Hills, CA 90212
310-278-7222

Craig Wyckoff and Gary Epstein each left careers as actors to become agents for different reasons. Craig felt agenting would be more of a challenge and Gary simply wanted to pay his rent on a regular basis.

Craig joined Los Angeles' William Felber Agency and began developing the television and film department while Gary answered phones for his own New York agent, Mort Schwartz before moving to one of Manhattan's old-line prestigious agencies, Hesseltine/Baker and becoming an agent.

Before long Craig and Gary each opened his own successful office. Functioning as liaison for each other for a while, Epstein and Wyckoff finally merged in 1991 in order to provide bi-coastal representation for their clients.

The literary department in Los Angeles is headed by Karen Wakefield. Karen joined Craig Wyckoff in 1988 after a career as an independent producer and as an executive in development. That background enables Karen to bring other-side-of-the-desk insights to the negotiating table. Karen's literary department continues to grow in size and prestige.

Clients from her list of 20 include Stephen Beck (*Murder, She Wrote* and two Nicholls Fellowship winners, Steve Garvin (*Status Quo*) and Steven DeKnight (*Wandering Grace*). Sounds to me as though if your name is Steve, you might have a shot here.

Karen also represent directors and producers. The select New York literary department is headed by Gary Epstein.

❖ Epstein/Wyckoff & Associates

311 W 43rd Street
Between 7th and 8th Avenues
New York, NY 10036
212-586-9110

Agents
Los Angeles: Karen Wakefield
New York: Gary Epstein
Client List
20
Clients
Stephen Beck, Steve Garvin, Steven DeKnight and others

❖ Favored Artists

122 S Robertson #202
btwn 3rd & Beverly Blvd.
Los Angeles, CA 90048
310-247-1040

Los Angeles native Scott Henderson always knew he wanted to be in the business. He's so affable that it's no surprise his first job was as a page at NBC in Burbank.

He joined the agent training program at Writers & Artists in 1987 and two years later was an agent at Favored Artists. Today Scott heads the literary department representing such prestigious writers as John Pogue who wrote *U. S. Marshalls*, the sequel to *The Fugitive*.

Scott's list of 25 clients also includes Phil Rosenberg (*Five Desperate Hours*), Quinton Peeples (*Joy Ride*), Brent Mote (*Atomic Train*) and writing team Shirley Tallman and Nancy Hersage (*Babysitter Seduction*).

Favored Artists sees new clients mainly through referral but, Scott does look at query letters and has called in writers from letters that interested him.

Although they have different names, this agency is the west coast arm of New York's Artists Agency. Since there was already a famous Los Angeles agency using that name when the agency opened here in 1985, Favored Artists became the west coast name.

The business is pretty evenly divided with the west coast handling nighttime writers and the east coast representing writers of daytime and reality shows with clients like James Reilly, Bob Villa, Gordon Elliot and Robin Leach.

Check the write-up on The Artists Agency, Inc. page 150 for information on their east coast counterpart.

Agents
Scott Henderson
Client List
25
Clients
John Pogue, Phil Rosenberg, Quinton Peeples, Brent Mote, Shirley Tallman, Nancy Hersage and others

❖ Field-Chech Agency

12725 Ventura Blvd. # D
btwn Coldwater & Whitsett
Studio City, CA 91604
818-980-2001

Although Maggie Field says she became an agent by mistake, I prefer to call it fate. From her first job typing *Ironside* scripts in the steno pool at Universal, she advanced to secretary/assistant through an instructive group of trainers: a literary agent at William Morris, a publishing company and another literary agent before finally becoming an agent at Zeigler Ross. She worked at Writers & Artists and Robinson Weintraub before suffering burnout and leaving the business altogether in 1984.

Burnout didn't last too long and Maggie decided to try the other side of the desk by joining Disney as a buyer. That experience focused her intentions to open her own office to protect and represent writers.

Fiercely vigilant for her clients, Maggie's list of lucky writers includes Virginia Brown (*The Guiding Light, Another World, Deadly Medicine, Mixed Blessings*), Babs Greyhosky (*Magnum PI, Xena*), Jenny Wingfield (*Man in the Moon*), and Sharon Elizabeth Doyle (*Stolen Babies*).

Maggie's partner, Judy Chech became an agent working with Maggie. Other agents at Field-Chech are David Murphy and Maggie Roiphe.

The agency represents 35 writers and producers, and one director, and only reads material recommended by someone they have already done business with: a client, producer, director, network or studio executive, so don't waste stamps, just get to know someone.

Agents
Maggie Field, Judy Chech, David Murphy and Maggie Roiphe
Client List
35
Clients
Virginia Brown, Babs Greyhosky, Jenny Wingfield, Sharon Elizabeth Doyle and others

❖ Film Artists Associates

7080 Hollywood Blvd.
btwn Highland & La Brea
Hollywood, CA 90028
213-463-1010

Penrod Dennis, president of Film Artists Associates, started as an agency producer of commercials for Young and Rubicam. After various agencies and cities, he arrived in Los Angeles and was persuaded by friends that his background would make him a terrific commercial agent. He started with Don Schwartz in 1967 and subsequently worked for Bernie Sandler at CTA.

Pen started the commercial department for Sid Craig, who originally created this agency in 1969. Through a series of name changes reflecting the comings and goings of various partners along the way, FAA has finally chosen a more generic name (saving considerably on the stationery bill, I'm sure).

Film Artists and Associates now represents writers, producers, actors, martial artists, variety artists and authors. The are also franchised by the DGA just in case one of their clients wants to direct, I guess.

Pen Dennis and Richard Heckenkamp preside over the small list of writers.

Agents
Penrod Dennis and Dick Heckenkamp
Client List
30
Clients
Confidential

❖ First Artists Agency

10000 Riverside Drive # 10
just E of Pass
Toluca Lake, CA 91602
818-509-9292

Bob Edmiston spent 25 years casting (at NBC, MGM, etc.) before he decided to shift gears and become an agent. He says now he wishes he had done it 20 years ago. His clients probably wish it too, for Bob is one of the nicest, most professional people in the business.

Bob worked with Sid Craig and for Bud Kenneally at Associated Talent before putting together his own list. He partnered with veteran agent Robert Raison in September, 1986, but Raison retired soon after, so now, Lee Demarche is Bob's colleague.

Agents
Bob Edmiston and Lee Demarche
Clients
32
Clients
Confidential

❖ The Barry Freed Company

2029 Century Park East
S of Little Santa Monica
Los Angeles, CA 90067
310-277-1260

In 1984, after 14 years of handling theatre, films and television at ICM, Barry Freed decided to start his own agency. In 1991, he sold that agency and immediately started another agency. This time, in addition to actors, Barry represents writers.

He does not, however represent writers for situation comedies or nighttime hours, his literary business consists solely of screenwriters of features or MOWs. When Barry finds a script that he likes, he signs the writer and seems to do well with them. A couple of clients from his list of 15 include Michael Meehan (*Reinventing Barking, Finders Keepers, The Share*) and Jeff Davis (*Stealing Manhattan, Carolina Moon, Tango Man*).

Barry is a one man office so he continues to be very selective about choosing his writers and actors.

Agents
Barry Freed
Client List
15
Clients
Michael Meehan, Jeff Davis and others

❖ The Gage Group

9255 Sunset Blvd. #515
just W of Doheny
Los Angeles, CA 90069
310-859-8777

A brilliant agent and a crazy human being, Martin Gage is someone you can't help but like. This affable/irascible man helms a homey successful agency that represents writers, directors and actors.

President of the literary department, Jonathan Westover was an assistant who helped cast commercials at JHR (Joseph Heldfond and Rix) and interned at Richland Wunsch Hohman before coming to the Gage Group and assisting previous literary department head, Caren Bohrman. When Caren left to pursue other interests, Martin offered Jonathan the chance to make the department his own.

Wanda Moore was an executive in development before she became Jonathan's colleague in 1995.

Gage Group clients write for theatre, film and television. A few from the list include Jane Anderson *(Baby Dance, The Positively True Adventures of the Alleged Cheerleader-Murdering Mom)*, Al Martinez *(Betrayal of Trust, Dancing Under the Moon)*, Eugenia Bostwick-Singer and Raymond Singer (*Nightscream, Beyond Obsession*) and Bryan Nelson. There are insightful comments by Jonathan elsewhere in the book.

Agents
Martin Gage, Jonathan Westover and Wanda Moore
Client List
17
Clients
Jane Anderson, Bryan Nelson, Al Martinez and others

❖ The Geddes Agency

1201 N Greenacre Ave.
E of Fuller/N of Santa Monica
Los Angeles, CA 90046
213-878-1155

Ann Geddes founded her agency in Chicago in 1967 and though she created her Los Angeles counterpart in 1983, she still thinks of the Chicago office as an important source of talent and continues to funnel clients from the Windy City into Los Angeles.

Ann brought a personal style of representation to her actors that she has never changed. She is closely plugged into her clients. Her sensitivity, support and perspective all work toward bringing the best from her clients.

Geddes literary department has been inactive the past few years, but Ann is in the process of resurrecting that division, so a query letter would not be out of order. If your material strikes Ann's fancy and her department is active, you couldn't do better.

Agents
Ann Geddes
Client List
Forming
Clients
Forming

❖ Laya Gelff Agency

16133 Ventura Blvd. #700
btwn Havenhurst & Woodley
Encino, CA 91436
818-713-2610

Executive director of the Emmys for ten years as well as associate producer of news for NBC, Laya Gelff became an agent because her actor husband was unhappy with his representation. Laya's background and connections enabled her to function as his agent, making phone calls and handling details of his career. It didn't take long for both Laya and her husband to decide that she should get an agency franchise and get paid for her expertise.

Since that time (1985), she has expanded her list to add 8 writers and 2 directors who function in both film and television. Client Malvin Wald conceived and wrote the original *Naked City* and will forever be famous for his line: *There are 6 million stories in the naked city and this is one of them.* He also won an Oscar for *Al Capone*.

Laya does not read unsolicited scripts and like most agents, prefers referrals. She will read a letter with a brief (two sentence) description of the piece along with a self-addressed-stamped-envelope and will let you know if it is something she would like to pursue further. She only responds with a request if she feels the material is viable, so only a small percentage receive a request note.

Agents
Laya Gelff
Client List
10
Clients
Barbara E. Azrialy, Malvin Wald, Ed Metzger and others

❖ The Gersh Agency

232 N Canon Drive
S of Little Santa Monica
Beverly Hills, CA 90210
310-274-6611

Phil Gersh has been part of the Hollywood scene since the days when agents were not allowed past the studio gates. A legend in the business well before he opened The Gersh Agency in the late 70s, his agency has become one of the most prominent and prestigious independent agencies in town. The Gersh Agency has a glittering list of writers, directors, actors and below-the-line personnel that quickly command attention and respect.

Always thought of as one of *the* places to shop for top literary talent, The Gersh Agency added new luster to its crown when Frank Wuliger joined Gersh as a vice-president in the middle of 1997. He brought with him clients, Simon West (*Con Air*), Kasi Lemmons (*Eve's Bayou*), Bob Comfort (*Dogfight*), Jeanne Rosenberg (*The Black Stallion*), Monica Johnson (*Mother*) and Robert Nelson Jacobs (*Out to Sea*).

Wuliger, traveled the route of many big time agents from the mailroom at The William Morris Agency on to assisting at a prestigious office before creating the literary department at APA in 1980. He was the senior executive in the motion picture department at ICM before producing for two years with Walter Mirisch. He was also an executive at DEG. Frank returned to agenting at The Agency in 1986 and started the literary department at Innovative Artists in 1991.

In addition to Wuliger, the Los Angeles literary clients are represented by Gersh son, David, Ron Bernstein, Richard Arlook, John Bauman, Lynn Fimberg, Lee Keele, Sandra Lucchesi (J. Michael Bloom, Susan Smith & Associates), Abram Nalibotsky and Ken Neisser.

Angela Cheng, who was exec assistant to Ron Bernstein has been promoted and is now a full agent repping film and TV rights of works by authors and journalists. Michael Seller was promoted to agent in the TV lit department. He represents writers, directors and producers.

❖ The Gersh Agency New York

130 W 42nd Street #2400
btwn 5th & 6th Avenues
New York, NY 10036
212-997-1818

Clients shared by both coasts include Bill Gerber (*Roseanne*) Marlane Meyer, Jeanne Betancourt (*Tattle: When to Tell on a Friend, Supermom's Daughter*), Ntozake Shange and others. The Gersh Agency New York was formed when David Guc (pronounce Gus), Scott Yoselow, Ellen Curren and Mary Meagher left Don Buchwald & Associates to form a New York office.

A significant agency for writers, directors, actors and below-the-line personnel, the bulk of the literary department is handled through the Los Angeles office, but the New York office manages to be busy enough to enlist the efforts of three literary agents, so Los Angeles is obviously not doing all the business.

Partner Scott Yoselow, the only founding member remaining with the company, heads the literary department in New York and is joined by colleagues Caroline Fitgibbons and Peter Hagan (Writers & Artists).

Agents

Los Angeles: David Gersh, Phil Gersh, Richard Arlook, Frank Wuliger, John Bauman, Ron Bernstein, Lynn Fimberg, Lee Keele, Ken Neisser, Abram Nalibotsky, Angela Cheng, Sandra Lucchesi and Michael Seller
New York: Scott Yoselow, Caroline Fitgibbons and Peter Hagan

Client List

220 combined coasts

Clients

Jan DeBont, Bill Gerber, Marlane Meyer, Jeanne Betancourt, Ntozake Shange, Simon West, Kasi Lemmons, Bob Comfort, David Arata, Robert Nelson Jacobs, Robert Resnikoff, Monica Johnson and others

❖ Gold/Marshak/Liedtke Agency

3500 W Olive #1400
at Riverside Dr.
Burbank, CA 91505
818-972-4300

In 1981 Harry Gold opened this agency and asked Darryl Marshak to be his partner, and in 1992, Darryl accepted. If Harry is as persistent getting his clients jobs, it's easy to see how this agency continues to thrive. The literary department at Gold/Marshak/Liedtke is headed by Jeff Melnick.

After years as a studio executive at Universal, Columbia and Metromedia, Jeff opened his first agency in 1989 repping such talent as John Patrick Shanley (*Moonstruck*) and Rob Epstein and Jeff Friedman (*Common Threads*). He worked for the noted literary office of Curtis Brown before joining GML where his clients include Charles Busch (*Vampire Lesbians of Sodom, Red Scare on Sunset*), playwright/screenwriter Lee Blessing (*A Walk in the Woods, Cooperstown, Steal Big Steal Little, Down the Road, Independence*), Mary Hanes (*Doing Time at the Alamo*), Larry Grusin (*Garbo Talks, Care and Handling of Roses*), James Duff (*Doing Time on Maple Drive, The War at Home*), Robert Lee King (*The Disco Years*), Kelly Masterson (*Into the Light, Dare Not Speak Its Name*) Bruce Newberg and Sam Harris (*Hurry Hurry Hollywood*), Jeff Bell (*Radio Inside*) and Laurie Hutzler (*Lorraine Loses It*).

Jeff proudly points out that every year at least one of his clients receives some industry nomination whether it be an Oscar, Emmy or Humanitas award.

Agent
Jeff Melnick
Client List
25
Clients
James Duff, Charles Busch, Lee Blessing, Kelly Masterson, Laurie Hutzler, Mary Hanes, Robert Lee King, Larry Grusin, Jed Tullett, Reggie Vel Johnson, Bruce Newberg and Sam Harris and others

❖ The Graham Agency

311 W 43rd Street
btwn 8th & 9th Avenues
New York, NY 10036
212-489-7730

Earl Graham was a music student when he took a job selling
tickets at the McCarter Theatre solely to make money. That first
exposure to the business proved prophetic and in the 60s, Earl found
himself managing Equity Library Theatre and running a placement
service for actors. Equity ran out of money for the project and someone
suggested that instead of getting civilian work for actors, Earl should
just go ahead and become an agent.

Ashley-Famous was the lucky agency that ended up with Earl as
their secretary. Ever entrepreneurial, Earl created a job for himself, that
consisted of viewing every play on Broadway and Off and writing
reviews of the talent and material for the agency.

One day, literary giant Audrey Wood stopped by to ask why Earl
was doing what he was doing and pointed out that his analytical skills
spotting material would be better served if he were a literary agent.
Wood became his mentor and Earl soon made that transition.

Earl was one of the casualties in 1971 when A-F reorganized,
becoming IFA (forerunner to ICM). Not to worry, IFA was fair and
allowed Earl to take all 50 of his clients with him. After opening his own
office, one of his first big finds was the prize winning play, *That
Championship Season* written by actor-turned-writer Jason Miller.

Just to prove that it wasn't a fluke, Earl also discovered another prize
winning play, *On Golden Pond* written by another actor-turned-writer
Ernest Thompson.

Earl reps about 35 writers. He says that plays need to be through
the developmental period before he is interested. He won't take on
screenwriters as such, or writers of musicals.

Clients include Leslie Steele (*Hide & Seek*), John MacNicholas
(*Dumas*), Richard Baer (*Mixed Emotions*), Michael T. Folie (*The
Adjustment*) and screenwriters Scott Steward Anderson, Stephan P.
Lindsay and David Ball.

Agents
Earl Graham
Client List
35
Clients
Leslie Steele, John MacNicholas, Richard Baer, Scott Steward Anderson, Stephan P. Lindsay, Michael T. Folie, David Ball and others

❖ The Charlotte Gusay Literary Agency

10532 Blythe Avenue
near Pico & Motor (by 20th Century Fox)
Los Angeles, CA 90064
310-559-0831

Charlotte Gusay's love of the literary has such deep roots that she founded and owned the prestigious George Sand Bookstore in Los Angeles. After 12 years selling books, she decided to switch to authors and opened her own agency representing fiction and non-fiction books, selected children's books with movie potential, entertainment rights, books to film, selected screenplays and screenwriters.

Among the agency's thirty or so clients are screen projects, novels and non-fiction books including film rights to works by authors Mark Sullivan (*The Fall Line*), Cynthia Bass (*Maiden Voyage*), David Shields (*Dead Languages*), Annie Reiner (*A Visit to the Art Galaxy, This Nervous Breakdown Is Driving Me Crazy*) and Miriam Marx Allen (*Love, Groucho*).

The Charlotte Gusay Literary Agency is looking for books, film projects and children's books. Send a brief query letter first.

Agents
Charlotte Gusay
Client List
30+
Clients
David Shields, Ken Grissom, Annie Reiner, Miriam Marx Allen, Leon Whiteson, Stephanie Wells-Walper, Judith Estrine, Ruben Mendoza, Eleanor Jacobs, Marsha McCreadle, Brian O'Dea, Jane Ransom and others

❖ Harden-Curtis

850 7th Avenue #405
btwn 55th & 56th Streets
New York, NY 10019
212-977-8502

When Mary Harden became an agent, she came equipped with a complete set of regional theatre contacts courtesy of her life as the dutiful wife of a regional theatre director. Traipsing about in her husband's wake, Mary met just about everyone and did every job you could do in the theatre before she and her husband finally put down roots and Mary began life as an agent working for Bret Adams. She became his partner in 1980.

In 1996, Mary felt it was finally time to open her own office and teamed with another agent who began her agenting career with Bret. Nanci Curtis helms the theatrical side of this agency while Mary represents the writers.

Harden-Curtis' list of 25 writers includes Mary Murfitt (*Cowgirls*) Joan Ackermann (*The Batting Cage, Arliss*), Jeff Baron (*Visiting Mr. Green*) and Jeff Kindley who writes for children's television.

Colleague Yvonne Kenney is also an Adams alumnae. Sara Rayer assists the agents.

This office represents writers and actors and sees new clients mainly through referral. Mary Harden is one of the most respected agents in the business.

Agents
Mary Harden
Client List
25
Clients
Mary Murfitt, Joan Ackermann, Jeff Baron, Jeff Kindley and others

❖ Barbara Hogenson Agency, Inc.

165 West End Avenue
near 66th Street
New York, NY 10023
212-874-8084

When Barbara Hogenson was leaving a position in advertising, she had the good fortune to become acquainted with literary great, Lucy Kroll. Barbara's background in the arts (an interdisciplinary graduate degree in Film, Photography, Art History plus a job at the Museum of Modern Art), appealed to Lucy and soon she and Barbara became partners. When Lucy died, Barbara opened her own office representing journalists, playwrights, authors and directors.

Associate Sarah Feider's path to agenting is also interesting. An undergraduate degree in English from Kenyon College in Ohio led Sarah to NYU's Tisch School of the Arts for a Masters Degree in Cinema Studies. Her experience interning at the Don Buchwald Agency focused her goal on being a literary agent.

Since Sarah's graduation in 1995, she worked for both Writers & Artists and with Barbara Hogenson, before becoming a full time agent at this office in 1997. Sarah now joins Barbara representing their varied client list of biographers, playwrights, screenwriters and directors.

Names from Barbara's list include Carol Brightman (*Writing Dangerously*), Penelope Niven (*James Earl Jones, Steichen*), Joanna Glass (*If We Are Women*), Tazewell Thompson and the estates of James Thurber and Thornton Wilder.

Sarah's clients include Scott Sickles, Julie Myatt and Sally Benner. Although this agency prefers referrals, they have read scripts from query letters. They haven't signed anyone from a blind query, but say they have read some quality work that way.

Agents
Barbara Hogenson and Sarah Feider
Client List
20
Clients
Carol Brightman, Penelope Niven, Joanna Glass, Tazewell Thompson, Scott Sickles, Julie Myatt, Sally Benner and others

❖ Hohman Maybank Lieb

9229 Sunset Blvd. #700
W of Doheny
Los Angeles, CA 90069
310-274-4600

Bob Hohman entered the agency business working at The Artists Agency and moved on to Stanford Beckett and Associates where he became an agent in 1983 and a partner in 1984. In 1985, Bob relocated to Triad and by 1988 was heading their motion picture literary department.

In 1991, Hohman, Bob Wunsch and Dan Richland united to provide a small agency environment with big agency entree. When Wunsch retired in 1996, Richland opened his own agency and Hohman joined Devra Leib (Broder Kurland Webb Uffner, Triad, Irv Schechter) and fellow RWH colleague Bayard Maybank to form HML.

Clients from this agency include Marisa Silver (*Permanent Record, Vital Signs*), Stephen Tolkin (*Daybreak*), Neal Jimenez (*For the Boys, Rivers Edge, The Waterdance*), Dean Pitchford (*Fame, Footloose*), Randy and Perry Howze (*Mystic Pizza, Chances Are*), Bob Tzudiker and Noni White (*Roger Rabbit* sequel, *Mrs. Faust*), Dan Petrie, Jr. (*Beverly Hills Cop*) and Mark D. Andrews.

Most of the list of 15 directors started with this agency as writers and have made successful transitions to writer/director status.

Agents
Bob Hohman, Bayard Maybank and Devra Lieb
Client List
50
Clients
Marisa Silver, Stephen Tolkin, Neal Jimenez, Dean Pitchford, Randy and Perry Howze, Bob Tzudiker, Noni White, Dan Petrie, Jr., Mark D. Andrews and others

❖ HWA Talent Representatives

1964 Westwood Blvd. Suite 400
at Santa Monica
Los Angeles, CA 90025
310-446-1313

HWA continues to grow in both size and scope. I first met Patty Woo (Bret Adams, Kass & Woo) in New York before she and Barbara Harter joined forces. Since then, the agency has opened a west coast office and doubled the size of their NY theatrical department.

Another change has been the creation of a literary division in the Los Angeles office, headed by Kimber Wheeler. Kimber was a New York gallery owner in 1991 when she decided to move to Los Angeles. Although she had no thoughts of choosing show business as a career, Kimberly ended up working for Columbia Pictures assisting Stephanie Allain (currently president of Jim Henson Productions) before entering the agent training program at UTA in 1994.

A year later she left the agency business to produce a project at Universal, but agreed to re-enter the agency business when Patty Woo gave her the opportunity to design her own boutique literary department.

Kimber prefers writers who have a strong original voice. Among her 20 clients are Silvio Horta (*Even Exchange*), Maisha Yearwood (*Friends and Lovers*) and writer-director Cheryl Dunye (*The Watermelon Woman*). Kimber has a handful of authors and the office has a reciprocal relationship with a New York book agency.

Kimber checks out query letters but, like most agents, prefers a referral from an industry professional.

Agents
Kimberly Wheeler
Client List
20
Clients
Silvio Horta, Maisha Yearwood, Cheryl Dunye and others

❖ Ellen Hyman

90 Lexington Ave. #10 J
at 33rd Street
New York, NY 10016-8914
212-689-0727

When she was an actress at Northwestern, Ellen Hyman's cohorts felt her *take charge attitude* would lead to a career as a director. She considered producing, but felt she didn't have enough self esteem to ask people for money. Instead, she has marshaled the abilities of both professions to become an agent.

Ellen learned the literary business *working with the best, Lucy Kroll.* Though her next job was representing actors at the Fifi Oscard Agency, Ellen was already working on her own time to establish a reputation as the agent who would champion the voices of women and black playwrighting clients.

When Ellen opened her own agency in 1989 to represent those clients, she already had the contacts and her clients were well on their way. Although Ellen represents her own writers as they transition to screenwriting, she has no interest in taking on new screenwriting clients.

Ellen never takes on more than 10 clients at a time. Her clients include Adriana Trigiani, Casey Kurtti, Leslie Lee and Charlotte Gibson. She reads all query letters, but rarely responds because of time constraints.

Agent
Ellen Hyman
Client List
10
Clients
Adriana Trigiani, Casey Kurtti, Leslie Lee, Charlotte Gibson and others

❖ Innovative Artists

1999 Avenue of the Stars #2850
S of Little Santa Monica
Los Angeles, CA 90067
310-553-5200

The prestigious talent agency that Gersh alums Scott Harris and Howard Goldberg created has transformed significantly since its 1982 inception as Harris & Goldberg.

Always respected for their impressive list of accomplished actors, Innovative added a literary department to their list some years ago. That department continues to evolve. Lit ace, Frank Wuliger was wooed away by The Gersh Agency in 1997, but the literary agents that remain, Todd Schulkin, Elana Barry and Jim Garavente have managed to steady the boat and keep the literary department on an even course.

Clients from their list of 50 include writer Rick Cleveland and Eric Simonson (both from the Stepenwolf Theatre company), Monica Johnson (Albert Brooks' writing partner, *Mother*), Stuart Urban (FAFTA award winning writer/director), Dorothy Fontana (one of the creators of *Star Trek*) and novelist/screenwriter, Andrew Klavan.

Innovative represents writers, directors, producers and below-the-line personnel. New clients usually come through industry referral.

Though query letters are discouraged, they are always read. Do not query this agency unless you have entree.

At this writing, the New York office does not have a literary department, but Scott has plans to add a lit department soon, so if you are in New York, you might want to call and ask.

Agents
Todd Schulkin, Elana Barry, Jim Garavente
Client List
65
Clients
Rick Cleveland, Eric Simonson, Andrew Klavan, Monica Johnson, Stuart Urban, Dorothy Fontana and others

❖ ICM/International Creative Management

8942 Wilshire Blvd.
just W of Robertson
Beverly Hills, CA 90211
310-550-4000

ICM was already in contention for the title of #1 well before CAA's founding fathers left the agency business for more lofty positions elsewhere. When Mike Ovitz and Ron Meyer left CAA, many high profile agents and clients were suddenly listening when ICM agents came to call.

Known to be less corporate than WMA and CAA (that means everyone in the corporation doesn't have to be called in to review your latest contract), ICM is described by insiders as a stylish, forward-thinking operation. Headed by president Jim Wiatts, dynamic ICM is intent on becoming the #1 talent agency in the world.

Formed when Ashley-Famous and CMA merged in 1971, this agency has many, many clients and many, many agents. The most famous are powerful Sam Cohn who heads the New York office and Los Angeles' charismatic Ed Limato. Limato was profiled in a *Vanity Fair article, The Famous Eddie L.* in January 1990.

The New York literary department led by Amanda Urban and Esther Newberg is seen by many to be a prime component in ICM's rise to power

Among many other distinguished writers and directors, ICM represents Neil Jordan (*The Crying Game*), Nick Enright (*Lorenzo's Oil*), Julie Brown (*Medusa: Dare to be Truthful*), Jeff Price and Peter Seaman (*Who Framed Roger Rabbit?, Doc Hollywood, Trenchcoat),* Jerry Zaks *(Marvin's Room)* and the team of Kevin Bright, Marta Kauffman and David Crane who created *Friends.*

Steve Rabineau and Rosalie Swedlin head the film/literary division. Other film/literary agents are Tricia Davey, Patty Detroit, Barbara Dreyfus, Michael Eisner, Richard Feldman, Todd Feldman, Amy Ferris, Stuart Fry, Alicia Gordon, Kristin Jones, Ken Kamins, Doug MacLaren, Cindy Mintz, Robert Newman, Nick Reed, Jim Rosen and Dave Wirtschafter.

Paul Haas heads the TV/literary division. Other members of the

❖ ICM/International Creative Management

40 W 57th Street
just W of 5th Avenue
New York, NY 10019
212-556-5600

TV/literary team are Steve Simons, Matt Solo, Richard Weitz and Jeanne Williams.
Maryann Kelly (Gersh Agency, Triad, William Morris) works with authors and ICM's New York's publishing operation.

Agents
Amanda Urban, Esther Newberg, Steve Rabineau, Rosalie Swedlin, Tricia Davey, Patty Detroit, Barbara Dreyfus, Michael Eisner, Richard Feldman, Todd Feldman, Amy Ferris, Stuart Fry, Jim Rosen, Alicia Gordon, Kristin Jones, Ken Kamins, Doug MacLaren, Robert Newman, Nick Reed, Dave Wirtschafter, Paul Haas, Cindy Mintz, Steve Simons, Matt Solo, Richard Weitz, Jeanne Williams and Maryann Kelly

Client List
Very large

Clients
Neil Jordan, Nick Enright, Ralph Bakshi, Rene Balcer, Peter P. Benchley, Woody Allen, Garry Marshall, Mike Nichols, Julie Brown, Cynthia Whitcomb, Greg Daniels and others

❖ Leslie B. Kallen Agency

15303 Ventura Blvd. #900
near Sepulveda Blvd.
Sherman Oaks, CA 91403
818-906-2785

Leslie Kallen says she is a cheerleader for new writing talent and
that this is why she became an agent. Starting in the business as a reader
and writing teacher, she also led scriptwriting seminars from a reader's
perspective. Finding herself with a client base of new screenwriters from
this experience, it was a short move to starting her own agency in 1987.
Leslie is known in the business as an alternative source for quality new
scriptwriters. Her stable of 25 plus writers include Allan Hollingsworth
(*Tswana, the Cat*), Paul Dreskin (*The New Count of Monte Cristo*), D. B.
Smith (*Red Rain*), Ron Clark (*Dead Run*) and Helene Wagner (*The Unseen,
Grey Matter*).

Agents
Leslie B. Kallen
Client List
25+
Clients
Paul Dreskin, Allan Hollingsworth, D. B. Smith, Ron Clark,
Helene Wagner and others

❖ Kaplan Stahler Gumer Agency

8383 Wilshire Blvd. #923
at San Vicente Blvd.
Beverly Hills, CA 90211
213-653-4483

Mitch Kaplan and Elliot Stahler graduated from the WMA mailroom, class of '74. After graduation, Mitch went into production and Elliot went to law school by night and worked as a literary agent at WMA by day. When Mitch decided that production was not his forte, he joined Progressive Artists Agency as a theatrical agent. Soon Elliot left WMA and, as he describes it, they *naively and successfully* started the literary department at PAA. In 1981, they opened their own offices and are now recognized as one of the most prestigious, tasteful and successful agencies in town. In 1997 the name of the agency changed to reflect new partner, Robert Gumer (ICM).

KSG believes in 30-year-careers for their clients and they invest the time to nurture beginners whether they are writers or directors. For all their success (and they have a lot of it), Elliot and Mitch still take time to read material and value new talent. In addition to Elliot, Mitch and Robert, writers at this agency are also represented by Andrew Patman. (The Artists Agency).

Clients include David Angell (*Wings, Frazier*), Ross Brown (*Kirk, Meego, Step by Step*), Shaun Cassidy (*Roar, American Gothic, Players*), and writing partners Dianne Messina Stanley and Jim Stanley (*Savannah, Pacific Palisades*) and Jeff Greenstein and Jeff Strauss (*Partners, Friends*).

Their list of 40 clients includes 22 writers and writing teams, line producers and Emmy award winning directors.

Agents
Mitch Kaplan, Elliot Stahler, Robert Gumer and Andrew Patman
Client List
22
Clients
David Angell, Ross Brown, Shaun Cassidy, Dianne Messina Stanley, Jim Stanley, Jeff Greenstein, Jeff Strauss and others

❖ Patricia Karlan Agency

2219 W Olive Ave. #222
near Pass Avenue
Burbank, CA 91506
818-752-4800

Since the network and studio business affairs folk negotiate all
the contracts, it seems as though a background in this field must be
second only to the conglomerate mailrooms as an educational
prerequisite for agents. It surely takes a lot of the praying and guess
work out of how far to push. This is exactly what Patricia Karlan's pre-
agent duties entailed.

At this point, Karlan has shrunk her list down to one writer,
Judith Guest (*Ordinary People*). She still represents some New York
publishers and agents for book deals. Please don't send Karlan any
scripts or she won't let me talk to her anymore!

Agents
Patricia Karlan.
Client List
quite limited
Clients
Judith Guest and publishers for book deals

❖ Kerin - Goldberg Associates

155 E 55th Street # 5D
between 3rd & Lexington Avenues
New York, NY 10022
212-838-7373

Charles Kerin's interest in the business was so strong that in his first job as a publicist for Scholastic Magazine, he managed to convince management to create a film award just so he could get to see free movies. That same kind of creative thinking led Charles to a job with prestigious old-line office, Coleman-Rosenberg where he became an agent. Charles left C-R to open his own literary agency representing soap writers in 1985.

Ellie Goldberg was an actress when old school chum, Gary Epstein (Epstein/Wyckoff) cajoled her into joining his office and becoming an agent. Goldberg's path has also included stints with Henderson-Hogan, Bonnie Allen and ultimately, Coleman-Rosenberg where she met Charles when he was called in to broker a deal for a literary client.

Kerin and Goldberg hit it off immediately and spoke often of opening their own agency *when the time is right*.

1995 turned out to be the magic year when Kerin and Goldberg got together to create this classy agency representing playwrights, directors, choreographers, scene designers, costume designers, art directors and actors.

Their literary list is select: 4-5 writers and 5-6 directors. Charles handles the literary clients at this agency and sees new writers only by referral. One of his clients is James Racheff (*Houdini, Abyssina*).

There are incisive quotes from Charles elsewhere in the book. Be sure to check them out.

Agents
Charles Kerin
Client List
6-7
Clients
James Racheff and others

❖ Joyce Ketay Agency

1501 Broadway #1908
at 43rd Street
New York, NY 10036
212-354-6825

Cancer Research Diagnosis and non-profit theatre have produced an unusually synergistic partnership. Joyce Ketay left the scientific community in search of a less depressing life. To sustain her during the search, a friend suggested work as an assistant to literary agent Ellen Neuwald. Dealing with Neuwald clients like David Rabe and John Guare helped clinch Joyce's decision to embark on a new life as a literary agent. When Ellen died in 1980, Joyce started Joyce Ketay Agency and ran it alone for 10 years.

Carl Mulert was a production and theatre manager for Arena Stage and Playwrights Horizons. Also burned out and seeking a new life, he confided to old friend Joyce that he was going to find a job as a secretary in a law firm someplace while exploring new options. Knowing how these things work, Joyce persuaded him to be her assistant and, of course, now he is her partner.

Carl joins a growing list of ex-production stage managers who find their backgrounds more valuable than they imagined. Stage managing includes a whole raft of valuable assets from resourcefulness to contacts from the other side of the desk, that are a great boon to any theatrically related business.

Joyce's and Carl's clients include Pulitzer Prize winner Tony Kushner (*Angels in America)*, Tony winner Michael Cristofer and writer/director Stuart Ross (*Forever Plaid*). They handle writers, directors and designers.

Recently, Joyce and Carl have entered into a partnership with Los Angeles megapower, CAA, allowing CAA clients access to Ketay's powerful Manhattan theatre connections.

Wendy Streeter is an associate agent at this agency.

Agents
Joyce Ketay, Carl Mulert and Wendy Streeter
Client List
50
Clients
Tony Kushner, Michael Cristofer, Stuart Ross, David Rabe,
Eric Simonson and others

❖ Paul Kohner, Inc.

9300 Wilshire Blvd.
just W of Doheny
Beverly Hills, CA 90212
310-550-1060

The late Paul Kohner built this prestigious agency into one of the most successful and famous boutique agencies in town. His list of writers, directors and actors is filled with famous names from Europe and America. In 1987, a year before Paul died, colleagues Gary Salt and Pearl Wexler bought the agency and they continue to deal in the old-world manner with which clients Billy Wilder and Ivan Passer are familiar.

While finishing a graduate degree at Stanford in the Drama Department in 1972, The Contemporary Korman agency presented Gary with an opportunity to enter the agency business. He was trained by ex-MCA agent, Ron Leif, at C-K (now Contemporary Artists). From there, he moved on to Smith Stevens Associates (now Susan Smith & Associates) where he inaugurated their literary department.

Since joining PKI in 1977, his focus in the literary marketplace has become more diverse as he carves out his own niche in a variety of endeavors. He reps publishers, authors, book material, composers, directors and producers as well as screen writers and television writers.

The agency continues to expand in all directions, particularly in the literary department where two new lit agents have joined the roster: Beth Bohn from The Turtle Agency and Stephen More who trained as an agent at Kohner.

The list of 20 writers contains names like Istvan Szabo (*Meeting Venus, Mephisto*), Donald Westlake (*The Grifters*), John Toles-Bey (*Rage in Harlem*), Tom Clancy (*The Hunt for Red October*) and Victor Nunez (*Ruby in Paradise, Ulee's Gold*) and others.

Gary not only heads the literary department repping writers, directors and producers, but also handles a few theatrical clients as well. For legal reasons, PKI accepts no unsolicited material, but does answer every query letter that is accompanied by self-addressed-stamped-envelope.

Agents
Gary Salt, Beth Bohn and Stephen More
Client List
20
Clients
Istvan Szabo, Donald Westlake, Ed McBain, Tony Huston, Victor
Nunez, Tom Clancy, John Toles-Bey, Denise Nicolos, Charles Marowitz
and others

❖ The Lantz Office

888 7th Ave. #3001
btwn 56th & 57th Streets
New York, NY 10106
212-586-0200

The Lantz Office is one of the class acts in the annals of show biz. When I quizzed New York agents as to other agents they admired, Robert Lantz was the name most mentioned. He started in the business as a story editor and on a Los Angeles business trip from his London home in 1950, Phil Berg of the famous Berg-Allenbery Agency made him an offer he couldn't refuse, *Don't go home. Come to New York and open our office there.* Mr. Lantz indeed did open the New York office at 3 East 57th Street representing Clark Gable, Madeleine Carroll and other illustrious stars until William Morris bought that company a year later.

Lantz worked for smaller agencies for a few years before opening Robert Lantz, Ltd. in 1954. In 1955, he succumbed to Joe Mankiewicz's pleas and joined him to produce films. It only took three years to figure out that he found agenting a much more interesting profession. In 1958, Lantz re-entered the field as a literary agent. Feeling a mix of actors and directors and writers gave each segment more power, his list soon reflected that.

Colleague Dennis Aspland worked for the legendary Sam Cohn before joining Lantz representing screenwriters and directors. The list of writers numbers about 20 and includes Jules Feiffer, Peter Shaffer, Anthony Shaffer, Bruce Wolf, Peter Feibleman and the estate of Sean O'Casey.

Agents
Robert Lantz and Dennis Aspland
Client List
20
Clients
Jules Feiffer, Peter Feibleman, Peter Shaffer, Anthony Shaffer, the estate of Sean O'Casey, Bruce Wolf and others

❖ Major Clients Agency

345 Maple Drive #395
S of Burton Way
Beverly Hills CA 90210
310-205-5000

Jeffrey Benson was an executive vice-president at Lorimar and Richard Weston was head of television production at Paramount before they teamed up in 1993 to produce one of the prime literary offices in Los Angeles. David McIlvain (Metropolitan), Ross Fineman, Stephen L. Rose, Michael G. Margules (Irv Schechter) Michael Van Dyke (The Agency), Andrea P. Newman (Amsel, Eisenstadt & Frazier), Jeff Wise (Vision Arts Management) and Tracy Murray (CAA) complete the agent roster at this now widely expanded agency.

In addition to their literary jewels, MCA represents important actors, directors and producers and has an important packaging department. Their clients include the executive director of *This Can't Be Love*, Billy Riback, Winifred Hervey who created *The Steve Harvey Show*, Lawrence Hertzog who created *Nowhere Man*, Tony DeSena (head writer on NBC's *Later*), Aaron Mendelsohn and Paul Tamasey (*Air Bud*) and writer-director Daniel Taplitz (*Commandments, Black Magic, Nightlife*).

Agents
Jeffrey Benson, Richard Weston, Stephen L. Rose, Ross Fineman, Michael G. Margules, Tracy Murray, Andrea P. Newman, Jeff Wise, David McIlvain and Michael Van Dyck

Client List
100+

Clients
Billy Riback, Winifred Hervey, Lawrence Hertzog and others

Ken Greenblatt 3/205-5099 cfax
Shelly Goldstein

❖ Media Artists Group/MAG

8383 Wilshire Blvd. #954
at San Vicente
Beverly Hills, CA 90011
213-658-5050

If Raphael Berko can't get you through the door, I don't know who can. A man brimming with ideas and passion, Raphael Berko became an agent because he was an enterprising and creative actor. Since he couldn't get an agent, Raphael took a job as an agent's assistant in order to submit himself for auditions. When *The Hollywood Reporter* wrote a story about his double life, the jig was up.

Screen Actors Guild told him he could be an actor or an agent, but not both. His choice has made his clients eternally grateful. When Raph was 29, he bought The Caroline Leonetti Agency and his fortunes have steadily risen.

Barbara Alexander heads the literary department and she's no slouch either. Alexander has been a writer/director/producer of short films, a VP of development at Odyssey Films, an independent producer and a production assistant. An agent for over 10 years, she's an empathetic and effective writer's advocate.

Her associate, Ellen Aaronson was in development at Renaissance-Atlantic before joining MAG.

Open and down to earth, this full service agency represents writers, directors, director-producers, writer-producers as well as both theatrical and commercial actors.

Barbara, Ellen and Raphael are dedicated to developing careers and taking clients on for the long haul. Their clients write for film and all areas of television, including interactive. The list of 30 writers includes Sheryl Hendryx (*Running Brave, The Jumping Fool, Final Jeopardy*), Paul Chitlik (*Youngsters),* Mark Zaslove (story editor on *Calamity Jane*) and Dave Finkel and Brett Baer (creators/producers, *The Monkey Days* at Disney).

Media Artists looks at new material only through industry referral. Although they do respond to some query letters, Barbara says the ratio is about 1 out of 200.

Agents
Barbara Alexander, Ellen Aaronson and Raphael Berko
Client List
30+
Clients
Sheryl Hendryx, Paul Chitlik, Mark Zaslove, Dave Finkel, Brett Baer
and others

323 - 658-7871 fax

❖ Helen Merrill

425 W 23rd Street #1F
btwn 8th & 9th Avenues
New York, NY 10011
212-691-5326

One of the most reputable literary agencies in New York and certainly one of the most difficult to penetrate is Helen Merrill, home to some of the most important writers, directors and set designers in the business. I was delighted to finally meet Ms. Merrill even if it was only on the telephone.

Originally a photographer, Merrill became an agent out of financial necessity and from the names on her client list (confidential), it's clear that money has not been a problem since she started her business in 1976.

Helen Merrill represents authors, playwrights and screenwriters and only considers query letters accompanied by self-addressed-stamped-envelopes. These letters should contain not only brief descriptions of the project, but information regarding any productions and/or published works with the publishers attached to it. Don't inundate this office with material unless you have the resume to back it up.

Agents
Helen Merrill and others
Client List
30
Clients
Confidential

❖ Metropolitan Talent Agency/MTA

4526 Wilshire Blvd.
3 blocks east of Highland at Rossmore
Los Angeles, CA 90010
213-857-4500   4509-fax

An actor and a writer in an earlier life, it only took Chris Barrett eight months working as an agent for J. Michael Bloom to decide he was ready to open his own first office, McCartt Oreck Barrett. That was in 1983 and MOB, as it was called, was known as one of the places to shop for interesting, unique actors, some of whom still grace Chris' client list today.

By 1989, Chris was ready to add other creative elements to his agency, so he formed Metropolitan and now represents a distinguished list of writers, producers, showrunners, directors, actors and comedians.

Most agencies ebb and flow with personnel, but Chris always seems to be flowing with great agents and clients, so it's no surprise that Deborah Miller (WMA) joined him in 1993 and has helped him pioneer some new-fangled-ideas on agent compensation that have helped build yet another important agency.

Chris's corporate concept works for the everyone involved, for the clients end up with the entire army of Metropolitan agents as their advocates as a result of Chris creative compensation idea that is so ground-breaking that *The Wall Street Journal* thought it worthy enough to write about:

For each commission dollar coming in from a deal, 30% is scored for the agent who originally brought in the client, no matter how long ago. The next 30% goes to the employee currently representing that talent. The final 40% goes to whoever has landed the deal in question. The same employee frequently performs all these functions, but many deals link two, three or more agents.

Talent Agency Shows Stellar Teamwork—in Hollywood, No Less
Thomas Petzinger, Jr.
The Wall Street Journal
January 26, 1996

Chris' vision, style, taste and emphasis on team effort result in an agency personality that attracted the head of his literary department, Marc Pariser.

Marc didn't start out to be an agent either. He was a layout artist at an animation studio and a fashion illustrator when his decision to change careers led to a job in the ICM mailroom. Thinking of the mailroom as merely an avenue into show business, Marc is as surprised as anyone that he ended up being an agent.

Not only has Marc worked at each of the conglomerate agencies (ICM, CAA, WMA), but he helmed his own production company before being recruited by Diane English as executive vice-president of Creative Affairs at Shukovsky English Entertainment.

Chris Barrett had wanted Marc to work with him for a long time and was just one of several agents who managed to call Marc during a time period when he was considering a return to life as an agent. Luckily for everyone at this agency, Chris won out and in August of 1996, Marc joined Metropolitan.

His distinguished crew of literary agents includes Andrea Newman (CAA), Pat Quinn (ICM, APA) and Steve Marks (ICM, Major Clients). Jeannie O'Brien who assisted at Susan Smith & Associates, The Gersh Agency and Metropolitan, and Bradley Glenn who was a commercial production coordinator and location manager before assisting at APA and at Metropolitan, both went through the agent-training program at Metropolitan and have now become colleagues in the literary division.

This agency is not for beginners, so unless you can get an industry referral, save your stamps. As your fortunes rise, this is a place to think about.

Representative clients from Metropolitan's distinguished literary list include William Link (*Columbo, Murder, She Wrote*), Phillip Railsback (*The Stars Fell on Henrietta*), Pamela Pettler (*Clueless*) and Chris Abbott (*Dr. Quinn, Medicine Woman*).

Agents
Chris Barrett, Marc Pariser, Steve Marks, Jeannie O'Brien, Pat Quinn, Andrea Newman and Bradley Glenn

Client List
85

Clients
William Link, Phillip Railsback, Pamela Pettler, Chris Abbott and others

❖ Monteiro Rose Agency, Inc.

17514 Ventura Blvd. #205
1½ blocks E of White Oak (Josh)—
Encino, CA 91316
818-501-1177

In an earlier life, Candy Monteiro wrote, produced, directed and hosted rock n' roll radio interview shows. She says she *knew more rock n' roll gossip than was good for her brain,* so she got a job as an assistant and reader for New York book agent Henry Morrison.

Fredda Rose wanted to be an opera singer, but became a Wall Street lawyer before joining ABC television business affairs. There, she learned *all those things* buyers do to writers, so she was a real asset at her next job at The Sy Fisher Agency where she became an agent.

When she arrived in Los Angeles, Monteiro assisted Bettye McCartt at MOB (now Metropolitan) and Sylvia Hirsch at Lew Weitzman (now Preferred Artists) before becoming an agent.

As a junior agent, Fredda drew the less financially viable animation writers, but as the status of animation grew, her writers became stars and graduated to features.

Candy and Fredda met when Fisher and Weitzman merged, and laid the foundation for Monteiro Rose which they opened in 1987. Their associate Milissa Brockish became an agent at this agency.

Their list of 50 + includes writers and producers for film, movies for television, series, animation and interactive. They also represent authors and they package.

Monteiro Rose is very selective about new clients. If you are already in the business in some capacity, your chances are better, but still, you'd better have many scripts and they better be good before you query this agency. Rose and Monteiro stress that any script ever submitted to an agent had better be the fourth or fifth pass, never the first.

Agents
Fredda Rose, Candy Monteiro and Milissa Brockish
Client List
50+
Clients
Confidential

❖ Omnipop

10700 Ventura Blvd.
1 block W of Lankershim
Los Angeles, CA 90046
818-980-9267

Who would ever think of Long Island as a spawning ground for an influential show-biz agency? My thought is that if you can have a hot personal appearance agency on Long Island, you could do just about anything.

The Omni partners are an eclectic lot. Tom Ingegno (pronounce engine-yo), Ralph Asquino and Bruce Smith were originally musicians, managers or stand-up performers. They booked themselves and their friends on college circuits and later clubs. As they graduated to bigger, more diverse venues and clients, starting an agency was a logical progression.

They created Omnipop in their current Long Island offices in 1983 and have been so successful that Bruce moved to Los Angeles to open an office there in 1993.

The partners' taste and savvy has led them to establish their own niche representing stand-up comics for personal appearances, television, film and commercials.

Clients routinely work *The Tonight Show, The Late Show with David Letterman, Late Night with Conan O'Brien* and *E Entertainment*, as well as clubs, film and theatre.

Don't send your film scripts for Omni is not basically a literary agency. They do, however, handle stand-ups who end up creating shows and/or become staff writers on comedy shows, so if you are a stand-up who is looking to crossover into comedy writing, this might be the place for you.

Omnipop's staff has been chosen for their skill and taste and because they all share some kind of performing background. The west coast clients are represented by Bruce, Tom Markwalter and Angela Davis while the east coast clients get partners Tom and Ralph as well as associates Simon Hopkins, Barbara Klein and Joan St. Onge.

❖ Omnipop

55 West Old Country Road
Hicksville, NY 11801
516-937-6011

Agents
West coast: Bruce Smith, Tom Markwalter and Angela Davis
East coast: Tom Ingegno, Ralph Asquino, Simon Hopkins, Barbara Klein and Joan St. Onge

Client List
40 both coasts

Clients
Adam Ferrara, Kathy Buckley, Steve O., John Wing, Andy Kindler and others

❖ Oppenheim-Christie Ltd.

13 E 37th Street 7th floor
just E of 5th Avenue
New York, NY 10016
212-213-4330

Oppenheim-Christie has long been known as an agency representing actors for commercials and voice overs but the recent merger with H. Shep Pamplin's Sheplin Artists extends the reach to include writers, directors, comedians, dancers, singers and variety artists.

Originally an actor-set designer-director-producer, Pamplin's frustration at his inability to get agents and casting directors to attend showcases led to a suggestion from his agent, Bob Donaghey at Talent East, that he might be able to be more effective if he just become an agent. Shep joined Bob as an agent and has never looked back. He opened his own office in 1994 and merged with Oppenheim-Christie in mid 1997.

The head of the literary department at Oppenheim-Christie, George Colucci, was also an actor-producer. With strong ties in the New York independent film community, he decided to use the inroads he had built for himself to help other independent filmmakers.

Good query letters actually get attention at this agency. Shep likes action/adventure, but George is the guy who works with the writers, so you will appeal to him best if you have the tightly written character driven piece that the New York independent market is looking for.

Agents
George G. Colucci
Client List
8
Clients
Confidential

❖ Original Artists

417 S Beverly Drive #201
S of Wilshire
Beverly Hills, CA 90212
310-277-1251
275-6725-fax

Jordan Bayer and Matt Leipzig were executives at Columbia Pictures in 1988. Jordan left to become an agent at ICM and started this agency in 1993. From Columbia, Leipzig traveled a different route, becoming president of Jerry Weintraub Productions and working with Roger Corman's New Horizons Pictures as head of production before deciding to join his old Columbia buddy and become an agent at Original Artists in 1997.

In a very short time, Original Artists has made a nice name for itself representing a stable of writers and directors for television and films. Names from their impressive list include Mark Feldberg and Mitch Klebanoff (*Beverly Hills Ninja*), Chris Hauty (*Homeward Bound II, Stretch Armstrong*), Doug Wallace (*Seven*), Will Aldis (*Back to School, Stealing Home, A Life in the Day of Tom Rowan*), David Weissman (*Guam Goes to the Moon*) and Joe Forte (*The Murderer Next Door*).

Both Bayer and Leipzig are committed to attention and personal service and feel the only place a writer can get that is at a small agency.

This information is based on research and not on personal interview.

Agents
Jordan Bayer and Matt Leipzig
Client List
40
Clients
Mark Feldberg and Mitch Klebanoff, Chris Hauty, Doug Wallace, Will Aldis, David Weissman, Joe Forte, Scott Freeman and others

❖ Fifi Oscard Agency, Inc.

24 W 40th Street
W of 5th Avenue
New York, NY 10018
212-764-1100

Fifi Oscard was a frustrated housewife and mother in 1949 when she began working gratis for Lee Harris Draper. When I asked her in what capacity she was working, she said, *mostly as a jerk*, but added that in nine months she was no longer inept and had worked herself up to $15 a week. Always interested in theatre and with the ability to do almost anything, Fifi has prospered.

From LHD, Fifi moved to The Lucille Phillips Agency, working three days a week. That inauspicious beginning led to Fifi's purchase of LPA in 1959 and the birth of The Fifi Oscard Agency, Inc. This agency deals with writers, directors, producers, singers, composers, actors — every arm of showbiz except the variety field.

Writers at this agency are represented by Carmen LaVia, Kevin McShane and Ivy Fischer-Stone.

Agents
Carmen La Via, Kevin McShane and Ivy Fischer-Stone
Client List
Confidential
Clients
Confidential

❖ The Daniel Ostroff Agency

9200 Sunset Blvd. #402
W of Doheny
Los Angeles, CA 90069
310-278-2020

Daniel Ostroff's advice to young scriptwriters is to *find a hot new agent and grow up with him.* He and client Richard Friedenberg (*A River Runs Through It*) have been together since Daniel made the journey from the ICM mailroom to agent, to Writers & Artists, a partnership with Robert Wunsch (Wunsch/Ostroff) and opening this agency in 1987.

Some of Daniel's other clients include Thom Eberhardt (*Night of the Comet, Captain Ron, Honey I Blew Up the Kids*), Ken Kaufman (*The Air Up There*), Helena Kriel (*Kamasutra*), Richard Franklin (*Brilliant Lies*), Tom Smith (*Honey, I Blew Up the Kids*), Dave Fuller and Rick Natkin (*Necessary Roughness*) and Josann McGibbon and Sara Parriott (*Runaway Bride*).

Originally from Washington, D. C., Daniel's introduction to the mailroom at ICM came about because his brother lived next door to a television producer.

Daniel tells an inspiring story about success: *Years ago, I read a profile in* The New York Times *about the world's greatest piano salesman. He worked long hours, played the piano, kept voluminous files...and knew everyone in the music business...I realized the key thing was left out: yes, he did all of those things but he also sold Steinways. Like him. I sell Steinways.*

Even if you feel you are a Steinway, don't compose a query letter. Daniel is highly committed to the list of clients he already has, but you can pick up some valuable information from his quotes throughout the book.

Agents
Daniel Ostroff
Client List
15
Clients
Richard Friedenberg, Thom Eberhardt, Ken Kaufman, Tom Smith, Helena Kriel, Dave Fuller and Rick Natkin, Josann McGibbon, Richard Franklin and Sara Parriott and others

❖ Paradigm

10100 Santa Monica Blvd.
at Century Park East
Los Angeles, CA 90067
310-277-4400

In 1969, after 21 collective years interning with various big agencies, Stu Robinson and Bernie Weintraub opened their own offices. Tired of endless staff meetings, wasted time and limited to coverage *west of La Brea*, they wanted to represent the whole town and do it their way. Ken Gross left his own business in 1985 to join RW and in 1990 a new name, Robinson Weintraub and Gross, reflected his accomplishments.

In 1993, their business changed dramatically when Gross left to became a manager/producer and Robinson and Weintraub joined forces with others to form a mini-conglomerate.

Their new partners were varied: STE and Gores/Fields were known primarily as a source for wonderful actors and Shorr, Stille & Associates was another prominent literary agency. The four agencies have become a distinguished and powerful presence in both New York and Los Angeles.

In 1997, TV literary powerhouse, Debbee Klein left the Irv Schechter Co. to join Paradigm and is now also a partner in the agency.

Founding partners at Paradigm are Sam Gores, Clifford Stevens, Stuart Robinson, Bernie Weintraub and Lucy Stille.

Paradigm reps 100-125 writers, directors and producers. Stu Robinson says, they don't represent books until they are movies and then they represent authors for movie rights.

Paradigm does not accept unsolicited material, so you'll have to find someone who knows someone to gain entree to this connected Los Angeles agency. In addition to partners Weintraub, Stille and Klein, others who represent writers at Paradigm are Matthew Bedrosian, Perre Brogan (Three Arts Management), Joe Gatta (ICM), Robert Golenberg, Valerie Phillips, Matt Rice, Andrea Simon, Sean Freidin (Irv Schechter Co.) and Sandy Weinberg (Innovative Artists, InterTalent).

❖ Paradigm

200 W 57th Street # 900
btwn 7th & 8th Avenues
New York, NY 10019
212-246-1030

The New York office specializes in actors for theatre, film, television, commercials and voice-overs and has no literary department.

Agents
Bernard Weintraub, Stu Robinson, Lucy Stille, Debbee Klein, Matthew Bedrosian, Perre Brogan, Joe Gatta, Robert Golenberg, Valerie Phillips, Matt Rice, Andrea Simon, Sandy Weinberg and Sean Freidin
Client List
100+
Clients
Confidential

❖ Pleshette/Millner Agency

2700 N Beachwood Drive
N of Franklin
Los Angeles, CA 90068
213-465-0428

Lynn Pleshette runs an agency strictly for writers. Respected in the business before she even had one, Lynn Pleshette has been extremely successful parlaying her background in publishing into one of the most admired literary agencies in Los Angeles. When she moved to Los Angeles in 1975, her best friend asked her to represent film rights to her novel. She figured she already knew how to *lunch* so why not?

Along with Lynn's prestigious list of scriptwriters, Lynn corepresents several novelist/screenwriters for distinguished New York book agents like Darhansoff and Verrill. Her deal for the film rights to Charles Frazier's novel *Cold Mountain* was for $1.2 million to be written and directed by Anthony Minghella. Other authors Lynn represents or corepresents include Jane Smiley (*Thousand Acres*), Scott Smith (*A Simple Plan*), Lawrence Wright (*Noriega, Bang*), Deena Goldstone (*Safe Passage*), Annie Proulx (*Shipping News*), John McLaughlin (*Magnet Head*), and Frank Parkin (*Krippendorf's Tribe*).

Producer Joel Millner became Lynn's partner in February 1997. Some of his clients include Chuck Pfarrer (*Jackal, Hard Target*) and Mark Verheiden *(Time Cop)*.

There are perceptive quotes from Lynn throughout the book. P/M is not in the market for new clients and discourages query letters and phone calls at this time.

Agents
Lynn Pleshette and Joel Millner
Client List
30
Clients
Jane Smiley, Scott Smith, Lawrence Wright, Deena Goldstone, Annie Proulx, Frank Parkin, John McLaughlin, Chuck Pfarrer, Mark Verheiden and others

❖ Preferred Artists

16633 Ventura Blvd. #1421
2 blocks W of Havenhurst
Encino, CA 91436
818-990-0305

Lew Weitzman somehow mutated from a UCLA student with a major in Russian into a major literary agent. His first exposure to the business was via the MCA training program in 1962. Already on the rise when government anti-trust laws forced the break up of MCA, Lew was invited to join prestigious Park Citron (which became Chasin-Park-Citron). He then spent 7 years in the motion picture and television literary department of The William Morris Agency before establishing Lew Weitzman and Associates.

Taft Broadcasting acquired that agency and Lew went with it. When American Financial bought Taft, Lew was legally free to start a new agency of his own again and created Preferred Artists with Roger Strull in 1988.

Sylvia Hirsch (WMA), Susie Weissman (ICM), Mary Kimmel, Brad Rosenfield and Lew's son, Paul, all join Lew in representing their list of between 90-100 writers, producers and directors. Writers from their list include Bob Bendetson (*Coach*), Stuart Raffill (*Passenger 57*), Pat Duncan (*Mr. Holland's Opus, Courage Under Fire*), Phil Lasker (*Identity Crisis*) and Ann Becket (*First Do No Harm, Mary & Tim*).

Agents
Lew Weitzman, Roger Strull, Sylvia Hirsch, Susie Weissman, Mary Kimmel, Brad Rosenfield and Paul Weitzman
Client List
90-100
Clients
Bob Bendetson, Stuart Raffill, Phil Lasker, Ann Becket, Pat Duncan and others

❖ Premiere Artists Agency

8899 Beverly Blvd. #510
near Doheny
Los Angeles, CA 90048
310-271-1414
205-3981-fax

Premiere Artists Agency was founded in January 1993 by Susan Sussman and John Ufland as a boutique literary agency. Six months later, Michael Packenham and Carolyn Kessler joined the agency as partners creating a prestigious talent division. Kessler has since left to become client Alicia Silverstone's manager/producing partner but Packenham remains to shepherd the acting clients.

In addition to Sussman and Ufland, the literary clients are serviced by Deborah Deuble (who trained at this agency) and Sheryl Peterson.

Premiere Artists represents scriptwriters, authors, actors, comedians, directors, producers, teenagers, young adults, below-the-line and new media. Of course, with all these components, they also package. As with most upper level literary agencies, new clients come to this office through industry referral, though they do read query letters.

Premiere was not available for an interview, so this information is based on research.

Agents
Susan Sussman, John Ufland, Deborah Deuble and Sheryl Peterson
Client List
80
Clients
Confidential

❖ Jim Preminger Agency

1650 Westwood Blvd. #201
S of Wilshire
Los Angeles, CA 90024
310-475-9491
470-2934-fax

One of the most elegant agencies in town is run by Jim Preminger. Jim's original show-biz goal was to become a producer. After spending three years optioning properties, working with writers on screenplay adaptations and generally trying to get into the business, the Artists Agency countered his offer of a project he hoped to package for Jack Nicholson, with an offer to open their literary department. Not only had show business opened its door to Jim, it invited him in, for just two years later in 1977, Jim became a partner.

In 1980 he decided to open his own agency with a dozen clients. Dean Schramm, a lawyer before becoming an agent with The Artists Agency, joined Jim in 1997. Together, they represent about 60 clients covering all principal literary areas: motion pictures, long form television, series television, plus animation and interactive media. These clients are writers, directors and writers/directors.

Writers from their list include Michael Butler (*White Mile, Pronto, Pale Rider, Against the Law*), Peter Casey and David Lee (creators of *Frazier* and *Wings*), Helen Plummer and Sherry Bilsing (on staff on *Veronica's Closet*), Geoffrey Neigher *(Total Security, Murder One, Picket Fences)* and Dave Hackel (*Wings, Frazier, Almost Perfect*).

The Jim Preminger Agency is one of Los Angeles' most respected and thriving independent agencies.

Agents
Jim Preminger and Dean Schramm
Client List
60
Clients
Michael Butler, Peter Casey, David Lee, Helen Plummer, Sherry Bilsing, Geoffrey Neigher, Dave Hackel and others

❖ Renaissance Literary Talent Agency

9220 Sunset Blvd. #302
W of Doheny
Los Angeles, CA 90069
310-858-5365

Although Renaissance Literary Talent Agency only opened its doors in 1993, it is one of the most effective, interesting, prestigious and historical agencies in town. Since partners, Joel Gotler, Alan Nevins and Irv Schwartz each carry mantles from earlier liaisons with the creme de le creme of Los Angeles and New York literary giants, Renaissance has a rich heritage.

Colorful Joel Gotler was in the garment business, the WMA mailroom, an agent at WMA, shared housing with Mama Cass and was an assistant to producer Jennings Lang before answering a blind ad from literary powerhouse H. N. *(Swanny)* Swanson that melded his love of reading with his gift of gab and beginning his literary agenting career.

His years with Swanny were happy and productive and resulted in a partnership in another agency that made his career. Whether he was in business with Swanny or not, they were always like family and after Swanny's death, his family turned to Joel to preserve the Swanson legacy by representing his clients.

Irv Schwartz also served time in the WMA mailroom before working for eight years with New York's most loved and respected literary agent, Robby Lantz. At The Lantz Office Irv represented clients like Jules Feiffer, Thomas Thompson and Milos Forman. Irv then worked for APA, The Agency and Metropolitan Talent.

Completing the scenario of the partners' immaculate literary bloodlines, Alan Nevins spent his formative years as the longtime associate of Irving *(Swifty)* Lazar, and was ultimately chosen by Lazar's heirs to carry on Swifty's agency after his death. When Joel and Irv decided to leave Metropolitan, they invited Alan to help them create Renaissance.

They started the business in a cottage on LaPeer, moved to the old H. N. Swanson office on Sunset and are just moving into their new offices at 9220 Sunset as this book is being written.

Renaissance represents authors, screenwriters, literary estates and a few budding directors. Their impressive client list includes John

Jakes (*Home Land*), Richard Russo (*Nobody's Fool, Magic Hour, Straight Man, Risk Pool*), James Ellroy (*LA Confidential*), Michael Connelly (*The Poet, Bloodwork*), David Stevens (*Breaker Morant, A Town Like Alice, Queen, Some of Us*) and Benedict Fitzgerald (*Wise Blood, Heart of Darkness, Zelda, Moby Dick, In Cold Blood*). This office doesn't really handle writers for series.

Because of their legacy with Swanson and Lazar, they also handle the estates of Truman Capote, Robert A. Heinlein, James Jones, Vladimir Nabokov, John O'Hara and many others.

Don't spoil your chances (and everyone else's) by querying Renaissance until you have appropriate material and/or entree.

Agents
Joel Gotler, Irv Schwartz, Alan Nevins, Brian Lipson, Steve Fisher and Alan Liebert
Client List
100+
Clients
John Jakes, Richard Russo, James Ellroy, Michael Connelly, David Stevens, Benedict Fitzgerald and others

❖ The Richland Agency

11777 San Vicente Blvd. #702
at Barrington
Los Angeles, CA 90049
310-571-1833

Dan Richland not only pilots his own jet, but was profiled in *Los Angeles Magazine* as ferrying around the likes of Burt Reynolds, Henry Winkler and such diverse Presidents as Ronald Reagan and Bill Clinton.

Richland ran his own agency before joining with Bob Hohman and Bob Wunsch in 1987 forming the prestigious Richland Wunsch Hohman Agency. When Wunsch retired in 1996, the remaining partners went their separate ways, Bob Hohman joined with Bayard Maybank and Debra Lieb to start their own office and Richland opted for a smaller environment and started his own one man office again.

Richland declined to be interviewed, so my information on this agency is spare

Agents
Dan Richland
Client List
Confidential
Clients
Confidential

❖ The Marion Rosenberg Office

8428 Melrose Place #C
just E of La Cienega Blvd.
Los Angeles, CA 90069
213-653-7383

In 1979 Marion Rosenberg was already a successful theatre and film producer both here and abroad when superagent Robby Lantz asked her to open his Los Angeles office. Working for Robby, she found her producer skills and contacts useful promoting one of the most luminous client lists in the world.

Ten years later, Marion opened her own prestigious office with a list of glittering clients. She's adamant about not printing clients' names, so if you have access, check the WGA lists. If you don't have a credible resume and entree, forget about this agency, but it's definitely something to aspire to.

Marion and colleague Matthew Lesher (Henderson Hogan) also represent directors, composers, actors and one costume designer. Marion handles the writers.

Agents
Marion Rosenberg
Client List
40
Clients
Confidential

❖ Rosenstone/Wender

3 E 48ᵗʰ Street
E of 5ᵗʰ Avenue
New York, NY 10017
212-832-8330

Howard Rosenstone started in the business with WMA in 1963. Originally an agent representing actors, Howard decided quickly that he preferred to handle directors and playwrights. In 1977 he left WMA to start his own agency and in 1980 he teamed with Phyllis Wender to form Rosenstone/Wender.

Partners, Wender and Rosenstone each maintain their own lists and function alone, so I assume that means that if you get Rosenstone, you don't get Wender and vice-versa.

Rosenstone represents directors, orchestrators, screenwriters, playwrights, composers and lyricists. He doesn't take on that many new clients so query letters need to be sensational and support high caliber work. Rosenstone represents writers from all over the world. Besides having such famous clients as David Mamet and Shel Silverstein, Howard represents the Tennessee Williams estate.

Agents
Howard Rosenstone, Phyllis Wender and Ron Gwiazda
Client List
Confidential
Clients
David Mamet, Shel Silverstein, the Tennessee Williams estate and others

❖ The Sanders Agency, Ltd.

8831 Sunset Blvd. # 304
E of San Vicente
Los Angeles, CA 90069
310-652-1119

Down to earth Honey Sanders is a born nurturer. When she was still an actress, she was always getting work for her friends. Her own agent, Francine Hinton at Richard Pittman Agency noticed and commandeered Honey to fill in for her when she became ill. Honey continued to work part-time as an agent until Francine's death when Honey decided to give up acting and concentrate on agenting.

The Sanders Agency has always represented actors, children, teenagers, dancers and young adults for theatre, film and television, but has recently added a literary department.

J. J. Kahn joined The Sanders Agency in 1996. Although her last job was at WMA, her most formative agenting time was spent at CAA during the Ovitz/Haber/Meyer regime. Her literary list is purposefully small, sporting only about five in the writing category. Two names from that list include Renny Temple (*Empty Nest, Growing Pains),* and Christopher Clark (*Star Trek, Chaos)* and several acting clients like Frank Stallone, who are beginning to submit scripts.

J. J. only looks at new writers via industry referral.

Agents
J. J. Kahn
Client List
5
Clients
Renny Temple, Christopher Clark, Frank Stallone and others

❖ The Irv Schechter Co.

9300 Wilshire Blvd. #201
at Rexford
Los Angeles, CA 90024
310-278-8070

In 1984, after 15 years at The William Morris Agency, Irv Schechter opened a celebrated literary agency that has grown to include not only writers and directors, but actors and below-the-line personnel.

The literary department at Schechter covers every base: Debbee Klein has moved to Paradigm, but the agency's strong base of agents and clients remains enviable.

Victorya Michaels handles game shows as well as writers and directors in off-network cable and talk shows while Irv presides over the film department. VP Don Klein heads the primetime television department. In addition to Irv, Don and Victorya, agents who handle writers at the agency are Irv's son, Josh, Frank Balkin and Abby Sheeline.

Agents
Irv Schechter, Don Klein, Victorya Michaels, Frank Balkin, Abby Sheeline and Josh Schechter
Client List
100
Clients
Confidential

❖ Richard Sindell & Associates

8271 Melrose Ave. # 202
btwn Sweetzer & Harper
Los Angeles, CA 90046
213-653-5051

Richard Sindell is a seventh generation agent. Although by my arithmetic that puts him back near Columbus or something, he says it only goes back to the Goldwyn era in the '40s. Richard (who is also a lawyer) opened this agency in 1991 after spending time agenting with Barry Freed and Robby Lantz.

Although this agency was created to represent actors, since Richard's background includes an association with literary legend, Robby Lantz, I didn't think it would take him long to open a literary department. Although their primary thrust continues to be representing acting talent, Richard and colleague Jeffrey Leavitt (David Shapira & Associates) represent a handful of writers, directors, composers and music editors.

Richard is another of those folk who are quite protective of their client list, but he wasn't shy about mentioning that he has acting clients on *Grace Under Fire* and *Dr. Quinn, Medicine Woman* as well in film and in the theatre.

Because Sindell & Associates carries a small list, they are rarely in the market for additions.

Agents
Richard Sindell and Jeffrey Leavitt
Client List
A handful
Clients
Confidential

❖ SGK & Associates

6391 Wilshire Blvd. # 414
at La Jolla
Los Angeles, CA 90048
213-782-1854

In addition to agenting, Arnold Soloway, who began his career in New York at The William Morris Agency, has managed and booked variety acts, packaged series, films and game shows, produced films, nightclub shows and infomercials and he has worked extensively in the agency business with agencies such as Lester Salkow, Kumin-Olenick and the Susan Smith Agency. He started his own successful agency, The Artists Group in 1975.

He sold that agency in 1993 and moved to Florida producing and packaging films and television projects. Arnold missed Los Angeles and the agency business, so he returned home to begin this new agency with old friends, Don Kopaloff and Susan Grant.

Kopaloff's job as a messenger for Twentieth Century Fox in New York launched him into show business. Helen Straus, head of the literary department at WMA, noticed Don and urged him to join the training program there.

After time out for the Korean war, Don returned to WMA until Freddy Fields and David Begelman invited him to join them at CMA (forerunner of ICM). Next, he was head of production at Avco Embassy, creating projects and matching them up with new writers and directors.

Following his job with Avco, Don created his own boutique agency, Donburry Management, Ltd. which was folded into IFA. Don remained with IFA until the IFA/CMA merger begot ICM. At that point, he started The Kopaloff Company which he ran until he decided to team up with Soloway and Susan Grant. Grant was a below-the-line agent and Arnold's colleague at The Artists Group.

SGK represents writers, novelists, playwrights, directors, editors and directors of photography.

Names from SGK's list include Dalene Young (*Cross Creek, Little Darlings, Summer in the Country*), Bill Sacks (*Leprechaun*), Victor Astrovsky (*The Spy Game, By Way of Deception*), Mel Shavelson (*Winds of War*) and Jack Olson (*Aphrodite, Desperate Mission, The*

Misbegotten Son).

The backgrounds of these agents and the diversified client list provide rich opportunities for packaging. All the partners at this agency handle literary clients. New clients come to SGK mainly through industry referral but they do look at all query letters.

Agents
Arnold Soloway, Susan Grant and Don Kopaloff
Client List
65
Clients
Dalene Young, Bill Sacks, Victor Astrovsky, Jack Olson and Mel Shavelson

❖ Susan Schulman Literary Agency

454 W 44th Street
btwn 8th & 9th Avenues
New York, NY 10036-5203
212-713-1633

Susan Schulman is pretty cool. Not only is she the only agent who ever told me that she is always looking for material, she tells me that she answers professional writers' query letters within two to three days.

Susan is focused on success. When she graduated from college and the job she sought as a professor of linguistics did not materialize, Susan just took her linguistics degree and started shopping for a new career. She began searching for a profession that would combine her love of reading with business.

That researched quest sent her to work at ICM where she learned from one of the most famous and effective literary agents of all time, Audrey Wood. Schulman points with pride to having worked with Wood and counts that training as part of her success, but all you have to do is experience Susan to know that whatever she sets her mind to, she accomplishes. She's a true entrepreneur who loves words.

Schulman started her own agency in 1980. Since she is based in New York, her main thrust is playwrights and book authors, but she also handles film and television.

When I asked Susan how many clients she represents, she said it's hard to determine since she represents clients in so many different ways. Walter Tevis (*The Color of Money, The Hustler, Queen's Gambit, The Man Who Fell to Earth*) has been dead since 1984, but she represents his estate which still needs attention. Robin Norwood's book *Women Who Love Too Much* is still a best seller after 14 years, but doesn't require the same kind of attention that breaking in a new writer demands.

Susan's list of stars is exceptional. She represents one of my favorite books, Julia Cameron's *The Artist's Way* which has sold 1.2 million copies in the United States alone. Susan represented the rights to the film *The English Patient* in tandem with Michael Ondaatje's book agent, Ellen Levine, so she obviously has a wide range of contacts.

Susan says she is *always looking for new material. I would be out of business if I weren't.*

Agents
Susan Schulman
Client List
Diverse
Clients
Julia Cameron, Robin Norwood, David Saperstein, Anne Michaels,
Walter Tevis and others

❖ David Shapira & Associates

15301 Ventura Boulevard # 345
W of Sepulveda
Sherman Oaks, CA 91403
818-906-0322

David Shapira's life was changed by an agent's pin-striped suit. En route to life as a lawyer, he encountered the celebrated agent, Jerry Steiner. David thought Jerry *looked so elegant in his pinstriped suit* that David (apparently not aware that he could have been a baseball player since the Yankees wear pinstripes) decided to be an agent. He quit school at 17 to work in the mailroom at General Artists Corporation where he was befriended by Rod Serling who helped him switch mailrooms (Ashley-Famous) with a hefty raise to $75 a week.

This was many years ago and the rest, as they say, is history. It took only seven months in the mailroom before David, figuring *this was going to take too long,* lied about his age (you had to be 21 to make deals) and became an agent. David has, at various times, worked with Marty Baum, Meyer Mishkin and Max Arnow (who cast *Gone with the Wind*). In 1974, David opened his first office (Goldstein/Shapira). David maintains a very select client list of actors, directors, writers and producers. Not for beginners.

Robert Littman handles the literary clients at this agency.

Agents
Robert Littman
Client List
Confidential
Clients
Confidential

❖ Shapiro-Lichtman-Stein

8827 Beverly Blvd.
W of La Cienega
Los Angeles, CA 90048
310-859-8877

If you become a client at Shapiro-Lichtman, rest assured that your phone calls will be returned. Martin Shapiro was still at the office at 8 o'clock at night when he returned my call. This is definitely the guy I would want representing me.

Shapiro and partner, Mark Lichtman met as colleagues at General Artists Corporation in 1968. Marty left when GAC merged with the forerunner of ICM, CMA. He worked at both the Gersh and William Morris Agencies before rejoining with Lichtman to open Shapiro-Lichtman on Independence Day in 1969.

In 1997 longtime Shapiro-Lichtman agent, Mitchell Stein's name joined the masthead as partner. In addition to Mark, Marty and Mitchell, agents representing writers at this agency are Christine Foster, Michael R. Lewis, Susan Salkow Shapiro, April Rocha and Lisa Sullivan.

Marty wouldn't name any clients lest he leave someone out, but gave me permission to peruse the list and name a few of his distinguished clients to give you an idea of who is on his list. They include David Webb Peoples (*12 Monkeys, Unforgiven, Hero*), Jim Carabatsos (*Hamburger Hill*), Garfield and Judith Reeves-Stevens (*Bloodshift, Nighteyes*), writer-director Gregory Goodell (*Beyond the Gate*), Emmy winning director Joseph Sargent (*Mandela, Miss Rose White*) and novelists Harlan Ellison (*I, Robot*) and William Gibson (*Neuromancer, Johnny Mnemonic*).

When I asked Marty the size of his list, he was both evasive and articulate, *Not too large to devote individual and personal attention to our clients and large enough that we can do all right.* In a constantly shifting marketplace, S-L-S clients write everything from film to reality programming to interactive projects.

Peggy Patrick and Laura Rhodes represent below-the-line clients. Respected theatrical agent Budd Moss has also joined the lineup bringing a list of eminent actors and expanding packaging capabilities.

Agents

Martin Shapiro, Mark Lichtman, Mitchell Stein, Christine Foster, Michael R. Lewis, April Rocha, Susan Salkow Shapiro and Lisa Sullivan

Client List

Not too large to devote individual and personal attention to our clients and large enough that we can do all right.

Clients

David Webb Peoples, Janet Peoples, Jim Carabatsos, Joseph Sargent, Gregory Goodell, Harlan Ellison, William Gibson, Garfield and Judith Reeves-Stevens and others

❖ Ken Sherman & Associates

Writers & Artists Bldg.
9507 Little Santa Monica Blvd.
at Rodeo Drive
Beverly Hills, CA 90210
310-271-8840

If you feel you can read people by their environment, you'd have to have Ken Sherman for an agent just on style, because his office is in the coolest building around. The legendary Writers & Artists building in Beverly Hills has Dan Petrie, Ray Bradbury and Digby Diehl (just for starters) as tenants and makes you feel like all the great screenplays from your past must have been written there.

A native Angelino, Ken says he always wanted to be in the business and though working toward a psychology degree from Berkeley, he managed to spend summers as a production manager for an Academy Award winning educational film company. Opting for life experience instead of the job the film company offered, Ken went to Europe, made crepes in a restaurant, dubbed English into foreign films, worked in film production, and wrote and researched a guide to Paris before returning to Los Angeles and becoming a reader for Columbia pictures.

In 1975, he was hired for a stint in The William Morris mailroom eventually becoming an agent there representing both actors and directors. Before opening his own office in 1989, he worked at The Lantz Office and Paul Kohner, Inc. His list of 25-30, features writers with famous names as well as writers with that potential.

Ken does not accept unsolicited material and is not interested in expanding his client list, but he has very instructive quotes throughout the book.

Agents
Ken Sherman
Client List
25-30
Clients
Confidential

❖ Susan Smith & Associates

121 N San Vicente Boulevard
S of Burton Way
Beverly Hills, CA 90211
213-852-4777

Many other independent agents in town aspire to be Susan Smith. Distinguished, elegant, and able to keep superstar clients like Brian Dennehy, Laura Dern and Kathy Bates happy while still maintaining boutique status makes Susan Smith a worthy prototype. She opened her first office in New York in 1970 and has continued to add distinguished actors to her list.

The literary department, though not as well known, is every bit as prestigious. In fact, it is so well thought of, that APA recently lured away previous literary department head, Justin Dardis.

Not to worry, the literary department now has more agents than the theatrical division. SSA represents writers, directors, producers and actors for stage, film and television. This agency also represents novelists.

Wendi Chasman, Stephen Gates and Deborah Obad represent clients like Nick Ross and Gary Auerback who wrote *Whiskey Down.*

The client list is purposefully select with first-class clients.

Agents
Wendi Chasman, Stephen Gates and Deborah Obad
Client List
40 writers and directors.
Clients
Nick Ross, Gary Auerback and others

❖ Miriam Stern, Esquire

303 E 83rd Street
Btwn 1st & 2nd Avenues
New York, NY 10028
212-794-1289

Miriam Stern is 75% entertainment lawyer and 25% agent. At present, she's full up on writing clients, but once she gets one project in the pipeline and on its way, she takes on another, so stay tuned.

When Miriam graduated from law school, she immediately set about to specialize in the part of the business that interests her most: entertainment law. Her mentor suggested that since this was her focus, she might want to represent some writers.

When I asked Miriam how she chooses clients, she told me the story of her first writer. After wading through a stack of manuscripts and selecting a work she felt worthy, she worked hard getting the writer placed at a major publishing house. While she was negotiating his second book, another agency stole the client away, so Miriam now adds character alongside talent when she is listing attributes she desires in clients.

Miriam represents a list of up-and-coming playwrights and authors of fiction and non-fiction. She reads all query letters carefully.

Miriam's enthusiasm, resourcefulness and ideas impressed me. If you catch her with an opening on her list, I think she would be an effective advocate.

There are quotes from Miriam elsewhere in the book.

Agent
Miriam Stern
Client List
6
Clients
Unnamed

❖ Stone Manners

8091 Selma Avenue
W of Crescent Heights & N of Sunset
Los Angeles, CA 90046
213-654-7575

Tim Stone, whose father is a famous British agent, brought his list of 50 British actors to Los Angeles and established UK Management offering services for British actors in this country in 1976.

Scott Manners was a business major with a talent for golf, who thought he might be a golf pro. The son of a stand-up comic and a June Taylor dancer, he never considered a showbiz career, until cast in a college play at UC Irvine where he became interested in acting.

As enthusiastic about acting as he was about golf, Scott began to study with Jeff Corey, who led him to truths which not only helped his acting, but also to agenting as a profession. His lucky clients benefit from the passion, drive, empathy and intelligence that Corey helped focus. Scott can sell anything to anyone.

His first agency job was for Fred Amsel, where he worked as a go-fer. After two months, Fred tossed him into the deep water of agenting. Not only didn't Scott sink, he appears to be a strong swimmer.

Manners worked with Rickey Barr at Richard Dickens Agency before joining Tim Stone and colleague Larry Masser in 1983. By April 1986, Larry Masser became a partner (Stone Masser) and by August of that year, Scott was the third partner (Stone Masser Manners). When Masser left to join APA in 1989, Scott and Tim became the sole partners.

Tim Stone heads the growing literary department. He is joined by colleague Casey Bierer. Bierer was in development at Imagine Films and an agent at APA before becoming a part of this dynamic agency.

Agents
Tim Stone and Casey Bierer
Client List
Building
Clients
Confidential

❖ The Tantleff Office

375 Greenwich St. #700
S of Houston & W of Hudson
New York, NY 10013
212-941-3939

Located in the same building as the trendy Tribeca Grill, just
visiting The Tantleff Office is enough to make you feel that you will be
a star immediately. With the connections and clients this agency has, if
you are talented, that might not be far off the mark.

Jack Tantleff really intended to be a doctor when he was
studying at Colby College in Waterville, Maine, but his extracurricular
theatre activities changed his thrust. The combination of seeing
Anthony Hopkins in *Equus* and hearing the legendary Ellen Stewart,
founder of New York's radical theatre, Cafe La Mama, speak on
campus, convinced Jack that he wanted some kind of life in the theatre.

Since Stewart was on campus for a while as a guest teacher, Jack
managed to ask for her guidance. He took his new mentor's advice and
enrolled at Sarah Lawrence where he was blessed with Wilford Leach as
his faculty advisor and teachers like Elizabeth Swados and Julie Bovasso.
His off-time was spent working at La Mama.

His first job after college was typing labels for Michael Harvey
and partner Peter Bobley, who were producing an evening of one act
plays by James McLure: *Lone Star* and *Pvt. Wars.* When financing fell out
shortly before opening, a call went out to everyone involved to raise
money. Jack (having no idea of what was involved in raising money)
naively volunteered to help. He was so successful that he shared an
associate producer credit with Stewart F. Lane.

Jack then worked for celebrated managers, Jack Schlissel and Jay
Kingwill as well as other management companies. He was the assistant
company manager on both *The Best Little Whorehouse in Texas* and *Sugar
Babies* and company managed *The Dining Room* as well as *American Buffalo*
starring Al Pacino.

Though agenting had never occurred to Jack as a career choice,
when he was offered the opportunity to be assistant to Clifford Stevens
(STE) who represented the likes of Jason Robards, Lauren Bacall,
Colleen Dewhurst, Glenn Close and Ellis Rabb, that option began to
look more interesting. From STE, he moved to Hesseltine-Baker and

was able to work with clients of a very high level until that agency closed in 1986.

Since at this point Jack was jobless, he decided to gamble on himself. He bought a computer, got a business line with three phone numbers and opened The Tantleff Office out of his apartment.

Jack's smarts and resourcefulness paid off and just three years later when *The Secret Garden* was still in the developmental stages, Jack's work load necessitated hiring some help and expanding to the spectacular space that The Tantleff Office occupies today.

Jill Bock came to Jack from ICM. She represents screen and television writers and has been successful with young film makers like Michael Shoob (*Driven*), Alan Madison (*Trouble on the Corner*) and Brian Sloane (*I Think I Do),* who just completed their first features.

Charmaine Ferenczi started with Jack as an intern years ago. Today, in addition to representing her own clients, she handles the huge job of tracking and negotiating foreign, stock and amateur rights for clients' plays.

Jack made a point to tell me that the three agents function as one team representing their clients.

Some writers from the team's list of scriptwriters, playwrights, directors and composers/songwriters, are Marsha Norman (*'night, Mother, The Secret Garden*), Brian Friel (*Dancing at Lughnasa),* Arthur Kopit (*Phantom, Nine, Wings*), Henry Krieger (*Dreamgirls*), Lucy Simon (*The Secret Garden*), lyricist Susan Birkenhead (*Jelly's Last Jam*), Ivan Menchell (*The Cemetery Club,* writer-producer on *The Nanny*)), Bob Goodman (a Warner Bros. Animation staffer who writes for shows like *Superman* and *Batman and Robin)* and Lucky Gold (*One Life to Live* and a multi picture screenwriting deal at Miramax).

The Tantleff Office is young, cutting edge and committed to representing not only the top of the list of the New York literary scene, but Los Angeles as well. They seek to be the new prototype agency for show biz talent on every level.

New clients come to this office strictly through referral although query letters are carefully read.

Agents
Jack Tantleff, Charmaine Ferenczi and Jill Bock
Client List
30
Clients
Marsha Norman, Brian Friel, Arthur Kopit, Henry Krieger, Lucy Simon, Michael Shoob, Alan Madison, Brian Sloane, Ivan Menchell, Bob Goodman, Lucky Gold and others

❖ The Turtle Agency

12456 Ventura Blvd.
at Whitsett
Studio City, CA 91604
818-506-6898

Cindy Turtle's background includes television production in New York and Los Angeles plus a stint at the distinguished Eisenbach-Greene-Duchow agency where she became their first female agent representing writers, producers and directors for features and television. She was Director of Development for Showtime from 1980-1983 before starting the literary department for LA agent Harry Gold.

She left Harry to form a partnership with Mike Rosen (The Rosen/Turtle Group). In 1990 Cindy started The Turtle Agency. Turtle and colleague Amy Dresner represent writers, directors and producers in all areas. Writers make up about two-thirds of their list of 45 clients.

Agents
Cindy Turtle and Amy Dresner
Client List
30
Clients
Confidential

❖ Twentieth Century Artists

15315 Magnolia Blvd. # 429
W of Sepulveda
Sherman Oaks, CA 91403
818-788-5516

Dynamic Diane Davis has been running this agency for over 20 years. Her late husband started Twentieth Century Artists and Diane, who had been a talent agent at Mary Ellen White, joined the agency about a year after it opened. The feedback on Diane from clients and colleagues has always been that she and her agency are effective, vital and strong. Agents who have trained with Diane and have gone on to open their own offices speak glowingly of their mentor.

Although, Twentieth Century was once known for its important literary division, placing writers like Stephen Cannell under contract at Universal (*The Rockford Files*), for the past few years, this agency has represented actors exclusively. Today, however, the agency represents writers, directors, choreographers, below-the-line personnel and comedians. With such an extensive list of talent, they are able to package quite effectively.

David Ankrum who heads the literary division was originally an actor and Diane's client. He became a writer (*Charles in Charge*) for several years and finally decided he wanted to become an agent. When he approached Diane, she felt he was the right person to put Twentieth Century Artists into the literary business again. David has about 30 scriptwriters for film and television. He reads query letters, but finds new writers mainly through industry referral and writers' workshops.

Agents
David Ankrum
Client List
125
Clients
Confidential

❖ United Talent Agency/UTA

9560 Wilshire Blvd. #500
at Rodeo Drive
Beverly Hills, CA 90212
310-273-6700

James Berkus (IFA), Robert Stein and Gary Cosay (WMA) founded Leading Artists in 1983, billing themselves as an intimate William Morris. When they merged with the important literary agency created by Marty Bauer (WMA) and entertainment lawyer, Peter Benedek (Bauer Benedek) creating United Talent Agency, they gave up all pretense at intimacy and moved shoulder to shoulder with WMA, ICM and CAA.

UTA grew even more powerful from the demise of InterTalent and the merger of Triad with William Morris, by picking up newly available top line talented agents and their clients.

The main strength at UTA is writers, producers and directors, but their list of actors continues to grow in stature and size.

Other partners at UTA are Jeremy Zimmer (ICM) and Martin Hurwitz (New World Entertainment).

Partner Jeremy Zimmer and Don Aloni head the motion picture/literary division. Other agents in the MP/literary division are Peter Benedek, Gary Cosay, Marty Bowen, Andrew Cannava, Sherwin Das, David Kanter, David Kramer, Josh Lesher, Billy Rose and Jessica Swimoff (Sanford-Gross & Associates). The TV/literary division is headed by Chris Harbert and Jay Sures with Chris Coelen, Cory Concoff, Dennis Kim, Robert Kim, Rick Lefitz, Leslie Maskin, Sue Naegle, Larry Salz, Ruthanne Secunda and Evan Weiss. Howard Sanders (Pleshette Green) and Richard Green (Pleshette Green) head up the book department.

UTA's commitment to independent filmmakers is led by agents, Howard Cohen and Charles Ferraro.

Literary clients include John Singleton, Vince McKewin (*Fly Away Home, The Climb, King of the Park, Samburu*), David O. Russell, Bruce Helford, Sy Dukane, Deann Heline and Eileen Heisler, Denise Moss, Lynn Latham (the pilot of *Homefront*), John Mattson (*Milk Money*), Alain Berliner (*Ma Vie En Rose*), Jonathan Nossiter (*Sunday*), Seth Zvi Rosenfeld (*A Brother's Kiss*) and Vin Diesel (*Strays*).

This agency was not available for a personal interview, so this information is based on research.

Agents

Jeremy Zimmer, Don Aloni, Peter Benedek, Gary Cosay, Marty Bowen, Andrew Cannava, Sherwin Das, David Kanter, David Kramer, Josh Lesher, Billy Rose, Jessica Swimoff, Chris Harbert, Jay Sures, Chris Coelen, Cory Concoff, Dennis Kim, Robert Kim, Rick Lefitz, Leslie Maskin, Sue Naegle, Larry Salz, Ruthanne Secunda, Evan Weiss, Howard Sanders, Richard Green, Howard Cohen and Charles Ferraro

Client List

Growing daily

Clients

Bruce Helford, Sy Dukane, Deann Heline and Eileen Heisler, Janice Jordan-Nelson, Denise Moss, Lynn Latham, John Mattson and others

❖ Warden White & Associates

8444 Wilshire Blvd. 4th Floor
near La Cienega
Beverly Hills, CA 90211
213-852-1028

Graduates from the famous William Morris mailroom agent-training-program form an elite corps that just about owns show business. Dave Warden is part of that alumnus and was in the same generation of agents as CAA's famous, Jack Rapke, so it was obviously a good year!

Before partnering up with Steve White in 1989, Dave worked as a motion picture literary agent at Eisenbach/Greene, APA and Susan Smith.

Steve White's pedigree is distinguished also. He was trained by Frank Cooper, a man who got his start in the business working as the secretary for William Morris himself. White left the business for a period of time but returned when the opportunity of teaming up with Dave presented itself.

Names from Warden White's client list include Sam Hamm (*Batman*), *X-Files* Emmy winner, Darin Morgan, *Viper* story editor and comic book illustrator, Howard Chaykin and Nicholl Fellowship award winner, Victoria Arch (*A Terrible Beauty*).

This office (David in particular) prides itself in developing writers and has signed a few whose work came to them *over the transom*.

Do not walk in this agency. Do not send unsolicited material. Do not fax. Contact this and other agencies only through brief query letters or through industry referral.

Agents
Dave Warden and Steve White
Client List
20
Clients
Sam Hamm, Darin Morgan, Victoria Arch, Howard Chaykin and others

❖ Peregrine Whittlesey Agency

345 E 80th Street #31F
at 1st Avenue
New York, NY 10021
212-737-0153

Although at first glance, one might think this is an agency run
by Mr. Peregrine and Mr. Whittlesey, in fact, this is a successful literary
agency run by one woman whose name is Peregrine Whittlesey. An
actress who continually found herself producing and working with
writers developing material, Peregrine was one of the founding members
of The Manhattan Theater Club.

The native New Yorker developed the voucher program for
TCG and was Elaine May's assistant for three years during which time
she read for Ms. May as well as helped edit material. From 1980-83,
Whittlesey was Literary Manager for The Goodman Theater in Chicago.
At the Goodman, she developed writers and arranged readings when
necessary.

After a go at producing and a successful experience helping a
friend get his play produced at Long Wharf, Peregrine decided to take all
her contacts, her ability to work with playwrights and her instincts and
open her own agency. An agent who does not *represent projects, but people,*
Peregrine only takes on those playwrights she believes in strongly.

Peregrine is drawn to people who have interesting lives rather
than people who are just good playwrights. She has a liaison with Curtis
Brown and The Agency, Ltd. in London. Since she is fluent in French,
she finds herself working with artists from that country as well. Her Los
Angeles connections are CAA and Jeff Melnick.

Peregrine responds to everything people send to her, but she
works alone, so be patient.

Agents
Peregrine Whittlesey
Client List
24
Clients
Darrah Cloud, Migdalia Cruz, Gary Leon Hill, Heather McCutchen,
Marlane Meyer, Sara Miles and others.

❖ The William Morris Agency/WMA

151 El Camino Drive
S of Wilshire
Beverly Hills, CA 90212
310-274-7451

There really was a man named William Morris who started this agency in 1898. During the 100 years since, although WMA has had it's ups and downs, down was never further than #3. Today, WMA, ICM and CAA are probably more equal in power and prestige than they have been in 20 years.

In late 1992 in a bid to regroup what many were describing as a has-been agency, WMA merged with the prestigious boutique agency, Triad in a bid to capture more big names. The Los Angeles Times states that *overall revenues at the agency have increased 65% since the Triad acquisition.*

Along with star clients who joined the agency at that point, WMA captured brilliant new agents, not the least of which was Triad partner and now head of the motion picture division and president of William Morris, Arnold Rifkin.

Credited with engineering the renewed visibility and power of John Travolta and Sylvester Stallone, Rifkin created an independent film department. He and his staff helped put together such films as *Pulp Fiction, The English Patient* and *Sling Blade.*

The other top dogs at WMA are Norman Browkow, chairman of the agency, Jerry Katzman, who packaged *The Cosby Show* and *Roseanne,* and Walter Zifkin, who played a big role in the acquisition of Triad.

The agency represents not only writers, directors, producers and actors, but athletes, newscasters, political figures and almost any other being of notoriety.

If having the most clients means you have the most power, WMA wins hands down. On a list of agents I looked at, WMA had 222 as compared to 94 at ICM and 113 at CAA. Of course, CAA only has the Los Angeles office, while WMA has offices on both coasts. In any event, the number of agents is pretty staggering. I'm not going to

The William Morris Agency/WMA

1350 Avenue of the Americas
at 55th Street
New York, NY 10019
212-586-5100

attempt to list all the names. Not only are the lists confidential, it's way too long. Although I will list a few names of literary agents that I have either picked up in the trades or other news stories.

Los Angeles motion picture/literary agents include Robert Stein, Joanne Roberts, Spencer Baumgarten, Jeff Field, Alan Gasmer, Todd Harris and Ron Mardigan. Los Angeles TV/literary agents include Lanny Noveck, Ann Blanchard, Renee Kurtz, Aaron Kaplan Rob Wolken, and Lee Cohen who does both motion pictures and television.

New York literary agents also handle a large book business and are led by Owen Laster and Brian Dubin. Some of the other agents who handle literary in New York are Bill Contardi, Mel Berger, Joni Evans Mary Meagher and Deborah Goldstein.

Agents

Los Angeles: Robert Stein, Joanne Roberts, Spencer Baumgarten, Jeff Field, Alan Gasmer, Todd Harris, Ron Mardigan. Lanny Noveck, Ann Blanchard, Renee Kurtz, Aaron Kaplan, Rob Wolken, Lee Cohen New York: Owen Laster, Brian Dubin, Mary Meagher, Bill Contardi, Mel Berger, Joni Evans, Deborah Goldstein and many many others

Client List

more and more every day

Clients

Tim Burton, Michael Tolkin, Peter Barnes, Henry Bromwell, Diane Wilk, Pamela K. Long, Anna Sandor, Bruce Vilanch, Noah Stern, Roger Wilson, John Dahl, Rick Dahl, David Wickes, Steven Soderbergh, Quentin Tarantino, Gus Van Sant and many others

❖ Ann Wright Representative

165 W 46th Street, #1105
just E of Broadway, in the Equity Building
New York, NY 10036
212-764-6770

When Ann Wright came to New York after training as an actress at prestigious Boston University, she joined the casting pool for CBS and cast soap operas. Like many other actors who have had an opportunity to explore other areas of the business, Ann discovered there were other rewarding ways to use her creative skills and decided to change career directions.

She trained to be an agent by assisting the legendary WMA agent, Milton Goldman and by casting television commercials at advertising agencies. Before opening her own agency, Ann worked for both Charles Tranum and Bret Adams.

Ann's commercial agency was legendary in the '60s and '70s, but she decided to close that part of her business and concentrate on handling talent for voice work. That wasn't quite interesting enough for Ann, so before long, she not only started repping talent for commercials, she added a theatrical division and began getting jobs for actors for theatre, film, radio and television.

Finally in search of a literary division, she enlisted husband, Dan Wright, who merged his own successful literary agency with this office, so now Ann has an agency that has the ability to package.

Dan represents about 25 clients for books, films, theatre and television. Many of his novelists have ended up with motion picture deals. His clients include Tom Dempsey, John Cooney, Ying Hzu and Brian Reich.

Queries with a self-addressed-stamped-envelope will receive a reply. Dan wants information about the author's background and a brief description of the property. Dan is particularly interested in material with strong film potential.

Agent
Dan Wright
Client List
80
Clients
Tom Dempsey, John Cooney, Ying Hzu, Brian Reich and others

❖ Writers & Artists

924 Westwood Blvd. #900
corner of Le Conte
Los Angeles, CA 90023
310-824-6300

Writers & Artists' name reflects the esteem in which this agency
(launched in New York in 1971) holds its writers. Since Rima Greer left,
they've become more confidential about their client list, so you'll either
have to take my word for it when I tell you they have Pulitzer prize
winners and important scriptwriters or else, if you have entree, check
the Writers Guild agency listings to see for yourself.

The literary department at W&A is headed by Jim Stein in Los
Angeles and Bill Craver in New York. Other agents for writers and
directors at this agency are owner Joan Scott, Michael Stipanich, Marti
Blumenthal, Larry Kennar (Maggie Field), Todd Koerner (Kaplan
Stahler), Evan Corday (Gold/Marshak) and Rick Berg. The recent
addition of Marjorie Skouras expands W&A's profile in the independent
marketplace. A heavy hitter in all departments, W&A combines prestige
with hands on service.

As with most of the other agencies I interviewed, although
W&A has stars, they also continually develop new talent. Michael
Stipanich stresses that it's not a good idea to submit your own material
to studios and producers without an agent as this will retard your
progress when you are represented.

❖ Writers & Artists

19 W 44th Street
just W of 5th Avenue
New York, NY 10036
212-391-1112

Agents
Los Angeles: Joan Scott, Michael Stipanich, Marti Blumenthal, Jim Stein, Rick Berg, Evan Corday, Larry Kennar, Todd Koerner and Marjorie Skouras
New York: Bill Craver, Rob Patillo
Client List
Confidential
Clients
Confidential

❖ Stella Zadeh & Associates

11759 Iowa Avenue
at Barrington
Los Angeles, CA 90025
310-207-4114

When Stella Zadeh was an executive for CBS years ago, several colleagues told her she had too much energy for CBS and suggested she start her own business. A year later in 1985 Richard Lawrence (Abrams, Rubaloff & Lawrence) gave her a start. In 1986 she acquired a Talent and Literary license and the world will never be the same. Somehow with the help of two assistants, she manages to represent a base list of 80 clients and helps many more.

The queen agent of reality-based producers/writers/directors, Stella didn't want me to name names, but says she has someone on almost every major talk or magazine show on television.

Don't rush to the mail box. She only accepts industry referrals, but she will read query letters. Although she handles a few traditional scriptwriters, they are all clients whose major thrust is reality-based programming. If you ask me, CBS should have harnessed the energy themselves.

Agents
Stella Zadeh
Client List
80+
Clients
Confidential

❖ Glossary

Above-the- line:

A budgetary term referring to talent, advertising and other negotiable expenses involved in making a film. This includes writers, directors, actors and producers.

Associate producer:

Performs one or more producer functions as delegated by the producer.

Below-the-line:

A budgetary term referring to production costs including such personnel as gaffers, grips, set designers, make-up, etc. Generally those fees that are non negotiated.

Bible:

Projected series story with ideas for progression from the television pilot forward.

Buzz:

Industry term meaning exciting information that everybody is talking about.

Calling card:

A spec script that gets you in the door. As *The New York Times* says, *Most often, a calling card is a script that everybody wants to read but nobody wants to make.*

Clout:

Power.

Connected:

To be in the system and to have entree to helpful relationships. If I am a powerful agent's secretary, I am connected to him and could get a project to him, etc.

Co-producers:
Two or more producers performing the producer functions.

Coverage:
Report supplied by reader to the buyer.

Development:
Process involving writers presenting work and/or ideas to producers who oversee the developing script.

The Dramatists Guild, Inc.:
Playwrights collective. Not a union in the strict sense of the word, the DG, Inc. protects members by offering collective bargaining agreements and contracts covering producers and theatre owners as well as providing guidelines relative to agency agreements and agents.

The Dramatists Guild Quarterly:
Provides information regarding agents, conferences and festivals, artists colonies, fellowships and grants, membership and service organizations, residencies, workshops plus an index of honors (Pulitzers, Obies, Oscars, etc.)

Element:
According to *The New York Times, an element is the basic building block of Hollywood, without which any project is simply an empty space pierced only by the phone calls of agents. Elements may be actors, directors, occasionally producers. They are never writers.*

Executive producer:
Supervises one or more producers.

Half-hour:
Situation comedy.

Interactive television:
Computer programming involving audience participation via computer/television sets. Still in its infancy. Said to be the next big thing. The jury is still out.

Line producer:
> Supervises physical production of project and is supervised by another producer who handles other duties.

Long form television:
> Movies of the week.

New Dramatists:
> Organization dedicated to finding gifted playwrights and giving them the time, space and tools to develop their craft, so that they may fulfill their potential and make lasting contributions to the theatre.

Outline:
> Written scene by scene diagram of script.

Pocket client:
> An agent feels you have promise, but that you are not far enough along, so he keeps in touch with you and monitors your work. When you have something he thinks he can sell, he submits it. If there is a sale, you would probably become a signed client. Sometimes called hip-pocket.

Pitch:
> Term used to define the process where a writer meets with producer(s) to tell the story (pitch) of his idea in hopes he will be hired to write a script.

Plugged in:
> Industry slang implying close associations or relationships with those in power.

Producer:
> A true producer initiates, coordinates, supervises and controls all aspects of a production from inception to completion. Frequently, the title is conferred to anyone who adds an important element to the project. That might be as simple, but important, as providing access to a star.

Many writers are given the title of producer which may give them more control over their material and demands more money than a just a staff writing position.

Query letter:
A brief letter that introduces the writer, synopsizes an idea a la TV Guide and invites further contact.

Reader:
A person employed by a buyer to weed through many scripts to select what the reader thinks warrants closer scrutiny.

Residual:
An re-use fee collected for writing an episode of a television series or when a film is sold to television. Every time your episode runs, you get a residual.

Royalty:
A re-use fee connected to a *Written by* credit for creating a television series. You are paid a fee every time any episode of the show you created runs since it is built on your original creation.

SASE
A self-addressed-stamped-envelope, which needs to accompany query letters and manuscripts if you expect a reply or to see your material again.

Showrunner:
Usually the executive producer of an hour-long show. Runs the show, hires and fires.

Spec scripts:
A script written on speculation without any financial remuneration up front or any prior interest from a prospective buyer.

Story analyst:
See reader.

Think:
> Industry slang term meaning a way of thinking.

The Trades:
> *Daily Variety, The Hollywood Reporter* and *Weekly Variety* are all newspapers that deal with the entertainment business. Available at newsstands or by subscription.

Treatment:
> A detailed written breakdown of a script, usually scene by scene.

The Writers Guild of America:
> Screenwriters guild — negotiates collective bargaining for screenwriters, arbitrates, provides services of all kinds.

WGA Directory:
> Listing of Writers Guild members delineating contacts (agents/managers/lawyers) and credits.

❖ Index to All Agents Mentioned

❖ Index to Book Agents

❖ Index to Los Angeles Agencies & Agents

❖ Index to Managers

❖ Index to New York Agencies & Agents

❖ Index to Resources

❖ Index to People, Topics & Everything Else